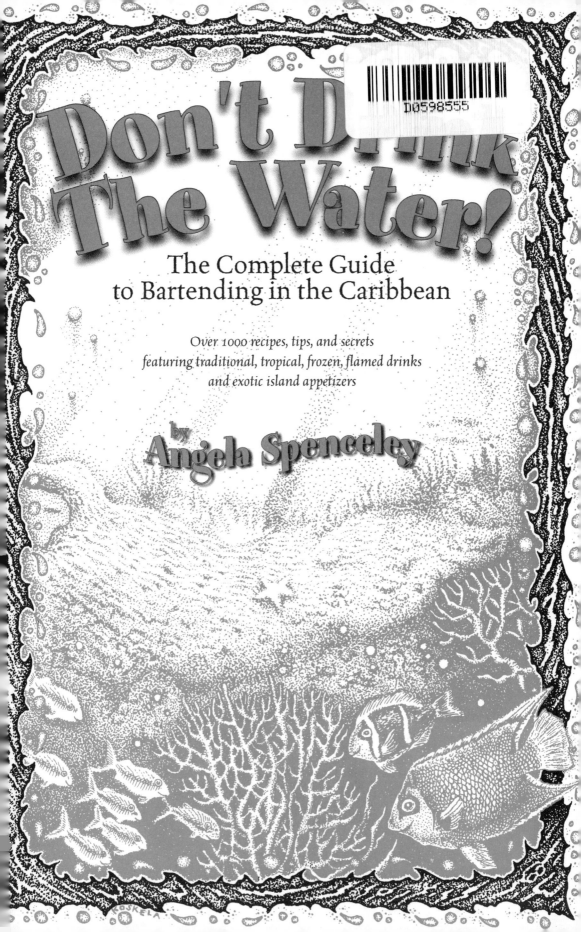

Don't Drink The Water!

The Complete Guide
to Bartending in the Caribbean

Over 1000 recipes, tips, and secrets
featuring traditional, tropical, frozen, flamed drinks
and exotic island appetizers

by Angela Spenceley

Acknowledgements

No man is an island.

Many thanks to my wonderful staff, Karma Nichols and Wilfredo Michaels, not only for their suggestions, but also for listening patiently. To Roxanne and Colby, whose writing is beginning to surpass mine.

Don't Drink the Water!

by

Angela Spenceley

Caribbean Press
U.S. Virgin Islands
Caribbean Press, St. Thomas, U.S. Virgin Islands
© 2002 by Angela Spenceley

Front & Back Cover Illustrations by Sean Koskela
Illustrations on pages 17 & 23 by Roxanne Spenceley

Printed & Designed by John Hinde Curteich, Inc., U.S.A.
710VI-3 / #7726

ISBN 0-9702168-2-3

Fifteen men on a dead man's chest

Yo, ho, ho, and a bottle of rum

Drink and the devil had done

    for the rest

Yo, ho, ho and a bottle of rum.

– Robert Louis Stevenson, Treasure Island 1883

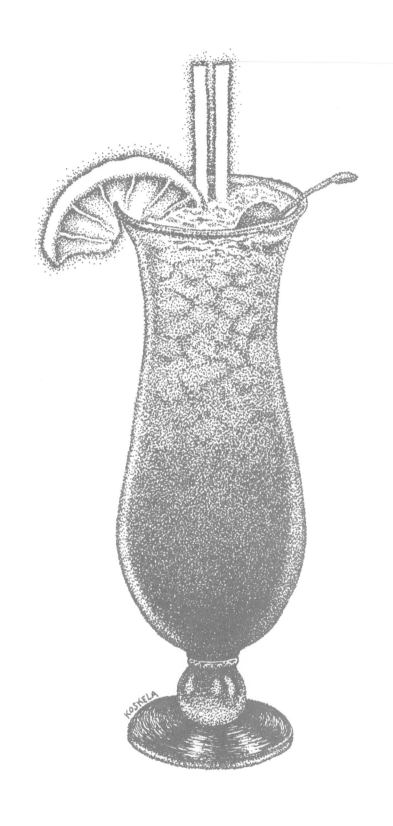

Contents at a Glance

Welcome to Paradise!

A ceiling fan lazily paddles air. A safari bus, overflowing with raucous tourists, shakes the mango-colored cottage and startles a lizard from its shaded hiding place. From behind a tangle of purple bougainvillea, Reggae music drifts up from cruise ships. It makes me smile and think of those faithful dreamers from forbidding climates. Just another day in paradise. Endless summer.

No worries. Play all day; party all night.

For centuries, the tantalizing concept of a tropical garden has captured the imagination. Nearly every civilization has its own myth about the Garden of Eden, Shangri-la, or Utopia. Countless books have been written on the subject. Milton, in *Paradise Lost*, stated that paradise was a state of mind. A setting of languidly swaying palms and an average temperature of 78° does help though.

Each year, millions of tourists visit our Caribbean islands to feel powdery sand beneath their feet on beaches that range in size from mile-long Magen's Bay in St. Thomas to Boca Prins beach in Aruba, the size of a Brazilian bikini. Or to read a book under a palm with a rainforest-cloaked volcano framing a white beach. Better yet, spend all their cash on our wonderful bargains on liquor (of course!), jewelry, watches, and perfumes. Maybe a little limbo under the stars.

Allow your heart to skip a beat and revel in the romance of the islands. Whether you are lingering on a sailboat set adrift on the aquamarine Caribbean Sea or having a summer cookout in Duxbury, Massachusetts, join us on our spirited tour of the Caribbean.

Bottoms up!

History and Geography of the Caribbean

If you have seen one Caribbean island, you have by no means seen them all. The more than a thousand islands range from remote cays, whose only inhabitants are geckos and wild parrots, to large islands whose glittering nightlife resembles Miami Beach or the French Riviera.

The Caribbean Sea, an arm of the Atlantic Ocean, is partially enclosed on the north and east by the Antilles chain of islands, a.k.a. The West Indies and is connected with the Gulf of Mexico by the Yucatan Channel. To the south lies Panama and South America, and Central America pulls in the West. Most of the islands are volcanic in origin with the exception of islands such as Anegada, which is a coral reef. Soaring volcanic peaks cloak lush rainforests, such as on Dominica, where Romancing the Stone was filmed. Guadeloupe, Martinique, and St. Lucia are also fertile with equatorial forest. Puerto Rico is a particularly varied island with its 100,000 acre Caribbean National Forest, the only tropical rainforest in the U.S. Forest system, a cacti forest to the south, and underground caverns, Camuy.

Many islands, including Puerto Rico, St. Thomas, St. Croix, and St. Kitts have ancient forts to see. The oldest synagogue building still in use in the Western Hemisphere is Mikveh Israel-Emanuel, located in Curacao, dedicated in 1732. Synagogue of Beracha Veshalom Vegmiluth Hasidim is the oldest synagogue in continuous use under the American flag since it opened its doors in 1833 and the second oldest building in the Western Hemisphere.

Each island is different from the other, but underneath it all, they hold many similarities. Most notable is the climate ranging from 78°F - 88°F. Eternal summer and unlimited beaches equal **island time!** Only the mongoose, which resembles a squirrel and devours snakes, and tradewinds move faster. Unlimited patience and a bottle of sunscreen are the only two prerequisites in the island, so no problem, mon.

History: The Arawaks, a peaceful, agricultural people, canoed up from South America more than 1,000 years ago. Between the cannibalistic Caribs and the gold-seeking Spaniards, with their host of diseases, the Arawaks and gentle Taino Indians became extinct. This is probably where the name Caribbean came from, i.e. the Carib Indians.

Columbus discovered the region in 1492 and named the numerous islands Los Virgenes after St. Ursula and her army of virgins. Between the 16th and 19th century the islands alternately flew the flags of the Danes, Dutch, Swedes, English, French, and Spanish. After wrestling control of the islands away from the Indians, Europeans established massive sugar cane plantations and imported slaves from Africa. With the abolishment of slavery in 1842, East Indians and Asian indentured servants replaced the labor force. Each wave of new immigrants, from European, African to Asian, brought not only its own culture, but foods and cooking customs as well.

To this day, rum, made from molasses, a by-product of sugar cane, is a major export from the islands. Despite this, nearly all the islands depend on tourism. Most islands are politically independent, while others have ties to the old country, such as the British Virgin Islands, U.S. Virgin Islands, and interesting St. Martin/St. Maarten with one side Dutch and the other French.

Geography: The Caribbean Sea encompasses more than a million square miles of multi-hued ocean beginning at the southern tip of Florida and extending to Venezuela, 1500 miles long and between 400 to 900 miles wide. The ocean is deep, between 6000 feet to 12,000 feet. **The Greater Antilles** consist of Hispaniola (Haiti and the Dominican Republic), Cuba, Jamaica and Puerto Rico. The Cayman Islands, close to Jamaica and south of Cuba, the Turks and Caicos, the Bahamas and Bermuda are in the Atlantic Ocean. Cruise lines often call Jamaica, Hispaniola, the Caymans, and Mexico the western Caribbean.

The Lesser Antilles compose a great many more islands, but are smaller than the Greater Antilles. This expanse is divided into three groups: The Leewards in the Eastern Caribbean and the Windwards in the southern Caribbean. The Leewards include the U.S. Virgin Islands, the British Virgin Islands, Saba, St. Barthelemy (St. Barts), St. Martin/St. Maarten, Saba, St. Eustatius (Staysha), Nevis, St. Kitts, Barbuda, Antigua, Montserrat and Guadeloupe. The Windwards consist of Dominica, Martinique, St. Lucia, St. Vincent, the Grenadines, and Grenada, with Barbados to the east. Off the coast of Venezuela in the Southern Caribbean are Trinidad and Tobago, Aruba, Bonaire, and Curacao.

Climate: The most popular time to visit the Caribbean is traditionally in winter when blizzards dump their snow in the north. Winter tradewinds cool the islands resulting in an average temperature between 78° and 88° F. July through October seem to be the most uncomfortably hot months. Keep in mind: It is the humidity that will kill you, not the heat.

Plan on shopping in the cool morning hours and hitting the beach in the afternoon. The Caribbean sun can be brutal, so use lots of sunscreen, wear a hat, and try to spend some time under a shaded palm.

Now, on to the important stuff. **How to become a Caribbean bartender of stature!**

Introduction to Bartending in the Islands

Rum was cheaper than water when I moved to the islands more than fifteen years ago. I recall going into the local grocery store, Pueblo, and purchasing a bottle of rum for less than $2.00. It's still a good buy at $3.99 during the time this book was written. Rum and the Caribbean have indeed become synonymous. But, let's for a moment examine the history of that favorite pastime – cocktail hour.

The cocktail's birth in the United States is of undetermined date and essentially an American invention. Cocktail hour has become synonymous with relaxation. Inventive bartenders acquired immortality with their signature drinks, many of which have become classics, such as the Martini, the Greyhound, or the Ramos Fizz. At the Planter's Hotel in St. Louis, Tom Collins invented the infamous tall libation that carries his name in 1858, as well as the Planter's Punch. Now that surprised me. Having lived in the Caribbean half my life, I thought a Planter's Punch referred to a drink concocted by plantation owners of the sugar cane era.

Vacationing in the Caribbean gained status and drinks mixed with rum, fruit juices and coconut gained popularity. With the advent of the Banana Daiquiri, the Painkiller, and the Piña Colada came other creamy, exotic drinks such as the Mudslide, the Bushwhacker, and the Screaming Orgasm.

In this book, you will find all the recipes you will need to serve traditional drinks and the latest exotic libations from the tropics. There is also a basic and advanced list of supplies, tools, and ingredients. I have purposely made the tip section concise, but do read it carefully for optimum results.

Go on and put in a Calypso CD, kick back and imagine yourself in a hammock, under languidly swaying palms, with a frosty Yellow Bird in hand. For those of you who have read my cook and guidebooks before, welcome back to Paradise!

Fun Facts and History of Alcohol

We have all seen the old-time comedies where the actor pours himself a glass of rubbing (isopropyl) alcohol and drinks it. Do not try this. Only ethyl alcohol (ethanol) is safe to drink.

Ethanol is a clear, colorless liquid with a fiery taste and heady vapor. It has a low freezing point, below -40°C and is often used in thermometers or as antifreeze in radiators. Vodka in the freezer is delightful and almost syrupy in its consistency.

Ethanol forms as the result of a chemical reaction – the fermentation of sugars. Yeast enzymes, zymase, decompose simple sugars from starches (grain-beer, fruit- wine) into carbon dioxide and ethanol. Impure yeast cultures often produce other byproducts, including glycerin, fusel oil, and various organic acids. It is these impurities, which impart the characteristic, and prized flavor of whiskies, wines, and brandies.

Civilization begins with distillation. --William Faulkner

Not exactly true, but the first alcoholic beverage was probably discovered by accident some 10,000 years ago when someone left out a bottle of grape or fruit juice in a warm room. What a find! By 4000 B.C., Mid-eastern and Asian societies discovered the use of grapes for wine making. By 1000 B.C., the Egyptians joined the party and only the temple priests were allowed to make beer. The Greeks were passed the secret, who in turn gave it to the Romans. Each society produced a different alcoholic beverage, depending upon what was available. The Japanese used rice to produce sake, Africans used millet to make beer, the English made mead from honey, others used barley for beer, and the Mediterranean used grapes for wine. Each type of liquor has the same physiological affect with an entirely different flavor, color, and consistency.

The alcohol content of fermented beverages is low, no higher than 12%. About a 1000 years ago the Irish and Scotch discovered distillation, the process of heating a substance and reducing the water content. The reduction in water resulted in a much higher proof. The resulting drink was a type of whiskey full of impurities. In the early 19th century, the patent still produced grain neutral spirits.

In the 20th century, we experienced prohibition in the United States which fueled the growth of organized crime bootlegging. Recently, the health benefits of a glass of wine a day are touted everywhere. Moderation indeed. Today, experts are saying it doesn't have to be wine to be beneficial to the heart, as any alcohol will do. At any rate, the last word is if you don't drink, don't start just for health reasons. Enough of that confusion!

Part One:
The Basics

CHAPTER ONE
The Right Tools
Utensils and Glassware

If you're going to do the job right, good quality tools are essential. The following is a basic list of bar tools:

Utensils:

1. **Bar spoon:** A long spoon with a twirled handle and a small scoop on the end. Indispensable for stirring drinks in a tall glass, pouring liquor down the twirled part or on the back of the spoon to keep layers variegated on layered drinks.

2. **Blender:** Essential for frozen drinks. For home use, there's no need to purchase a costly $200 blender. They sure do look nice though. I splurged and spent $50 on my last blender because it claimed to crush ice. I was sorry I threw out the old one. Always put in the liquid first to the save the blade.

3. **Cocktail shaker set:** Includes a 16-ounce heavyweight mixing glass and a steel cup-like insert.

4. **Corkscrew:** There are four types of corkscrews: **double-action corkscrew,** which I prefer, locks onto the top of the bottle and as you turn the cork is extracted; **wing-type corkscrew** has two arms that lift as you turn the coil into the cork, push down on the arms and the cork comes out; **sommelier's corkscrew** resembles a Swiss Army knife and has the nice additions of a small knife and bottle opener; and the **old- fashioned wood on the bottom corkscrew** where you hold the bottle between your legs. The choice is yours.

5. **Ice bucket, scoop, and tongs:** A metal bucket is nice, but a small pail in a tropical color works also. Never, ever dig a glass into the ice bucket or use a scoop or tongs. Hands are off-limits.

6. **Jigger or pony:** Two-ended device measuring a 1/2 ounce on one side, the pony and 1 1/2 ounces, jigger, on the other.

7. **Knife or cutting board:** Many cocktails, especially island drinks, require fresh fruit. Purchase a small paring knife and a cutting board. After each use, dip the board in a mild bleach and water solution, rinsing well.

8. **Speed pourers:** These fit right into the mouth of a liquor bottle. Count one, two, three for a generous 1-1/2 ounces of liquor.

9. **Strainer:** This fits into the mouth of the shaker, holding back the ice, allowing you to pour the chilled drink into a glass.

10. **Water jug or pitcher:** It's a good idea to offer water to guests. Keep plenty on hand.

Glassware:

The following diagram is a partial list of all the glassware available for drinks. Few of us have room in our homes for all of them, so feel free to pick and choose. Be aware that using the correct glass makes all the difference to the flavor and presentation of drink. Imagine a champagne cocktail served in a clunky ceramic beer stein or a Piña Colada served in a rocks glass.

1. **Beer glasses:** These can hold as much as a liter. Chill in the freezer to frost the mug. Pilsner glasses, footed and shaped like a 'v' are used for bottled beer.
2. **Brandy snifter or balloon glass:** Classic, globular shape designed to funnel the bouquet of an exquisite cognac, brandy or armagnac. Sized from 4 to 24 ounces.
3. **Champagne:** Tall and narrow to conserve the bubbles.
4. **Cordial glass:** Useful for serving liqueurs straight up
5. **Highball or Highball glass:** Tall, narrow, and versatile glass holding between 8 and 12 ounces used for Singapore Sling, Sloe Gin Fizz, Collins's, etc.
6. **Martini or martini glass:** Martinis, Manhattan, or other cocktails served straight up.
7. **Old-fashioned or rocks glass:** Perfect for serving a drink on-the-rocks or with just a splash of soda or water, holds between 5 and 10 ounces.
8. **Shot glass:** Also used as a measuring device, 1 to 2 ounces in size.
9. **Wine/ white:** Comes in 5 to 10 ounce size. I prefer the larger size and not refill constantly. Of course, a chilled wine will warm more quickly in a larger glass; therefore, it's a trade-off. Usually narrower bowl than the red.
10. **Wine/ red:** Available in 5 to 16 ounce size. The wide bowl allows the wine to mix with the air, i.e. breathe.

CHAPTER TWO

Setting Up Your Home Bar: A Checklist

Basic Bar :

- ❑ One 750-ml bottle of aperitif such as: Pernod, Campari, Jagermeister, Lillet
- ❑ One 750-ml bottle of bourbon
- ❑ One 750-ml bottle of brandy or cognac
- ❑ One 750-ml bottle of scotch
- ❑ One 750-ml bottle of gin (domestic or imported)
- ❑ One 750-ml bottle of rum (light)
- ❑ One 750-ml bottle of tequila
- ❑ One 750-ml bottle of dry vermouth
- ❑ One 750-ml bottle of vodka (domestic or imported)
- ❑ One 750-ml bottle of whiskey (domestic or imported)
- ❑ One 750-ml bottle of Grand Marnier
- ❑ One 750-ml bottle of Sambuca or other anisette-flavored liqueur
- ❑ One 750-ml bottle of Bailey's Irish Cream Liqueur liqueur
- ❑ One 750-ml bottle of Kahlua or other coffee liqueur
- ❑ One 750-ml bottle of white crème de menthe
- ❑ One 750-ml bottle of Amaretto or other almond liqueur
- ❑ Six bottles of beer (domestic or imported)
- ❑ Six bottles of light beer (domestic or imported)
- ❑ One 750-ml bottle of champagne
- ❑ Two bottles of domestic chardonnay or white wine of choice
- ❑ One bottle of red wine

Hint! Use mostly better brands. You don't want your guests to think you're cheap.

Better-stocked Bar :

Add the following to the above:

- ❑ One 750-ml bottle of aperitif
- ❑ One 750-ml bottle of flavored rum, i.e. coconut, pineapple,
- ❑ One 750-ml bottle of flavored vodka, i.e. lemon, orange, coconut
- ❑ One 750-ml bottle of Canadian whiskey
- ❑ One 750-ml bottle of Irish whiskey
- ❑ One 750-ml bottle of 12-year-old scotch
- ❑ One 750-ml bottle of single-malt scotch
- ❑ One 750-ml bottle of sweet vermouth
- ❑ One 750-ml bottle of gold tequila
- ❑ One 750-ml bottle of V.S.O.P. cognac
- ❑ One 750-ml bottle of Peach Schnapps
- ❑ One 750-ml bottle of Galliano
- ❑ One 750-ml bottle of B&B

Deluxe Bar :

Add to the above two lists:

- ❑ One 750-ml bottle of armagnac
- ❑ One 750-ml bottle of Blue Curacao
- ❑ One 750-ml bottle of Chambord
- ❑ One 750-ml bottle of imported brandy (Portugal, Spain, etc.)
- ❑ One 750-ml bottle of Cointreau
- ❑ One 750-ml bottle of Chartreuse
- ❑ One 750-ml bottle of Frangelico
- ❑ One 750-ml bottle of imported premium gin
- ❑ One 750-ml bottle of dark rum
- ❑ One 750-ml bottle of aged rum
- ❑ One 750-ml bottle of 151° rum
- ❑ One 750-ml bottle of flavored rum (different from above)
- ❑ One 750-ml bottle of flavored vodka (different from above)
- ❑ One 750-ml bottle of imported premium vodka
- ❑ Twelve bottles of imported beer
- ❑ One 750-ml bottle of imported champagne
- ❑ Two bottles of imported white wine
- ❑ Two bottle of imported red wine

The following is needed for all bars:

Mixers :

One bottle each:

- ❑ Orange juice
- ❑ Cranberry juice
- ❑ Pineapple juice
- ❑ Tomato juice
- ❑ Grapefruit juice
- ❑ Coca-cola
- ❑ Lemon-lime soda
- ❑ Ginger ale
- ❑ Tonic water
- ❑ Sparkling water or seltzer

Garnishes, condiments, etc :

- ❑ Lemon twists
- ❑ Lemon and lime wedges
- ❑ Lime slices
- ❑ Orange slices
- ❑ Pineapple slice
- ❑ Cherries
- ❑ Olives
- ❑ Onions
- ❑ Rock salt, crushed
- ❑ Simple syrup
- ❑ Superfine sugar
- ❑ Celery Stalks
- ❑ Salt and Pepper
- ❑ Tabasco™
- ❑ Horseradish
- ❑ Worcestershire
- ❑ Bitters
- ❑ Grenadine syrup
- ❑ Rose's Lime syrup

Hint! Use white pepper as it will be invisible in drinks.

CHAPTER THREE

Parties: How Much to Buy

Step 1: Getting the Right Supplies

LIQUOR CHART:

Booze 750-ml bottles	4-8 guests	8-15 guests	15-25 guests	25-35 guests	35-55 guests	55-75 guests
White wine, domestic	2	4	6	8	10	14
White wine, imported	1	2	2	3	4	6

Hint! Each bottle of wine serves four glasses. Adjust amounts according to whether your guests are wine or liquor drinkers. Estimate at two glasses of wine per wine drinker.

	4-8 guests	8-15 guests	15-25 guests	25-35 guests	35-55 guests	55-75 guests
Red wine, domestic	1	1	2	2	3	3
Red wine, imported	1	1	1	1	2	3
Champagne, domestic	2	3	3	3	4	4
Champagne, imported	1	2	2	3	4	4
Vermouth, dry	1	1	1	1	2	2
Aperitifs, your selection	1	1	2	2	3	4
Bourbon	1	1	1	1	1	1
Brandy or cognac	1	1	1	2	3	3
Cordials, your selection	1	2	2	3	3	3
Gin	1	1	2	2	2	3
Rum	1	1	2	2	3	3
Scotch	1	1	2	2	3	3
Vodka	1	2	2	3	3	4
Whisky, U.S. or Canadian	1	1	1	1	2	2
Whiskey, Irish	1	1	1	1	2	2
Beer (12 ounce bottles)	24	36	60	78	120	168

MIXERS, FRUITS, CONDIMENTS, ETC. CHART:

Item	8-10 guests	8-15 guests	15-25 guests	25-35 guests	35-55 guests	55-75 guests
Juices (quarts)						
Cranberry	1	2	2	3	3	4
Orange	1	2	2	3	3	4
Grapefruit	1	2	2	2	3	4
Tomato	1	2	2	2	3	4
Soda (2-liter)						
Club soda	3	3	4	4	5	6
Cola	3	3	3	4	5	6
Diet Cola	2	3	3	4	4	5
Ginger ale	1	2	2	2	2	3
Lemon-lime soda	1	2	2	3	3	4
Tonic water	1	2	2	3	3	4
Assorted necessary extras:						
Milk (quart)	1	1	1	1	2	3
Mineral water (1-liter)	2	2	3	4	5	6
Ice (5 lb. bag)	1 1/2	3	5	7	10	15
Napkins	25	45	75	100	150	225
Stirrers (1000/box)	1	1	1	1	1	1
Superfine sugar (box)	1	1	1	1	1	1
Simple syrup (quart)	1/2	1/2	1	1	1	1
Tobasco (bottle)	1	1	1	1	1	1
Worcestershire	1	1	1	1	1	1
Horseradish (jar)	1	1	1	1	1	2
Salt, rock crushed (box)	1	1	1	1	1	1
Pepper, small tin	1	1	1	1	1	1
Cream of Coconut (can)	1	1	2	2	3	3
Grenadine (bottle)	1	1	1	1	1	1
Rose Lime juice (bottle)	1	1	1	1	1	1
Lemons	2	3	4	5	6	7
Limes	1	2	3	4	5	6
Maraschino cherries (jar)	1	1	1	1	1	1
Olives, green (jar)	1	1	1	1	1	1
Oranges	1	1	2	3	4	4
Pineapple (garnish)	1/2	1	1	2	2	3

Five Things That Will Influence Your Purchases

Age: Amount and type of liquor to purchase will fluctuate with the age of the partiers and time of year. For the under 35 crowd, decrease the hard liquor and beer by one half. Increase the white wine by half. For older guests, purchase more dark alcohols. They will also appreciate better brands.

Season: In cooler weather, reduce the beer. Stock up on darker alcohols, coffee drinks, red wine, etc. Summer revelers will drink lighter drinks, spritzers, light-colored alcohols, i.e. vodka, gin, etc.

Special Occasions and Holidays: Expect to serve eggnog at Christmas, champagne at New Year's and weddings, etc. For Caribbean or island-themed parties, stock up on light and dark rums.

Guests Preferences: It is often difficult to prejudge a crowd. If you do know your guests tastes, adjust your purchases accordingly. There is no sense stocking a full bar, if all your friends prefer California chardonnay.

Time of Day: Start morning brunches with Mimosas, Bloody Marys, Sloe Gin Fizzs and Screwdrivers. As the day progresses, add more liquor and variety. Before dinner cocktails should be light, stimulating to appetite, not knocking guests out. Serve after dinner alcoholic coffees, brandies, and liqueurs.

Liquor

For the average four-hour cocktail party, purchase one liter of hard alcohol for every six guests. Do not be tempted to purchase the larger bottle because they are a better buy. You will need two hands to pour these oversize bottles and be miserable.

Think about your budget and the quality of liquor you wish to purchase. Who will attend this party? Your future mate, boss, client, or in-laws? In that case, buy the best quality you can afford. For a neighborhood party, buy cheaper, recognizable names. For a large block party, choose the least expensive brands. You can get away with just about anything if making punch. Mixed drinks go hand in hand with less expensive lighter-colored alcohols, vodka, rum, gin, etc.

Wine

This varies from party to party. Younger guests will drink more wine. White wine predominates in summer, a bit less so in winter. Never serve anything without a cork in it. Know your crowd.

Beer

For the average four-hour cocktail party, purchase one case of beer for every ten guests. Adjust accordingly if you have advance knowledge of their preferences. The under 35 crowd will drink more beer. Consider purchasing a keg for more than 70 guests. A keg will serve about 165 12 ounce bottles of beer.

For peak flavor, place the keg in a large tub and pack with chunks of ice. Cover with a towel to keep the ice from melting too quickly. Be sure to ask for instructions on how to work the keg as they all vary somewhat.

Mixers

Plan on two quarts of mixers for every liter of alcohol. Older guests tend to drink darker alcohols, straight. Less mixers are needed depending on the age of the crowd. The most popular mixers are fruit juice, cola, and water. Don't forget diet soda.

Punch

For more than 12 guests, try serving a punch. Many of the Caribbean mixed fruit drinks in this book will lend themselves to a larger recipe. Estimate about four servings per guest.

Ice

For the average four hour cocktail party, have on hand 1 lb. of ice per person. See Bartending 101 for more tips on ice.

Food

You must have food at a cocktail party. Period. I made this mistake the other day. My assistant, her landlord, and another sales rep of our company came over for cocktails before Thanksgiving Dinner. I had assumed it would be a quick glass of wine or two, then off to dinner. The girls neglected to mention that dinner had been moved back an hour. We had terrible hangovers the next day, which we barely managed to hide from our only male employee. See the chapter on Exotic Appetizers, Bar Munchies and Finger Food.

Step 2: Setting Up

Once you have made all your purchases, you will want to set up the bar in an attractive and efficient way. Be sure the table can support the weight of liquor bottles. Cover with a colorful plastic tablecloth and top with a white linen one if desired. Spills are easier to clean if the bar is located near the kitchen.

For parties under 20 guests, no designated bartender is required. See the diagram to set up a self-service bar. You will need one bartender for up to 100 guests. See diagram for one-person bar. For parties over 100 guests, two bartenders are necessary. See diagram. Note there are two sets of liquor bottles, one for each bartender. Mixers are shared.

Be sure to set the bar in an area away from traffic, preferably against a wall. Tipsy guests, you know.

Step 3: Party's Over!

This is very simple. Take a few tips from professional bars. First, announce last call at least 45 minutes before the designated end of the party. Then just pack up the bar. If you have any extra light switches to throw on, do so.

Keep an eye out for guests who have had too much to drink. When in doubt, do not let an intoxicated guest drive home. You can even be legally liable and sued. Either drive the guest home yourself or call them a cab.

Diagram 1: A self-service bar

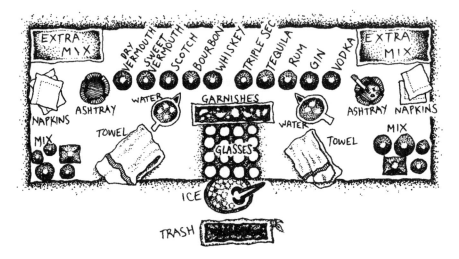

Diagram 2: A one-person bar

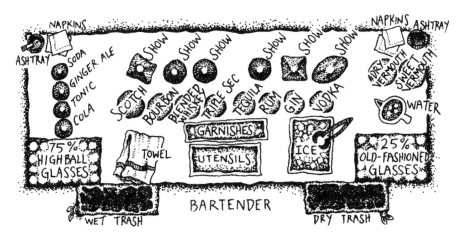

Diagram 3: A two-person bar

CHAPTER FOUR

Bartending 101
Secrets & What To Do With Everything

The Two Secrets of Every Good Drink

Ice. Pure and fresh. You've seen old ice with its fur, ice-crystal ridge. Ugh! It tastes horrendous to boot. Poor quality ice can impart an off or foreign taste to drinks. Tap water will often have minerals or chlorine added. Ice will absorb the flavors of foods stored in the vicinity. Can you imagine storing fish bait or liver next to the ice?

Choose a quality grade of bottled water with a low mineral content. A strong mineral water may be nice to drink straight, but will ruin a cocktail. Pure, unadulterated ice will bring a clean and sparkling flavor and appearance to drinks. The raves from your guests will be worth the extra care.

Many bartenders are under the erroneous assumption that they are being generous when pouring drinks with little ice. Every good drink must have enough ice to cool it sufficiently. This does not mean making watery , weak, unappetizing drinks. To avoid melting, especially in the heat of the tropics, mix your drinks using adequate amounts of ice, quickly.

A last word on ice. Be prepared with at least twice as much ice as you think you will need. An extra bag of ice, can save a party .

Be sure to chill all glasses. As mentioned, heavyweight beer mugs may be kept in the freezer. Lukewarm drinks are mediocre and a warm glass will melt the ice, resulting in a diluted drink.

Mixers. Water, sodas, juices and syrups are the least costly part of your bar ingredients. So, purchase high-quality ingredients for optimum results.

Mixers, especially carbonated ones, lose their sparkle and freshness after a day. Always open fresh, chilled bottles. I prefer the smaller 12 ounce bottles of soda to the larger ones, unless of course you're entertaining a crowd.

Never open a warm bottle of soda. Most of the fizz will be all over you, possibly the guests and the floor instead of in the drink.

Fruit

Garnish and Garbage: The right glass can do much to improve the appearance of a drink. Equally important to taste and appearance are the little extra's a bartender garnishes or drops into a drink.

Bartenders, to denote fruits and vegetables, use the words garnish and garbage interchangeably. In reality, they mean two entirely different things. A garnish changes the taste of a drink, such as a lime wedge in a rum and coke, a.k.a. Cuba Libre, or a lemon twist in an Old Fashioned. Garbage is meant to make the drink look appealing, i.e. olive in a Martini or pineapple and cherry on a Piña Colada.

Here are some common garnishes and garbages and how to handle them:

Lemon twists:
See illustration

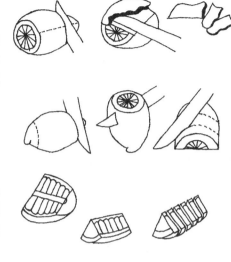

1. Cut off the two lemon ends.
2. Make a lengthwise cut between the two ends you just cut off. Use a spoon and insert it between the rind and the fruit, separating them.
3. Cut the rind into 1/4 inch strips.

Lime wedges:
See illustration

1. Cut the lime in half through its equator. Place the exposed fruit flat on a cutting board and slice from top to bottom. Then repeat, cutting into quarters. You should have eight wedges.

Orange slices:
See illustration

1. Starting at stem, not at the equator, cut fruit in half.
2. Cut in half again, length-side.
3. Slice into wedges.

Pineapple slices:
See illustration

1. Slice off top and bottom of fruit.
2. Cut in half length-wise.
3. Lay fruit flat side down and cut in half again, length-wise.
4. Place fruit on end and slice off fibrous core.
5. Slice into wedges.

Maraschino Cherries:
Always use stemmed cherries. Drinkers like to pick up the cherry by the stem and either pop it into their mouths or play with them.

Olives:
Olives should be green, pitted and minus the pimento.

Onion:
Purchase tiny cocktail onions. Do not use fresh onion in Gibsons.

A few more tips:

Bloody Mary Condiments: Always have fresh celery on hand for these drinks. Keep any or all-on hand for these drinks: Tabasco™, Worcestershire, horseradish, white and black pepper.

Nutmeg: Purchase fresh nutmeg wherever possible and a tiny grater for Bushwhackers, Painkillers, Brandy Alexanders and eggnogs.

Salt: Keep a plate of crushed rock salt on hand for Margaritas, Salty Dogs, etc.

Sugar: Use the superfine granulated kind. It will dissolve quicker.

Shake or Stir?

Never shake a carbonated drink. I'd like to say that clear drinks are stirred and cloudy drinks are shaken. unless otherwise instructed. However, you will find extensive use of a cocktail shaker in this book. I just like the way it chills the drink to an appropriate temperature for best taste.

To shake a drink in a bar shaker, half fill the glass portion of the shaker with ice, pouring the cocktail ingredients over the ice. Place the metal container over the glass. Be sure to hold the bottom and top together firmly and shake. Point away from people and furniture!

If the two pieces become stuck, tap gently. Fit a strainer over the glass if the drink is desired without ice. Always pour from the glass not the metal.

How to Pour

Method 1: Insert a speed pourer into the end of a 750-ml liquor bottle and count one, two, three. Practice until you can measure out 1-1/2 ounces consistently.

Method 2: Measure the liquor into a jigger (1 1/2 ounces). Accurate, but slow.

Removing Corks from Wine and Champagne Bottles

Wine:

1. Use a sharp knife or the blade on a wine opener and cut off the foil.
2. Wipe the top of the bottle with a clean damp cloth.
3. Center the corkscrew over the cork and insert. There is no need to come out at the other end of the cork. Go in far enough (about 3/4) to extract the cork.
4. Attach the lever of the opener to the lip of the bottle. Either push the wings down or pull out the cork depending on the style of opener.
5. Wipe the top of the bottle again.

Champagne:

1. Remove wire and foil from bottle.
2. Hold the bottle away from people, yourself and furnishings.
3. Hold the bottle in one hand, grab the cork with the other hand and twist the bottle gently.
4. Keep a cloth handy to wipe up spills. Remember the contents are under pressure.

Simple Syrup

Dissolve one pound of sugar in one quart boiling water, until thickened. Keep refrigerated. Discard after one month.

A Few Basic Measurements

Measurement	Metric Equivalent	Standard
1 teaspoon	3.7 ml	1/8 ounce
1 tablespoon	11.1 ml	3/8 ounce
1 jigger	44.5 ml	1 1/2 ounces
1 pony	29.5 ml	1 ounce
1/2 pint	257.0 ml	8 ounces
1 pint	472.0 ml	16 ounces
1 quart	944.0 ml	32 ounce

Servings Per 750-ml Bottle

1 ounce	25 servings
1 1/4 ounce	20 servings
1-1/2 ounce	17 servings

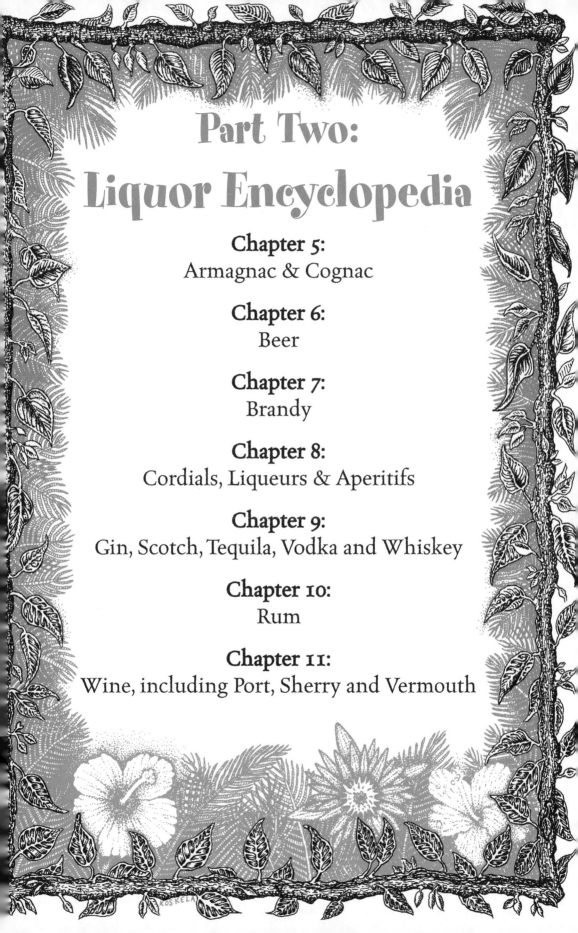

Part Two:
Liquor Encyclopedia

CHAPTER FIVE
Armagnac and Cognac

Armagnac is France's oldest brandy made in the Armagnac region of southwestern France since the 15th century. Two delicate stages encompass distillation. White wine is heated in a continuous still at a low temperature. The alcohol vapor passes through coils, resulting in a 63 percent alcohol spirit. It is then aged in oak barrels from Armagnac, Trancais, or Limousin. Aging can last up to sixty or seventy years. Any more than that, and it deteriorates in flavor. After bottling, unlike wine, the Armagnac stops aging. A fifteen-year-old Armaganc bottled in 1890 is still only a fifteen-year-old Armagnac.

There is a great deal of confusion over how to read Armagnac labels.

V.S. or Three Stars	the youngest brandy in the blend is at least 3 years old
V.O.	very old supposedly, but at least 4 1/2 years old
Extra, Napoleon, X.O. Vielle Reserve	at least 5 1/2 years old
V.S.O.P.	very superior old pale, as long as 10 years

Popular Armagnac

Sempe	6 to 15 years old, Extra Grand Reserve 35 to 50 years, blended
Janneau	aged 8 to 10 years
Aramagnac Lapostolle X.O.	fine brand, aged over 30 years

Cognac is made only in Cognac, France and is considered the champagne of the brandies. The distillation process is similar to Armagnac. All cognac is aged at 30 months. The labels are similar to Armagnac, with a couple of additions.

Grand Fine Champagne	made from grapes grown in the Grande Champagne region of Cognac
Petite Fine Champagne	made from a blend of grapes between Grande Champagne and Petite Champagne region of Cognac.

Popular Cognac

Courvoisier
Hennessy
Martell
Remy Martin

All produce various labels, such as V.S., V.S.O.P., Napoleon, X.O, Grand Champagne, etc.

Storing and Serving

Both Armagnac and cognac are known as after-dinner drinks, usually served neat. Smoothly aged cognacs vary in aroma and flavor. Some have a mild vanilla flavor, others grape, some have a caramel hint. All are 80 proof. Serve at room temperature in brandy snifters.

Storage in a cool dry place will ensure that an opened bottle will last for two years.

CHAPTER SIX

Beer

Beer is made from a variety of grains including hops, barley, corn, and even rice. Mostly it is made from malted barley, corn, and water. Barley, which has been soaked in water, germinates. Didn't know you were drinking sprouted beer, did you? The resulting malt is added to corn grits, cooked, and blended. Wort, a sweet liquid, is removed from the mash, where it is boiled. Hops are added to the wort, and then cooled. Sugar is converted into alcohol and carbon dioxide when yeast is added. If bottom yeast is added, the result is lager. Top yeast produces ale. Fermentation is carefully timed.

Different Beers

Ale	slightly bitter, with a higher alcohol content-top fermented
Bock	my parents enjoyed this; caramel hint, dark, slightly sweet
Ice	brewed with very cold water, then frozen; when the ice crystals are removed, it leaves a higher proof and smooth taste
Lager	stored at very cold temperatures for an extended time, bottom fermented
Lambic	lovely ingredients such as raspberries, peaches and cherries are added
Light	while I enjoy this, I truly think this is watered down beer
Malt	higher alcohol content from fermenting at warmer temperature
Pilsner	light beer, strong hop overtones
Sake	learn something new everyday; sake is not a rice wine-it's Japanese beer made from rice!
Stout	bitter, made from roasted barley
Trappist	dark, high proof, made by Trappist monks in the Netherlands

CHAPTER SEVEN

Brandy

Finally, I know what "weinbrand" means in German. My parents would use this word with reverence and allow me sips of apricot, pear and cherry brandies from Austria (highly prized by them) and Germany. Meaning burnt wine, brandy is distilled from wine or fruit, and then aged in oak barrels.

Brandy was most likely the first product of the still. Called "Eau-de vivre," meaning water of life, it replaced foul, disease-carrying water prevalent during the Middle Ages. It was also thought to alleviate illnesses and prolong life. Four processes are involved: fermentation of the fruit, distillation, aging in oak barrels and blending.

American brandy accounts for one out of every four bottles of brandy sold in the U.S. Most are made from Thompson Seedless and Flame Tokay grapes using continuous stills. All California brandy must be aged at least two years in oak barrels. The longer the aging, the more mellow the brandy.

French brandies are usually clear. Well known is Calvados, made from apples and aged ten to fifteen years. Pear brandy is made from the Williams or Bartlett pear. Framboise comes from raspberries, fraise from strawberries, Mirabelle from plus, and Kirsch from cherries. Do not confuse kirsch with cherry liqueur or cordials. It does get confusing when in the U.S. fruit brandies are treated as cordials and have sugar added to them. They are still high in proof – 70. The kirsch, a brandy, is much higher in proof! Other countries such as Austria, Germany, Greece, Holland, Peru, and Switzerland also produce fine, exotic brandies.

Popular brandy

Applejack	apple brandy, U.S.
Calvados	apple brandy, France
Framboise	strawberry brandy, France
Kirsch	cherry brandy, France
Poire	pear, Switzerland, Austria, France
Slivovitz	plum, Germany or Hungary

CHAPTER EIGHT

Cordials, Liqueurs, Aperitifs

Folklore abounds when it comes to aperitifs and liqueurs. Some say they were originally intended as appetite enhancers. Many liqueurs were originally created as medicines. Curacao was thought to prevent scurvy. The word aperitif comes from Latin and means to open. Others say liqueurs were originally intended as aphrodisiacs. There is some debate over that.

For the sake of conciseness, we will call all aperitifs and cordials liqueurs in this chapter. Most liqueurs are made from various herbs, fruits, berries and spices. All have at least 2.5% sugar and most are much sweeter than that. Liqueurs make excellent flavor enhancers for ice cream toppings, soufflés, sauces, and deserts.

Liqueurs are made by infusion (steeping in water, like tea), maceration (steeping in alcohol), percolation (like making coffee) or distillation (mixing with alcohol in a still). Cream liqueurs are homogenized with alcohol, which also preserves the liqueur.

There are hundreds of different liqueurs. Do not confuse the fruit brandies produced in the U.S. with the brandies produced in Europe, such as kirshwasser, which uses no sugar. For instance, a cherry liqueur, cherry-flavored brandy, and cherry brandy are as different as night and day. A cherry liqueur has a low alcohol content (48 - 60 proof) and is sweet and syrupy. A cherry-flavored brandy has about 70 proof alcohol and is not quite as sweet as the former. A cherry brandy has a high proof, 70 to 100 and is not sweet or made with sugar.

To make things simple, the liqueurs have been loosely grouped by their flavors and some are interchangeable within the same group.

Berries

Blackberry Brandy (American): Very popular in the U.S.

Black Haus: Blackberries

Boggs Cranberry Liqueur: Cranberry

Chambord: Black raspberry, various fruits and botanicals. Purple in color. Very nice at the bottom of a glass with a champagne or wine float.

Coing: Rare, clear spirit made from quince.

Cordial Medoc (France): Made in Bordeaux from raspberry, orange, cacao and other botanicals with a brandy base.

Cranberria: Cranberry

Crème de cassis (French): Black currant, various fruits and berries.

Echte Kroatzbeere: Blackberries

Fraise: Strawberry

Framberry: The Alsatian firm of Dolfi produces this raspberry liqueur.

Framboise: Clear strawberry brandy.

Groseille: Clear distilled spirit made from currants.

Guavaberry: Rum and local berries only made on St. Maarten. Fruit found high in hills on center of island. Woody, fruity, bitter-sweet.

Himbergeist (German): I used to drink this as a child. O.K. just a little bit. Means spirit of the raspberry.

Houx: Rare, clear spirit made from holly berries in Alsace.

Kirsch: Cherries.

Kirshwasser: Brandy made from fermented cherries.

Lakka (Finland): Made from Arctic cloudberry by the firm of Marli in Turku.

Maraschino: Cherries

Mure: Clear spirit made from blackberry or mulberry.

Myrtille: Clear spirit made from whortleberry or bilberry. Can be called airelle.

Prunelle: Sloeberry, similar to Sloe gin.

Sloe gin (France): Made from the sloeberry, a small purple plum and a bit of gin.

Sureau (Alsace): Made from elderberries

> **Did you know?** GUAVABERRY is the legendary island folk liqueur made on St. Maarten in the West Indies, first made hundreds of years ago. Distilled from the finest rum, cane sugar and wild local berries found high in the warm hills of St. Maarten.
>
> Guavaberries are not like the guava fruit at all. There are two species of guavaberry, black and orange fruit, with a slight difference in taste between the two.
>
> The aged liqueur has a woody, fruity, spicy, and bittersweet flavor.-courtesy of Sint Maarten Guavaberry Company *www.guavaberry.com*

Cacao or Chocolate

Afri-Koko (Africa): Made in Sierra Leone, chocolate-coconut flavored.

Cacao Creole (St. Lucia): Rum and chocolate.

Calypso Island Amaretto Chocolate: fabulous, almond-chocolate

Calypso Island Banana-Chocolate Liqueur: reminiscent of chocolate-covered bananas

Calypso Island Chocolate Liqueur: nice finish, not too sweet

Calypso Island Chocolate-Mint Liqueur: like a peppermint patty

Calypso Island Coconut-Chocolate Liqueur: like a Mounds' candy bar

Calypso Island Raspberry-Chocolate Liqueur: out of this world!

Choclair: Another coconut and chocolate liqueur.

Crème de Cacao: Available in clear or dark. Blend of vanilla and cacao beans.

Droste Bittersweet Chocolate Liqueur: Chocolate, not too sweet.

Godet Belgian White Chocolate Liqueur: Aged cognac and Belgian White Chocolate.

Godiva Cappuccino Liqueur: Luscious, creamy coffee-flavored liqueur

Godiva Liqueuer: chocolate liqueur

Godiva White Chocolate Liqueuer: Rich, decadent white chocolate liqueur

Marmot (Switzerland): Has little pieces of chocolate in the liqueur.

Mozart Chocolate Liqueur (Austria): I had Mozart chocolates for the first time while on a trip with my attorney. They were divine. The chocolates are praline-nougat and chocolate. The liqueur is blended with kirsch. Fabulous.

Royal Mint-Chocolate Liqueur: self-explanatory

Sabra (Israel): A chocolate liqueur flavored with orange. There is also a coffee orange version.

Vandermint (Dutch): Chocolate with a hint of mint.

Wild Spirit: High in alcohol, herbs and an undertone of cacao.

Cinnamon

Goldschlager (Switzerland): This packs a punch. Cinnamon with 24-karat gold flakes.

Coconut

Beach Comber: fresh cream, rum, coconut

Malibu: white rum and coconut liqueur

Coffee

Coffee Brandy: Brandy and coffee

Coffee Espresso (Italy): Coffee

Crème de mocha: Coffee

Gallway's Irish Coffee Liqueur: Coffee

Kahlua: There is some dispute about the origins of this liqueur made from coffee and alcohol distilled from cane sugar. Rumors of Middle East abound, Morocco, Arabia, or Turkey. Made in Mexico today. Hint of chocolate as well.

Nassau Royale: Strong citrus flavor with a touch of coffee. Mmm.

Pasha Turkish Coffee Liqueur: Coffee

Rumba: Caribbean coffee liqueur made with rum

Tia Maria (Jamaica): Made from Blue Mountain Coffee, rum and spices.

Ti Tase (St. Lucia): Coffee

You can interchange these if you run out of one (except the Nassau Royale).

Cream

Amaretto Cream liqueur: Amaretto and cream
Bailey's Irish Cream Liqueur: Cream and Irish Whiskey and assorted other flavors
Belle Bonne:
Carolan's:
Crème de la Cave (St. Lucia): Rum and cream.
Cruzan Rum Cream (St. Croix, USVI): Rum and cream.
Devonshire: Irish Cream liqueur
Dunphy's:
Emmet's:
Heather Cream Liqueur: Cream and Scotch Malt Whiskey
McGuire's Original Cream:
Myer's Rum Cream:
O'Darby's:
St. Brendan's:
Toasted Almond Cream:
Tropical Lady (St. Lucia): Coconut milk, cream, rum, and spices.
Venetian Cream:
Waterford:

These liqueurs contain cream, alcohol and other flavors. They go well in coffee drinks. The alcohol keeps the cream from spoiling.

Fruits

Abricotine (French): Apricot liqueur
Airelle: Cranberry or bilberry
Alize: Passion fruit juice and cognac.
Amer Picon (French): Smooth blend of African oranges, gentian root, quinine. Low in alcohol. Serve with sparkling water over ice.
Applejack: Apples and brandy.
Apricot Brandy (American): Apricots and brandy.
Apry: Made by the firm of Marie Brizzard, apricot cordial.
Aurum (Italy): Golden orange flavored liqueur.
Barak Palinka: Clear spirit distilled from apricot fruit and pits.
Bergamot (Germany): Brandy-based made from bergamot which has an intense citrus taste.
Blackberry Strasberg: blackberry by Bols
Bohemian Raspberry: made by Bols, raspberry liqueur
Calvados: An apple brandy made in Normandy, France that is aged about four years.
Cerasella (Italy): Cherry
Cerise: Cherry
Cheristock (Italian): Cherry
Cherry-Flavored Liqueur: cherry by Bols
Cherry Heering (Denmark): Very rich and powerful cherry flavor.
Cherry Marnier (France): Cherry
Cocoribe (Virgin Islands): Coconut blended with rum. Delightful.
Cointreau (French): Blend of sweet and bitter oranges. Nearly clear in color. Excellent flavoring for baking as well.
Crème de banane: Banana
Crème de d'anana: Pineapple
Crème de Grand Marnier: cream-based Grand Marnier
Crème de Grand Passion: cream-based passionfruit liqueur
Cuarenta Y Tres: Mediterranean liqueur made from citrus, vanilla, herbs and other fruits.
Curacao: Comes in orange and blue. Be sure to use the blue when color is specified. Made from bitter oranges grown on the Caribbean island of Curacao.
DeKuyper (The Netherlands): Cherry
Forbidden Fruit (American): A rare grapefruit liqueur.
Grand Marnier: Oranges and cognac.
Grant's Morella Cherry Brandy (England): Cherry
KoKonut Rum (St. Lucia): Coconut and rum
Lile Supreme: An assortment of fruits including orange, lime, mango, lychee, goyavier combined with rum.
Malibu: Caribbean rum and coconut.
Mandarin Napoleon (Brussels): Tangerine-flavored liqueur with cognac base.
Melon: green melon liqueur by Bols
Midori: Made from green honeydew melons.
Mirabelle: Clear spirit made from yellow plums.
Old Sint Maarten Lime Liqueur: rum/lime St. Maarten
Old Sint Maarten Mango Liqueur: rum/mango St. Maarten
Old Sint Maarten Passionfruit Liqueur: rum/passionfruit St. Maarten
Orange Bliss (St. Lucia): Bitter liqueur for an older drinker.
Passoa Passion Fruit Liqueur: I see this all over in the Caribbean. From Brazil, contains passion fruit, berries, citrus and other island fruits.
Peach Schnapps: Peach
Persico (Dutch): Made by Bols, peach liqueur with shades almonds and other flavors.
Pisang Ambon (Dutch): Green, bitter orange and spice flavored.
Poire Williams: Excellent clear spirit made from Williams or Bartlett pears.
Quetsch: Purple plum.
Rochet Cherry Brandy (France): Cherry
Slivovitz (Croatia): Plum brandy reminiscent of Quetsch, aged in wooden barrels.
Southern Comfort: Peaches, herbs, brandy and bourbon. Really nice.
Touee: Caribbean island key lime and rum liqueur
Triple Sec: This liqueur has three distillations and is a

combination of Curacao oranges and Valencia oranges.

Tuaca: Oranges and other herbs native to Tuscany, Italy blended with an aged brandy.

Van Der Hum (Dutch South Africa): Tangerine and brandy.

Yukon Jack (Canadian): Whiskey with citrus and botanicals.

Wisniak (Poland): Cherry.

Cocoribe and Malibu are used in tropical drinks or on the rocks.

Cointreau is clear and bittersweet and is not easily interchangeable with the orange-colored and much heavier Grand Marnier. Curacao comes in numerous colors, such as blue, yellow, green, red and clear. Be sure to use the blue only if specified. Cointreau may be substituted for triple sec.

Recently there have arrived many new melon liqueurs. Taste them first if possible.

Herbs, Spice and Botanicals

Aquavit: Caraway and potato.

B & B: Benedictine and cognac.

Benedictine: Contains in excess of 27 herbs, botanicals and spices, including: cloves, nutmeg, cardamom, myrrh, vanilla. Cognac based. The monks will also kill you if the recipe is stolen.

Bronte (English): Made from herbs, fruits and spices. A.k.a. Yorkshire liqueur.

Byrrh (France): Aperitif with a hint of orange and quinine.

Bunratty Meade: Herbs, honey and wine.

Cachaca: Distilled from sugarcane sap. Rum flavor and background of vanilla and other botanicals.

Calisay (Spain): Quinine-flavored liqueur from Barcelona.

Campari (Italian): A bright red aperitif made from spices, fruits, herbs and roots.

Canton Ginger: ginger-flavored liqueur

Certosa (Italian): Similar to Chartreuse.

Chartreuse: Made by the Carthusian monks near Grenoble since the seventeenth century. See below.

Crème de menthe: Mint, comes in clear and green.

Crème de violet: Violet

Crème de Yvette: Another violet colored and flavored liqueur.

Danziger Goldwasser: Spicy, citrus flavor with gold flakes.

Der Lachs Goldwasser: Contains 22-karat gold flakes, 25 herbs and spices

Drambuie: Herbs, honey, and 15-year-old malted whiskey

Estomacal-Bonet (Spain): Similar to Izzara.

Fernet Branca (Italian): Heady, aromatic resulting in a bitter blend of 40 botanicals and spices including: rhubarb, chamomile, cardamom, saffron and myrrh.

Fior d'Alpe (Italy): Characterized by a twig in the bottle decorated with rock candy. Herbal.

Fleurs d'Acacia (Alsatian): Clear spirit made with acacia flowers.

Galliano: Another lovely liqueur. Pale yellow with over 30 botanicals, including: vanilla, juniper, yarrow musk, anise, and lavender.

Gilka (German): Reminiscent of Kummel with a cumin-caraway flavor.

Ginger Liqueur: ginger liqueur by Bols

Glayva (Scottish): Similar to Drambuie, but made with Scotch.

Grand Gruyere (Switzerland): Herbal.

Izzara: Produced by the Basques with an armagnac base blended with herbs. Available in green and yellow.

Jagermeister (German): More than 56 assorted fruits, herbs, roots, and spices, including: ginseng, juniper berries, ginger, saffron, anise, licorice, poppy seed and citrus peel.

Liqueur d'Or: Similar to yellow Chartreuse in flavor.

Kummel: Anise, caraway, cumin.

Mazarine: Similar to yellow Chartreuse. Made by the house of Cusenier from a recipe dating back to the seventeenth century.

Mesimara (Finland): Made in Turku by Marli from Arctic bramble.

Old Sint Maarten Spice Liqueur: rum/spices St. Maarten

Parfait Amour: Violet

Pernod (French): Interesting aperitif made from anise star, mint and balm.

Pimento Dram (Jamaica): Spicy, made from flower buds of pimento tree.

Punt e Mes (Italian): Bitters, vermouth, orange, quinine, and other botanicals.

Pimm's No. 1: Herbs, spices and fruits.

Peppermint Schnapps: Peppermint

Roiano (Italian): Interesting liqueur made from herbs, anise, and vanilla. Similar to Galliano.

Rumple Minze (Germany): Peppermint Schnapps with high alcohol content.

Seventh Heaven (St. Lucia, WI): A liqueur made with ginger and the aphrodisiac Bois Bande, highly-prized by the locals.

Sommer Garden (Denmark): Perfect for the calorie conscious. Made with saccharin. After dinner liqueur.

Strega: Meaning witch in Italian, made from more than 70 herbs, roots, and botanicals

Suze (French): Gentian root bitters, distilled.

Swedish Punsch: Similar to Batavia arak, the Indonesian aromatic rum.

Verveine du Velay (France): Made from botanicals of the genus Verbena.

Vieille Cure (Bordeaux): Aged liqueur with over 50 ingredients, similar to Chartreuse-also available in yellow in green.

Benedictine and Chartreuse are exotic blends of botanicals, herbs and spices dating back to the 16th century. Green chartreuse is flavored with chlorophyll and yellow is flavored with saffron.

Did you know? Dr. Johann Siegert, Surgeon General in Simon Bolivar's army in South America, created angostura bitters. Sailors would pick up bottles of the blend of tropical herbs and spices to improve their appetite.

Licorice and Anise

Absinthe: Made from wormwood and high in alcohol content.

Anisette: Anisette, Ouzo and Sambuca come from the Mediterranean and are made from anise. Very sweet.

Anesone (Italy): Anise

Herbsaint (American): Another absinthe substitute similar to Pernod. Made in New Orleans.

Liqueur d'Anis: Made from anisette.

Mastikha (Greece): Made from anisette.

Mistra (Italian): Anise flavored

Ojen (Spain): Anise flavored

Old Sint Maarten Anis: anise St. Maarten

Opal Nera: Nice. Black sambuca with a hint of lemon.

Ouzo(Greece): Anise

Pastis de Marseilles (France): Anise flavored

Sambuca (Italy): Anise, the black has a more intense licorice taste

Samcafe: Licorice and coffee liqueur, very nice

Raki (Turkey): Sweet licorice flavor.

Ricard (France): Anise-licorice

Some people would put Galliano and Pernod on this list. You will find them under herbs above.

Absinthe contains a dangerous narcotic called wormwood and is 136 proof. It is illegal in the United States. Pernod makes an adequate substitute. Supposedly turns brains to soup.

Nuts

Amaretto (Italy): Made from apricot pits and herbs, resulting in an almond flavor.

Amontillado: Sherry-based with a nut flavor.

Crème de noisette: Hazelnut

Crème de noyaux: Almond, sweet and bitter

Crème d'almonde: Almond

Frangelico: Hazelnuts, berries and flowers. Delicious.

Liqueur Nutz n Rum (St. Lucia, WI): Peanuts, spices, cream and rum

Moringue Pistachio Cream Liqueur: Rum, crushed pistachios, almonds, and sugar.

Old Sint Maarten Almond Liqueur: almond, St. Maarten

Pistacha: Cointreau produces this pistachio-flavored liqueur in the U.S.

Praline (American): Made in New Orleans similar to those delicious pralines. Butter, pecan, dark sugar, and vanilla.

Amaretto de Saronno is an expensive liqueur that tastes wonderful over ice cream, neat, over the rocks or mixed. Crème d'almonde and crème de noyaux are interchangeable.

Frangelica tastes entirely different as it is made from hazelnuts. There is no substitute for it.

Other

Licor 43: vanilla-flavored, mix with milk for a vanilla-caramel shake

Butterscotch Schnapps: butterscotch liqueur

Whiskey, Rum, Scotch, Brandy-based

Advocaat (Dutch): Sort of like an over-proof eggnog made with brandy.

Aguardiente (South America and Spain): Cheap brandy aptly named "burning water." For the more adventurous.

Batavia Arak (Indonesia): Heady, aromatic rum blended from malted rice and molasses. Aged in barrels like cognac.

Batida (Brazil): Name given to any fruit and rum drink.

Celtic Crossing: Cognac and Irish malt whiskey.

Irish Mist: Heather honey, sweet and spicy with Irish whiskey base.

Glenfiddish: Malt whiskey liqueur

Lochan Ora: Scotch whiskey and honey.

Rock & Rye: U.S. product made from fruit juices and aged rye whiskey.

Wild Turkey Kentucky Bourbon Liqueur (American): Sweet liqueur made from Bourbon.

Yukon Jack can also be put under this heading. Find it under Herbs in this book.

Wines and Miscellaneous

Cynar (Italian): Made from artichokes. Bittersweet, serve over ice.

Crème de celery: Celery based sweet liqueur.

Crème de rose: Vanilla and roses

Crème de the: Tea

Dubonnet (American): Originally French in origin, now made in California. Available in red and white, wine base with quinine.

Lillet (French): Popular aperitif wine available in white and red. Made from 85% Bordeaux wine and 15% fruit liqueurs. Lillet Blanc is made from Sauvignon Blanc and Semillion.

Metaxa (Greek): Sweetened brandy.

Okolehao (Hawaii): Distilled taro root, rice and molasses.

Pineau des Charentes (French): Grape juice to which alcohol has been added. Aperitif.

CHAPTER NINE

Gin, Scotch, Tequila, Vodka, and Whiskey

Gin

A finely-crafted gin is like a Monet painting. It is unaged liquor dependent on the blender's ability and skill to find just the right **combination of botanicals.** Every gin distiller has his own highly prized and guarded secret recipe. Ingredients range from juniper berries (main ingredient in all gins), angelica root, orris root, licorice, caraway seeds, anise, coriander, fennel, cassia bark, cinnamon, cocoa, bergamot (strong citrus taste) lemon and orange peel and other botanicals. Without the addition of these other ingredients, the gin would be flavorless. It would be vodka.

Gin manufacture goes through numerous steps. First, grains, such as corn and rye, are distilled in a patent still. This neutral spirit is diluted with water, flavored with juniper berries and herbs, and distilled once more, resulting in 80 to 100 proof liquor. Some American gins are only distilled once. The essences of the various flavoring agents are added after the first distillation. Other firms will add the botanicals before the first distillation. Each distiller uses a slightly different method to obtain the coveted flavor.

Flavors vary because of the different quality botanicals or flavorings used. Even impure water will affect the taste. Cheap gin tastes like disinfectant and may be used as such in a pinch. Always use high quality gin to make drinks. It is one of the most versatile alcohols, next to vodka. Save the costliest gins for on the rocks or gin and soda.

The word gin comes from the French genievre-juniper berry. Dr. Sylvius, physician at the University of Leyden, invented it in Holland. Originally, gin was used to cure sailors on Dutch East India company ships of strange tropical diseases. While gin did not affect the maladies, it reduced fever and was used as a mild sedative, diuretic, appetite stimulant, and a vasodilator. Juniper also has antiseptic properties. When British soldiers returned from the war in the Netherlands, they brought back the "Dutch Courage" to England. At one point, there were more than 7,000 gin bars in London.

Gin does spoil quickly, so keep the bottle capped tightly. If it tastes off or turns milky, discard. Store in a cool, dry place. Keeping gin in the refrigerator is not a bad idea.

Some of the more **common types** of gin include:

London dry gin (English): All gins today are considered dry. This mixture contains more barley than corn.

Dutch or Holland gin: This is distilled at a lower proof than the London gin and has a sweeter flavor. Made from barley, malt, corn, and rye.

Flavored gins: Living in the Virgin Islands in close proximity to huge duty-free liquor palaces, I see an influx of flavored alcohols. Gin has been the latest to join vodka and rum. Expect to see lemon, lime, and orange. I am sure coconut, pineapple, and cranberry will be next.

Scotch

I found the manufacture of Scotch very interesting. For openers, Scotch Whisky is spelled without the "e" in whiskey. It must be distilled in Scotland to be called Scotch. However, it may be bottled elsewhere.

Scotch malt whisky is made from barley, yeast, and water. Grain whisky combines malted barley with unmalted barley and corn. The barley is soaked in water for several day and dried, where it germinates. The starch in the barley has now turned into fermentable sugar-the enzyme diatase is released. Careful watch must be kept over the germination and temperature.

At the correct time, drying the green malt in a kiln fired by peat stops the germination. This is what gives Scotch its smoky taste. The malt is then ground, poured into large tanks filled with hot water. After eight hours, the wort is transferred to fermentation vats. Yeast is added and the mixture is allowed to ferment for two days. The sugar in the wort becomes low-proof alcohol (wash). Impurities are filtered out.

Malt whiskey is distilled twice in copper stills. After this process, the raw whiskey is poured into used or new American oak containers, wine barrels, or bourbon barrels for at least three years by law. Some are aged as long as fifteen years. After this period, the distiller blends fifteen to fifty different whiskies.

There are over 2,000 different Scotch whiskies from over 100 distilleries, each with its own mysteriously derived flavor. Mysterious? For example: picture two identical casks of whiskey aging in the same warehouse, one on a clay tile floor, the other on warehouse shelving. Each will end up tasting different-probably because of air circulation. Whisky likes to breathe in its barrels.

Not to be unmentioned is the distillery on the Isle of Islay. In the ninth month of aging, this single malt whisky takes on a seaweed taste, which disappears when it is twelve years old. Interesting.

Single Malt Whiskies

There are over 100 distilleries of this Scotch. The many different climates, water, raw materials, and variations of stills contribute to the individuality of this whisky.

Popular Blended Whiskies

Ballantine	Grant's
Chivas Regal	Johnny Walker
Cutty Sark	Teacher's
Dewar's	

Serve Scotch over ice, neat, with water or sparkling water. It can also be made into mixed drinks. Store in a cool, dry, and dark place.

Tequila and Mezcal

Tequila has unfairly acquired a bad reputation. Probably some tourists in Mexico were served cheap Tequila. Traced back to the Aztecs to 1,000 A.D., it was originally known as *pulque*. The Mexican government has issued strict controls on Tequila. It must come from the area known as Tequila, in the state of Jalisco-an area of volcanic soil in the Sierra Madre. About forty to fifty distillers grow the blue agave plants and produce Tequila.

The heart of the blue agave, *Agave tequilana Weber*, is known as the head, and weighs between 80 and 100 pounds. After growing for ten years, the heart is roasted in large ovens, shredded and the juice pressed. The juice is combined with sugar and yeast. The fermentation continues for three to four days. After a double distillation in copper pots to bring the alcohol level up, the spirit is ready for drinking. Some of the Tequila will be aged and called Tequila Anejo. This mellow spirit is costly and compares to fine cognac. Tequila is usually 90 proof or more; it must be at least 51 proof.

There are **four different types** of Tequila:

Tequila Blanco: Sometimes diluted with water. Comes directly from the still. Clear.
Tequila Joven Abocado: Same as above with additional flavors and coloring agents added.
Tequila Reposado: Briefly aged for a couple of months to one year with additional flavors and coloring added.
Tequila Anejo: Aged at least one year in government sealed barrels.

Popular Tequilas:

Jose Cuervo   Sauza
Patron   Two Fingers
Pepe Lopez

Mezcal

Mezcal is potent with a smoky flavor. It is not under strict government guidelines. It is exclusive to the region of Oaxaca. Originally, distillers put the worm in the bottle as it spent its entire life in the agave.

Popular brands:

Gusano Rojo Mezcal   Monte Alban
Miguel de la Mezcal

Vodka

Both Russia and Poland claim the invention of vodka, perhaps as early as the 10th century. The Russian word *vodka* means "dear little water."

Vodka is now the most popular hard liquor in the United States. Due to liquor shortages of old favorites after the wars, vodka became well known. The Moscow Mule was created, i.e. Smirnoff Vodka, limejuice, and ginger beer. At one time, there were over four thousand vodka distilleries in Russia.

Originally made from potatoes, it can also be made from wheat, rye, or corn. The better vodkas are no longer made from potatoes. The spirit, unlike whiskey, is distilled at 190 proof and filtered through charcoal, like Cuban rum. The neutral spirits are diluted with distilled water so as not to impart any foreign tastes. Expensive vodkas may be triple or quadruple distilled. Some are filtered through fine sand or charcoal.

Flavoring vodka is not a recent invention. For decades, Russian housewives, not liking the taste of straight vodka, have flavored with herbs, fruits, and berries. Recently, vodka has been filtered through juices adding lovely overtones of citron, cranberry, jalapeño, and others.

Popular brands:

Absolut	Skyy
Finlandia	Smirnoff
Glacier	Stolichnaya
Gordon's	Tanqueray Sterling
Ketel One	

Flavored Vodkas:

Brand	Flavor
Absolut Citron	Lemon, lime, grapefruit and madarin
Absolut Kurant	Black currants
Absolut Mandrin	Mandrin Orange
Absolut Pepper	Jalapeño and paprika
Artic	Banana
Finlandia Pineapple	Very rich and heady
Finlandia Cranberry	Cranberry
Gordon's Wildberry	Blend of berries
Okhotnichya	Herbs and honey
Stoli Kafya	Coffee
Stoli Ohranj	Orange
Stoli Okhotrichya	honey
Stoli Persik	Peach, nice
Stoli Pertsovka	White and black pepper, chillies
Stoli Razberi	Raspberries
Stoli Strasbert	Strawberry
Stoli Vanil	Exotic vanilla beans
Stoli Zinamon	Cinnamon and cassis-hot

This is by no means the entire list. There are probably new flavors being created as I write this book.

Store vodka in the refrigerator or freezer. It becomes a little slower pouring when kept very cold.

Whiskies-American and Canadian

Whiskey is distilled from grain and involves four steps: malting, fermenting, distilling, and ageing. It's the ageing in wooden barrels, which provide flavor, aroma, and color to an otherwise clear liquid.

Grain is first ground and cooked to bring out the starch. Malt is added which converts the starch into sugar. After cooling, yeast is added, and the mash is poured into fermenters. The fermented mash is conveyed to a still and heated. Vaporized alcohol is caught and trapped. Water is added to reduce the proof and the whiskey is transferred to barrels.

After aging, the whiskey is placed in tanks to be bottled. For **blended** whiskies, different whiskies are combined, neutral spirits added or additional filtration processes implemented. **Straight** whiskies are not mixed. Country of origin plays a large part in the whiskey process. As previously discussed, Scotch, and Irish whisky differ entirely from each other as do American and Canadian whisk(e)y.

American whiskeys include blended, bourbon, bottled-in-bond, corn, rye, and sour mash. **Bourbon**, named for Bourbon County, Kentucky, is the most popular whiskey made in the United States. In 1789, Rev. Elijah Craig, a Baptist minister, discovered that corn whiskey aged in charred barrels had a smoother and mellower taste. The superior tasting whiskey was later called Bourbon. There are over 500 brands of straight and blended bourbons.

Amber and slightly sweet, it is distilled from at least 51% corn by law. The balance of ingredients usually includes rye and barley. It must then be aged at least four years in new, charred oak barrel.

Early in the eighteenth century, farmers discovered that while they could carry to barrels of grain to market, they could also carry two kegs of whiskey. Whiskey became an important cash crop and at one point, there were over 5000 stills in Western Pennsylvania.

In 1791, Alexander Hamilton, Secretary of the Treasury, imposed an excise tax on whiskey to pay off debts from the American Revolution. This resulted in the Whiskey Rebellion of 1794, quickly put down by President George Washington.

Kentucky Bourbon popular brands:

Baker's Kentucky Straight Bourbon: 7 years old, 107 proof, Small Batch

Booker's Kentucky Straight Bourbon: 7 years & 8 months old, 93 proof, Small Batch

Jim Beam: 4 years old and 80 proof; 5 years old and 80 Proof; Black Label: 8 years old and 90 proof.

Old Crow Bourbon: 8 years old and 80 proof; 10 years old and 86 proof; The Classic: 12 years old and 90 proof

Old Grand Dad: 86 proof, Bottled in Bond: 100 proof; 114 Barrel Proof

Rock Hill Farms Single-Barrel Kentucky Straight Bourbon: 100 proof

Wild Turkey Kentucky Bourbon: 80 proof

Wild Turkey Kentucky Bourbon Old Number 8: 101 proof

Wild Turkey Kentucky Bourbon Rare Breed: a blended whiskey of 6, 8 and 12 year olds, from 109 to 112 proof

Other primitive methods of distilling included added gunpowder to the whiskey and igniting to "prove" it. If a yellow flame resulted, the alcohol was too low in proof. If a rapid blue flame burned, it was too high. A steady, bright blue flame was perfect, i.e. 100 proof.

Tennessee bourbon is straight whiskey made from at least 51% corn or *any other grain* and then filtered through sugar-maple charcoal. This filtering process gives Tennessee whiskies its unique flavor. Most Tennessee whiskies follow the same guidelines, though not legally required, as Kentucky Bourbon.

Tennessee Bourbon popular brands:

George Dickel Tennessee Whiskey: Old No 8. Brand, 80 proof; Old No. 12 Superior Brand, 90 proof; Barrel Reserve, 10 years old, 86 proof

Jack Daniels Tennessee Sour Mash Whiskey: Black Label, 86 proof; Green Label, 80 proof; Gentleman Jack, 80 proof

Rye Whiskey contains at least 51% rye. The flavor is quite individual.

Rye Whiskey popular brands:

Bellows & Co.: 80 proof

Mount Vernon: 80 proof

Canadian whiskies are all blends made from an assortment of grains such as corn, barley, rye, and wheat. Legally, they must be at least three-years old, but most are at least six. Lighter and more delicate in flavor than American whiskies, they also have a lighter body.

Canadian popular brands:

Black Velvet: six years old, 80 proof
Canadian Club: six years old, 80 proof
Canadian Mist: six years old, 80 proof

Crown Royal: six years old, 80 proof
Seagram's V.O.: six years old, 80 proof

Blended American whiskies contain at least 20-percent 100-proof whiskey combined with neutral spirits or grain whiskey. Additional colorings and flavor enhancers improve taste. They are all at least 80 proof.

Blended popular brands:

Barton Reserve
Carstairs
Imperial

Mattingly & Moore
Seagram 7 Crown

The Seagram 7 Crown is used in what is known as a "14", i.e. Seagram's 7 and Seven-Up soda.

On a final note, many people are confused between "sour mash" and "sweet mash." This refers to the yeasting process used during distilling, sour mash being the more common. A certain percentage of the mash used must contain stillage, which are liquids without alcohol, left over from the previous distillation. Sweet mash is made without stillage.

Bottled-in-bond refers to the Bottled-in-Bond Act passed in the 1890's. Distillers were not required to pay excise tax until the whiskey was actually sold, not just warehoused. The requirements were that only straight whiskey be used, be 100 proof and aged in wooden barrels for four years.

CHAPTER TEN

Rum

Just say rum and immediately Caribbean and Robert Louis Stevenson come to mind. Pirates singing "Fifteen men on a dead man's chest and a bottle of rum ..." while burying chests of treasure on deserted islands. Picture oak barrels piled high in brick warehouses traded alongside spices, cotton, indigo and other luxuries from all over the world.

Caribbean rum got its start when **Columbus brought sugar cane** from the Azores to Puerto Rico on his second voyage in 1493. Ponce de Leon, the first governor of Puerto Rico planted the cane and his legendary search for the "fountain of youth" was more like a search for pure water for rum distillation. The first Puerto Rican rum was shipped to the United States over one hundred years ago in 1897-nearly 18,000 gallons.

Unlike spirits made from grain such as whiskey or gin, the sugarcane juice and molasses can be fermented directly into alcohol. Grain spirits must first be converted from starch into sugar. Sugarcane is pressed, boiled, reduced, and strained for clarification. A bit of yeast is added to some molasses, allowed to ferment for a few days, and then added to the sugarcane juice. Every distiller has his own unique brand of yeast. It is said that Barcardi's yeast is over a hundred years old.

The first distillation results in a crude rum between 130 and 180 proof. The continous-column stills are often four stories high. The rum is then aged in oak barrels for two to ten years. If charred oak barrels are used, the rum is dark. Sometimes caramel color is added as well. I have tried some dark rum from down island that was nearly black in color with a syrupy texture. Some rum is aged in stainless steel casks and of course is clear. After the **proper aging** process, the distiller "marries" rums of various ages and batches, producing lovely blends with **distinctive bouquets and smoothness.**

Each island in the Caribbean has its own unique rum. Puerto Rican rums such as Barcardi, Don Q, and Captain Morgan are light and dry. They are also the most popular in the world. Virgin Island rums such as Cruzan and Paradise (actually manufactured by the same company that make Cruzan) are a bit heavier. Mount Gay is a Barbados rum with a hint of smoke. It is heavier than Puerto Rican rum and has an amber color. Jamaican rum such as Myer's is known to be dark and rich. It is fermented naturally instead of using yeast. Bermuda has a lovely smooth rum called Bermudez. Pusser's Rum from the British Virgin Islands was the official rum of the Royal Navy for 300 years.

Most light rums come from Puerto Rico and the Virgin Islands. Generally, darker rums come from Barbados, Jamaica, Haiti, and Martinique.

Rum also comes from unusual places such as Brazil, Nicaragua, Panama, Columbia, and Venezuela. New England has a rum called Caldewell's Newburyport. Despite the vast brands of rum, Puerto Rican rum account for more than 77% of all rum sold in the United States.

Quick Quiz:

How many different rum labels are produced?

❏ 200
❏ 300 to 500
❏ 500 to 1000
❏ over 4000

How many different countries and islands produce rum?

❏ 25
❏ 40
❏ 75
❏ over 86

For the answers, go to the end of this chapter.

Rums of the Caribbean and Central America

(listed by country or island and brand)

Anguilla:
Anguilla Rums Ltd.

Antigua & Barbuda:

Cavalier Antigua Rum	Angelo Barreto	Jumby Bay

Aruba:

Aruba Trading Company	Hansen Caribbean Rum Company	LTD.

Bahamas:

Alvarez Camp & Co., Ltd.	Bacardi & Company, Ltd.	Bahama Blenders Ltd.
Burns House Ltd.	Ron Matusalem Ltd.	

Barbados:

Alleyne Arthurs' Special Old Barbados Rum	Caribbean Spirit	Cockade Fine Rum
Gosling's Choicest Barbados Rum	Cockspur 5 Star	Foursquare Distillery
Johnson & Redman	Hanschell Inniss Ltd.	Huncol Ltd.
Old Brigand Rum	Lamb's Navy Rum (blended and bottled in London)	Lightbourn's Selected Barbados Rum
Malibu	Martin Doorly & Co. Ltd.	Mount Gay "Eclipse" Rum
Mount Gay Sugar Cane Brandy	R. L. Seale & Co., Ltd.	Twelve Islands Shipping Co. Inc.
West Indies Rum Distillery Ltd.		

Belize:
Travellers Ltd.

Bermuda:

Bermudez	Barcardi & Company Ltd.	Gosling's Black Seal
Todhunter-Michell Distilleries Ltd.		

Cayman Islands:

Blackbeard's Liquor/Grand Cayman	Bottler's & Blenders	Tortuga Rum Company Ltd.

Cuba:

Alzola Distillery	Barcardi & Co.	CIMEX, S.A.
Casa Merino 1889	Cuba Ron SA	Destileria Nauyu

Destileria Sevilla   Incera Hermanos, S. en C.   Havana Club
Ron Matusalem   Sloppy Joe's Bar

Dominican Republic:

Barcelo & Co.   Brugal & Co.   J. Armando Bermudez & Co.
Macorix   Siboney   Vinicola del Norte

Grenada:

The Best of Grenada Ltd.   Dunfermline Estate   River Antoine Rum Distillery
The Grenada Sugar Factory Ltd.   Westerhall Distillery

Guadeloupe:

Distillerie Beauport	Roger Beuzelin	Distillerie Bielle
Ste. Civile Agricole de Bologne	Distillerie de Bonne Mere/ S.I.S	Chrispac
Damaoiseau	Darboussier/S.I.S	Desmarets
SARL Domino	Claude Dormoy	Jean Dormoy
Gaston Fremon	Gabriel Godefroy/Maria Galanda	Distillerie de Grand'Anse/
SOSUMAG	C. de Grandmaison	M. de Houselbourg
Pere Labat/ Distillerie Poisson	Le Rhum Agricole	Leader Price
Littee	Longueteau/ Mon Repos	Madras/ Liquoma
Claude Marsolle	L. Marsolle	G. Maston
Montebello/ A. Marsolle	Musee du Rhum/ Bellevue Reimonenq	J. Nouy
La Pirate	F.A. Polka-Safrano	C. Preira
Punch Case	Primisteres Reynoird	Rhum Agricoles de
Rhum Bologne	S.C.O.D.A.G.	Bellevue Marie-Galante
Domaine de Severin/ Joseph Marsolle	Charles Simonnet	SODAF
SODIPA/ SDPM	Sotrarhum S.A.R.L.	Distillerie St. Louis
Felix Vartin		

Guatemala:

Ron Botran   Ron Zacapa   Industria Licorera Quezalteca

Haiti:

Rhum Barbancourt   Rhum Barbancourt Liqueur

Jamaica:

Appleton Estate	Bonded Warehouses	C.J. Wray
Coruba	Daniel Finzi Fine Old Rum	Dr. Ian Sangster & Co. Ltd.
Edwin Charley (Jamaica) Ltd.	Fred L. Meyers & Son Ltd.	Hudson's Bay Jamaica Rum
Grange Hill Products Co.	Karbyl & Sons	(bottled in U.K.)
Kelly's Jamaica Rum	K.R. B. Lea & Co.	Captain Morgan
Myer's Rum	Rumona Jamaica Rum Liqueur	Sugar Mills Ltd.
Skol	The Rum Company (Jamaica) Ltd.	Wray & Nephew

Martinique:

Andre Dormoy/ La Favorite	Clement	DePaz
Dillon	Distillerie Neisson/ Domaines	Thieubert
Distillerie des Rhums Agricoles	D.R.A.S.A.	Duquesne
Fonds Dore	G. & P. Dormoy	G. Hardy
J-C. B. Distribution	J. Bally	Kanichie Rum Martinique
La Favorite Eight Year Old	La Mauny	Madkaud Pere & Fils
Martinique Agro Industrie	Rhumerie du Simon	Rhum Survi
Rhum J-M	SAEM du Galion	S.G.D.A.
Saint Etienne	Saint James	Trois Rivieres
William Charleston		

Mexico:

Barcardi y Cia.	Bodegas Capellania	Destileria Huasteca
Licores Veracruz, S.A.	Casa Madero	

Netherlands Antilles:

Busco N.V.	Caribbe Rum Company	Sint Maarten Guavaberry Company
N.V.	St. Martin Spiced Rhum	SugarBird Rum Factor

Nicaragua:

Ron Flor de Cana — Compania Licorera de Nicaragua

Panama:

Abuelo (meaning grandmother) — Barcardi Centroamericana, S.A. — Bodegas de America, S.A.
Caribbean Spirits — Carta Viejo — Cichisa
Cortez — Cuba Libre Products, Inc. — Destiladora Nacional, S.A.
Admiral Nelson

Puerto Rico:

Bacardi Corp. — Barcelo Marques & Co. — Bugalu LTD
Calypso — Captain Morgan Rum Co. — Caribe Distillers
Compania Ron Llave — Compania Ron Merito — Destileria Ron Grando
Destileria Serralles — Distilleries V.M. Ramirez — Edmundo B. Fernandez, Inc.
Ron Carioca — Ron de Castillo (I've been to the — Boca Chica
Don Q (also made by Ron Castillo) — Serralles castle in Ponce and — Grenardo
Palo Viejo — it's gorgeous) — Ronrico
Ron del Barrilito — Ron Matusalem — Trigo Corp.

St. Kitts & Nevis:

Baron Edmond de Rothschild Distilleries

St. Lucia:

Jos. Jn. Baptiste Crystal — Bounty Rum — Clear White Rum
Denros Strong Rum — Kweyol Spice — Old Fort
Ron D'Oro — St. Lucia Distillers — Wilco Ltd.

St. Maarten:

Blackbeard's Sint Maarten — Cariba Native

St. Vincent & the Grenadines:

After Our's — Golden Eagle Refreshment — Kim's Plaza
M. Matheson — St. Vincent Distillers Ltd — Sunset St. Vincent Rum

Trinidad & Tobago:

Angostura Bitters (Dr. J.G.B. Siegert — Caroni (1975) Ltd. — Fernandes Distillers (1973) Ltd.
Sons) Ltd. — Trinidad Distillers Ltd.

Virgin Islands (British):

Aristocrat — Callwood Distillery — Caribaya
Carnival — Carta Vieja — Foxy's
Pusser's Rum — Styles Callwood

Virgin Islands (U.S.):

Calypso Island, see A.H. Riise — Cruzan Rum — Carioca Rum Co.
Gold Award — Hobson's Rum — Laird's Five O'Clock
McCormick — Old St. Croix — Paradise Rum
Pott Rum — Redrum — Ron Chico
Ron Popular — A.H. Riise

Trinidad:

Fernandes "Vat 19" — Ferdi's 10-Year-Old — Old Oak Rum
Royal Oak — Siegert's Bouquet Rum

North America

Canada:

Acadian Distillers Ltd. — Alberta Distillers — Arctica Distilling Corporation
Captain Morgan Rum Distillers Ltd. — Compania Ron Carioca/Schenley — DeKuyper
Diamond Rum Company — Distilleries, Inc. — Dumont Vins & Spiritueux
FBM Distillery Co., Ltd. — Glenora Distillers Ltd. — Highwood Distillers Ltd.
Hiram Walker & Sons — International Distillers of Canada — Kittling Ridge
Lamb's Rum Company — Maraca Rum Merchants — Marine Rum Distillers
Newfoundland Liquor Corporation — OK Liquor Stores — Old Havana (Bacardi)

Palliser Distillers Ltd.
Rosswog Farm Distillery
Twelve Islands Shipping Company
Yukon Liquor Corporation

Potter Distilling Corp.
Schenley Canada
Venada

Rieder Distillery Ltd.
The Governor General Rum
    Company

United States:

A. Smith Bowman Distillery
Albertson's Inc.
American Liquor Co.
Badger Liquor
Bellow & Company
Body Crystal
CBP Spirits Ltd.
Conch Republic Rum Co./
    Old Florida Rum Co.
Famous Imported Brands
Franco's Cocktail Mixes
Gray Wine and Spirits
Indies Distilled Products
Laird & Co.
The Liquor Mart
Mc Donough's Liquors
Mohan's Liquor Store
Monarch Import Company
Montego Bay
Muskie Mels
OAK Park Distilling Co.
Pearson's Liquor Annex
Pioneer Distillers Company
Randall Foods
Ron Diaz Rum Co.
Saint James Spirits
Munson Shaw Co.
Springfield Liquor Market
The Daiquiri Factory Ltd.
United States Distilled Products Co.
Vanguard, LTD.
Wide World Importers

ABC Distillers Co.
Allen's Ltd.
Associated Liquor Products Co.
Barton Brands
Bill's Place
Caldwell's Newburyport
Celebration Distillation
David Sherman Corp.
Distiller's Best, Ltd.
FedCal
General Distillers Corp.
J. Harrison Company
K.R.W. International Ltd.
Leather Stallion Saloon
Majestic Distilling
Mc Cormick Distilling Co.
Mohawk Distilled Products
Montana Distillery
Monumental Distilling Co.
Nelson Distributors
Odenton Liquors
Phillips Beverage Company
Portside Distilled Products Co.
Redrum
Ron Roberto Rum Co.
Sazerac Company
Sir James Pub
State Line Liquors
Towne Wine & Liquor
Universal Distilling Co.
V. G. Corydon Distilling Products, Ltd.
World Wide Distributors Co.

A. & G. J. Caldwell Company
American Distilling Co., (Inc.)
Associated Rum Importers
Beach Road
Bishop Wines and Spirits
Castle Bay Distillers
Cocoribe Co.
DeKuyper
Distiller's Serving Co.
Florida Distillers Company
W & A Gilbey
Hawaiian Distillers
Kings Distilling Products Ltd.
De Leon Importers Ltd.
Matusalem & Co.
Meier's Distilled Products
    Company
Montebello Brands Inc.
Mr. Boston Distiller
North Shore Dist. Co.
Paramount Distillers
S.S. Pierce Company
Quality Foods
Rom Conga Distilleries, Inc.
Ronrico Rum Company
Schenlet International Corporation
Smith's LTD.
Sterling Distilling Co.
Trader Vic's Products Co.
Univeral Importing Co.
Le Vecke Corporation

South America:

Argentina:
Peters Hnos, C.C.I.S.A.

Porta Hermanos

Bolivia:
Ingenio Azucarero Guabira

Brazil:

Janeiro Cachaca
Amarantina
Artesanal Mineira
Cande Ind. E. Com. LTDA
Claudio
Coral Cachaca do Brasil
Fazenda Boa Esperanca
Fazenda Vale Verde
Aguardente Ferreira Comercio
Tatuzinho-3 Fazendas Ltda.
Marquesi - Destilaria de Aguardente
    Ltda.

Toucana Cachaca
Amburana
Artesanal Quinta do Minho
Carlao Agropecuaria Ltda.
Coqueiral
Destilaria Mendes Ltda.
Fazenda Cana Verde & Cia
Fazenda Vista Longa
Industria
Caninha Jamel
Pitu LTDA

Alambique Santa Luzia Ltda.
Antonio Amorim
Bebidas Santa Clara Ind. Com. Ltda.
CATEDRAL Industria e Comercio
    de Aguardente Ltda.
Dias & Soares Ltda.
Fazenda Conquista
Fer Agroindustrial LTDA
Industrias Reunidas de Bebidas
Januaria Centenaria
Princesa Januaria

| Industria e Comercio de Aguardente Schmith Ltda. | Cachaca Tabaroa Valter Lopo Lisboa | Armazenda em Toneis de Carvalho Viti Viniicola Cereser S.A. |

Chile:
Martini & Rossi

Columbia:

| Ron Viejo de Caldas | Ron Medellin | Tres Esquinas |
| Fabrica de Licores y Alcoholes de Antioquia | Licores de los Andes, S.A. | |

Costa Rica:
Ron Viejo Especial

Ecuador:

| Ron San Miguel | Embotelladora Azuaya S.A. | Desarrolla Agropecuario C.A. |
| ILA - Industrias Locorereas Asociadas S.A. | Licoresa S.A. Destileria Zhumir | (D.A.C.A.) |

Guyana:

| Lemon Hart & Sons Finest Demerara Rum (bottled in U.K.) | Hudson's Bay Demerara Rum (bottled in U.K.) | Rhum Ste. Maurice El Dorado Special Reserve |

Peru:
Maloca S.R.L.

Uruguay:
ANCAP

Venezuela:

Cacique Ron Anejo	Destilerias del Penedes	El Muco
Industrias Pampero C.A.	Licorerias Unidas/Seagram	Ocumare Amazonas
Pampero	de Venezuela	Santa Teresa

Ok, if you've peeked at the quiz answer, you'll know why I'm getting tired of typing.

Europe - abbreviated

Austria:

| Gautier Muckstein | Lehar | Purkhart |
| S. Spitz | Sebastian Stroh | |

Belgium:

| Battard | Mestdach | Neycken |
| St. Pol | Leon Wathelet | |

Bulgaria:
Vinprom

Croatia:

| Badel | VINARIJA IMOTSKI | ISTRAVINO |
| Maraska | | |

Cyprus:
Keo Ltd.

Czech Republic: I counted over 144 distilleries here!

| Danek, Ostrava | Flirt CB, s.r.o., Cerna v Posumavi | Glen Hill, Dolni Bousov |
| Jan Kozak | MIKI, Petrvald | Scuba Diving |

Denmark:

| George Lorange & Cos | Vingaarden a/s |

Estonia:
AS Ofelia

Finland:
Primalco Oy

France: I counted over 100 here.

Archambeaud Freres	C.M.I.	Chevalier & Cie
Dufaur & Co.	Cie des Grands Rhums	Old Nick
Distillerie Wolfberber		

Germany:

Adolf Richter	Bremer Rum Contor	Red Fox Markenvertrieb
Viktor Riegger	Ludwig Schwartz Co.	Weinbrennerei Meerane

Hungary:

Angyafoldi Rum es Likorgyar	Royal Likorgyar, Budapest	Zwack Unicum

Ireland:

Grant's of Ireland

Italy:

Antiche Distillerie Triestine	Barbero 1891 S.P.A.	Nuova Curti'r
Giarola	Rum Nation/Rossi & Rossi	Distillati San Giorgio

Netherlands:

Meyer Baggers	Bootz Distilleries	Coopconsult
Simon Rynbende & Zonen	Wenneker Distilleries	

Poland:

Polmos Bialystock	Polmos Bielsko Biala	Polmos Poznana

Portugal:

Cave Central da Bairrada S.A.

Slovakia:

Aquila	Frantisek Dubecky	Fatra
Intergal	Kvestor	Slopak, Malacky

Slovenia:

APIS, Sentilj	Dana, Mirna	Slovenijavino, Ljubljana
TOZDALKO		

Spain:

Bacardi y Cia, S.A.	Vicente Bernabeu, Jativa	Carlos Montfort
Antonio Nadal, S.A.	Salvador Tarraso	

Sweden:

V & S Vin & Spirit AB

Switzerland:

Lateltin, LTD

United Kingdom:

Glen Adam Distillers	Bacardi & Company	Buccaneer Vitners
William Cadenhead	Captain Morgan Rum Distillers	Crown & Co.
Walter Hicks & Co.	Lamd & Watt	Prince Consort
Rigby & Sons	Rum Trading Company Ltd.	Tanqueray, Gordon & Co. Ltd.
Twelve Islands Shipping Company	United Rum Merchants Limited	

Yugoslavia:

SP PIK Kovin	Suboticanka Su

Asia - abbreviated

Bangladesh:

Carew & Co (Bangladesh) Ltd.

India:

Ajudhia Distillery	Amrut Distilleries Ltd.	Army Welfare Project
Carew & Co. Ltd.	McDowell	Rampur Distillery
Shiva Distilleries Ltd.	South Seas Distilleries & Breweries	

Indonesia:
Three Corner Distilleries   Luiz Valenta

Japan:
Suntory Limited

Jordan:
Eagle Distilleries & Co.

Lebanon:
St. Nicolas Co.

Nepal:
Snow-Land Sons Ltd.

Phillipines:
Central Azucarera de Tarlac   La Tondena Distillers, Inc.

Sri lanka:
W.M. Mendis & Co. Ltd

Thailand:
Sang Som Co. Ltd.

Australia and Oceania - abbreviated

Australia:
Bundaberg Distilling   Cawsey Menck Pty. Ltd.   Miranda
Seagram Australia   Tucker & Co.

Fiji:
South Pacific Distillers

French Polynesia:
Distillerie a Moorea

New Zealand:
Abacus Liq./Federal Liq.   Bishops Wood Estate ltd.   Bondpak Centre
Seagram (New Zealand) Ltd.   South Pacific Distillery

Africa - abbreviated

Cape Verde:
Joao A. Monteiro 7 Filhos, LDA.

Egypt:
Distillerie Zottos & Co.

Ghana:
Gihoc Distilleries Co. Ltd.

Madagascar:
Ath. Mellis et Cie   Melvino   Vidzar de Nosy Be

Mauritius:
Grays & Co.   Medine Sugar Estates Co.   United Spirits Producers

Reunion:
Distillerie Societe J.Chatel & Cie   Distillerie Riviere du Mat (SORACO)   GIE Rhum
Isautier

South Africa:
Aroma   Ricardominion Rum Company   Gilbey Distillers & Vintners
Glendale Distilling Company   Totpak   Montego Bay Rum Co.
                                                                    (bottled in S. Africa)

Zimbabwe:
Caribbean Rum Importers (African Distillers Distillers Ltd.)

Answer to quiz: There are over 4000 rum labels produced in over 86 countries.

Whew! And to think I was going to type them all! I changed my mind midway through. What a geography lesson. I didn't even know some of these countries existed, never mind made rum.

Rum is synonymous and indigenous to the Caribbean. Therefore, I have devoted an entire chapter to Rum Drinks.

Of special interest, rum is available in many new and exotic flavors: orange, coconut, banana, pineapple, vanilla, citron and spiced.

Did you know? BLACKBEARD THE PIRATE, a.k.a. Edward Teach, Thatch, was a fearsome giant of a man who wore his beard braided to his waist. He would light tapers and stick them under his three-pointed hat, causing an awe-inspiring swirl of smoke around his head. He sported two cutlasses and six cocked pistols worn in a scarlet bandolier across his chest.

Between 1716 and 1718, he terrorized coasts from Boston to Bonaire in the West Indies, taking dozens of prizes, burying tons of treasure, and thoroughly mistreating his wives and crew. *How'd he get these women to marry him in the first place?*

Most pirate stories and movies are now based on the romantic, fearsome, and swashbuckling Blackbeard. Larger than life, he had a bloodthirsty zest for life. Blackbeard drank only the finest rums, and before battle would drink large quantities laced with gunpowder and spices.

CHAPTER ELEVEN
Wine
including Port, Sherry and Vermouth

The earliest records of wine making go back to 3000 B.C. Wine is mentioned numerous times in the bible, from Daniel attending a dinner by Belshazzar, King of Babylon to Jesus Christ when he turned water into wine for the poor.

It is beyond the scope of this book to fully discuss wine and I strongly suggest you purchase a book on devoted to wines. In the meantime, the following is a simple guide and commentary.

Good wine depends upon several things. I've noticed that wines produced in cool or coastal areas have an entirely different taste from those produced in warmer areas. **Climate** plays a major role in the production of wine. Extreme temperature swings must be avoided. The delicate grapes prefer temperate summers and cool autumns. Rain should be heavier in winter and spring.

Different grape varieties contribute to the distinguishing taste of wines. Certain types only grow in particular areas and climates. **Soil** is another important factor. Chardonnay wine from California tastes entirely different from that made in France. Most wine in the U.S. is made in California.

Popular white wines:

Alsace	France
Bordeaux	France
Burgundy	France
Chardonnay	United States, France, Argentina, Australia
Chenin Blanc	United States, France
Gewurtztraminer	Germany
Pinot Griogio	Italy
Reisling	United States, France, Germany
Sauternes	France
Sauvignon Blanc	United States, France
Semillon	United States, France, Australia
Soave	Italy
Zinfandel	United States

Popular red wines:

Barbera	Italy
Beaujolais	France
Bordeaux	France
Burgundy	France
Cabernet Sauvignon	United States, France
Chianti	Italy
Merlot	United States, France, South America
Pinot Noir	United States, France
Rhone	France
Zinfandel	United States

Sparkling wines and champagne

Dom Perignon, a French monk, invented champagne in the 17th century. Carbon dioxide, a by-product of fermentation, was cleverly trapped in the bottle.

Champagne is made from a variety of grapes from the Champagne region of France. Sparkling wines are made in the United States and other countries.

Serving and Storage

Champagne is often served before dinner and for festive occasions. Serve in a tall glass, which will preserve the bubbles, at approximately 45(Fahrenheit. Tilt the glass to not break the bubbles, pour in a small amount, and allow settling and then filling two thirds.

Keep sparkling wines in a quiet, cool, dark place. Champagne may be stored for a few years.

Bartender's Secret-Temperature of Red Wine

Every good sommelier knows that red wine served slightly chilled pops its flavor. Serve at 50 degrees as opposed to room temperature.

Port

The first time I purchased a bottle of port, it was a gift for a friend. I was in Nantucket at the liquor store and didn't understand why the bottle was so dusty. Apparently, the dust on the bottles is prized. True port comes from Portugal. Port is a sweet wine with the addition of brandy. The higher proof brandy raises the alcohol content of port and improves the taste of the grapes.

Type of port:

Ruby   dark and sweet
Tawny   aged longer than the others, lighter and drier
Vintage port   rare, and sweet

Popular port:

Cockburn's
Croft

Serving and Storage:

Use port as an after-dinner drink. After opening, keep only 4 to 6 months.

Sherry

Sherry is similar to port in that it is a fortified wine to which brandy has been added. Produced all over the world, it originally came from Spain.

Types of sherry:

Fino	dry, serve chilled before dinner
Manzanilla	light, dry, serve chilled before dinner
Amotillanda	not as dry, full, serve between courses
Oloroso	stronger than Amotillanda
Cream	Oloroso blended with Moscatel wine. Sweet, rich. Serve before, during, or after dinner

Popular brands:

Dry Sack
Harvey's Bristol Cream

Vermouth

Vermouth is a complex wine flavored with sweeteners, botanicals, spices, flowers, peels, and seeds with a high alcohol content-approximately 18%. Some of the agents used are cardamom, cloves, orange peel, and nutmeg.

Popular vermouth:

Cinzano
Martini and Rossi
Stock

Serving and Storage:

Vermouth is added to a multitude of drinks, the most popular, of course, the martini. Store opened bottles in the refrigerator as vermouth quickly loses its aromatic qualities. Purchase the smaller 375ml bottle to avoid it going stale quickly.

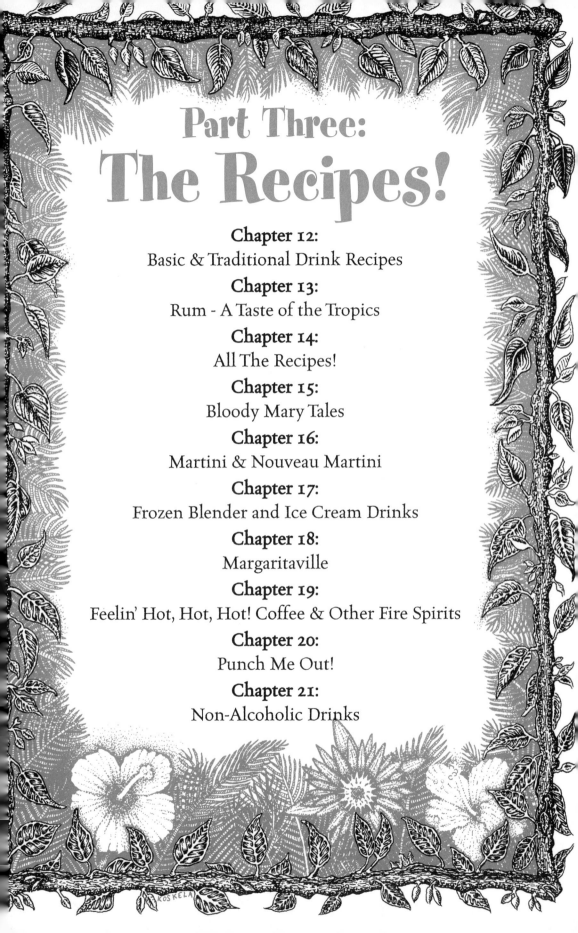

Part Three:
The Recipes!

CHAPTER TWELVE

Basic & Traditional Drink Recipes

Alexander

1 1/2 oz. liquor, such as brandy   1 1/2 oz. white or dark Crème de Cacao
1 1/2 oz. light cream or milk   rocks glass

Shake all ingredients in a cocktail shaker filled with ice. Strain into a rocks glass filled with ice.

Collins

2 oz. liquor, such as gin   3 oz. sour mix
1 oz. club soda   highball glass

Fill a highball glass with ice. Stir in all ingredients.

Cooler

2 oz. liquor, such as vodka   ginger ale
lime wedge   highball glass

Fill a highball glass with ice. Pour in liquor and fill with ginger ale to top. Stir gently. Garnish with a lime wedge.

Daiquiri

2 oz. light rum   1 1/2 oz. fresh limejuice
1/2 oz. simple syrup   cocktail glass

Shake all ingredients in a cocktail shaker filled with ice. Strain into a cocktail glass.

Fruit Daiquiri

2 oz. light rum   1/2 oz. white Crème de Cacao
1/2 oz. fruit liqueur   1/2 cup fresh fruit
1/2 cup crushed ice   hurricane glass

Blend in electric blender until smooth. Pour into a hurricane glass.

Gimlet

2 oz. gin or vodka   1 oz. Rose's Lime Juice
splash of fresh lime juice cocktail glass

Shake all ingredients in a cocktail shaker filled with ice. Strain into a cocktail glass.

Highball

1 1/2 oz. liquor, such as whiskey   ginger ale
highball glass

Fill a highball glass with ice. Pour in liquor and fill to top with ginger ale. Stir gently.

Manhattan

2 1/2 oz. whiskey   1/4 oz. sweet vermouth
Maraschino cherry juice   splash of simple syrup
Maraschino cherry   low ball glass

Fill a low ball with ice. Stir in all ingredients. Garnish with cherry.

Margarita

2 oz. tequila   splash of Triple Sec
1 oz. limejuice   splash of simple syrup
salt   lime wedge
cocktail glass

Wet the lip of the cocktail glass with the lime wedge and twist in a plate of salt. Shake all ingredients except salt and lime wedge in a cocktail shaker filled with ice. Strain into the cocktail glass.

KOSKELA

Mint Julep

2 oz. Kentucky bourbon or brandy
1 tsp. powdered sugar
drop of bitters
highball glass

4 to 5 fresh mint leaves
splash of water
mint leaf for garnish

Place the mint leaves in the bottom of the highball glass. Add sugar and water, grinding leaves. Fill glass to top with ice. Add liquor and stir. Garnish with mint leaves

Rickey

2 oz. liquor, rum, or vodka
highball glass

club soda

Fill a highball glass with ice. Pour in liquor and fill to top with club soda. Stir gently.

Sling

1 1/2 oz. liquor, such as gin
2 oz. sour mix
Maraschino cherry
highball glass

1/2 oz. cherry brandy
1 oz. club soda
orange slice

Shake all ingredients, except orange slice, cherry, and club soda in a cocktail shaker filled with ice. Strain into a highball glass with ice. Fill to top with club soda. Garnish with cherry and orange slice.

Sour

1 1/2 oz. liquor, such as whiskey
orange slice
rocks glass

3 oz. sour mix
Maraschino cherry, plus a little juice

Shake all ingredients, except cherry and orange slice in a cocktail shaker filled with ice. Strain into a rocks glass with ice. Garnish with orange slice and cherry.

Spritzer

1 1/2 oz. liquor, could be wine also
lemon twist

club soda
highball glass

Fill a highball glass with ice. Pour in liquor and fill to top with club soda. Garnish with lemon twist.

Stinger

2 oz. brandy or other dark liquor
lowball glass

1 oz. white Crème de Menthe

Fill a lowball glass with ice. Stir in liquor.

CHAPTER THIRTEEN

Rum-A Taste of the Tropics

Rum is one of the most popular liquors on earth. There are over 4000 rum labels manufactured in over 86 countries. Surprisingly, over 77% of all rum imported into the United States is Puerto Rico's Barcardi rum. From the classic summertime Tom Collins to traditional eggnog during the winter holidays, rum is a versatile liquor.

While a rum and coke will never lose popularity, many new exotic drinks have been created recently. Jump Up and Kiss Me, A Day at the Beach and Big Bamboo are just a few.

High proof rums such as 151 work well for flaming deserts or to add an extra kick to drinks. The new flavored rums such as orange, pineapple, coconut, banana, and chocolate add intense flavor to drinks. Be adventurous and experiment with this versatile tropical liquor.

A Day At The Beach
ST. MARTIN, FRENCH WEST INDIES

1 oz. Cruzan Coconut Rum
1/2 oz. Amaretto
splash of grenadine

1 oz. Cruzan Orange Rum
4 oz. orange juice
Highball glass

Fill a cocktail shaker with ice. Shake all ingredients and strain into a Highball glass filled with ice.

Ankle Breaker
ST. KITTS

1 oz. 151 proof rum
1 oz. cherry brandy
rocks glass

1/2 oz. Cruzan Lime Rum
splash of Triple Sec

Fill a rocks glass to the top with ice. Stir all ingredients into glass.

St. Kitts is south of St. Martin, between St. Eustatius (Staysha) and Montserrat, island of the erupting volcano.

Apple Pie
CLASSIC DRINK

1 oz. light rum
1/2 oz. Calvados
splash of fresh lemon juice

1/2 oz. sweet Vermouth
splash of grenadine
rocks glass

Fill a cocktail shaker with ice. Shake all ingredients and pour into an old-fashioned glass filled with ice.

Bahama Mama #1
Nassau, Bahamas

1 1/2 oz. white rum
2 oz. pineapple juice
1/4 oz. fresh lemon juice
dash of Angostura Bitters
Highball glass

1 oz. Crème de Cassis
2 oz. orange juice
splash of grenadine
orange slice

Fill a Highball glass with ice. Pour all ingredients into glass and stir. Garnish with orange slice.

Nassau is the most frequented cruise ship port of call in the world.

Yeah, mon! Anguilla is synonymous with deserted tropical island. Endless stretches of powdery beaches, azure waters and tropical tradewinds supply this island with enough peace and tranquility you'll forget the office back home. Slender and relatively flat, made of limestone and coral, Anguilla is the northernmost of the Leeward Islands. The island has a reputation not only for its blinding white beaches, but also for its fabulous luxury resorts which attract many celebrities. Despite its arid terrain, the island is abloom with brilliant fuscia, orange and white bougainvillea, oleander, and hibiscus.

The least you need to know:

Capital: The Valley
Population: 12,000
Money: Eastern Caribbean Dollar, US$1=EC2.68
Official Language: English and a bit of Patois
Political Status: British Independent Territory
Just for Fun!: Exploring the islands dozens and dozens of varied beaches, coves, mile-long stretches of sand, dunes, waves; visit Wallblake House, an island plantation; shop at the Anguilla Arts and Crafts Center for a wide selection of local handiwork.
Tidbit: Archaeological evidence points to inhabitation by Indians 2,000 years ago.

Bahama Mama #2
St. Croix, U.S. Virgin Islands

1 1/2 oz. pineapple rum
2 oz. pineapple juice
2 oz. orange juice
Highball glass

1 oz. Kirschwasser (or Cherry Brandy,
    not liqueur)
orange slice

Fill a Highball glass with ice. Pour in all ingredients and stir. Garnish with orange slice.

Another good use of flavored rums. The reason to use cherry brandy instead of cherry liqueur is that the brandy is less sweet and a much higher proof.

Banana Daiquiri
St. Thomas--Mountaintop

1 1/2 oz. white rum
1/2 oz. Rose's lime juice
1/2 cup crushed ice
hurricane glass

1/2 oz. Crème de Banana
1 banana
splash of Triple Sec

Put all ingredients into blender until smooth. Pour into hurricane glass.

To think-when I first moved to St. Thomas many moons ago, World-Famous Mountaintop served banana pancakes. Mountaintop has a fabulous and huge oval-shaped bar overlooking Magen's Bay. A visit here is a must.

Banana Man
Martinique

1 oz. white rum
1/2 oz. Rose's limejuice
sugar

1/2 oz. Crème de Banana
1 oz. light cream
martini glass

Wet the lip of a martini glass with water and twist in a plate of sugar. Fill a cocktail shaker with ice. Pour in remaining ingredients and shake. Strain, neat into a martini glass.

The Arawak Indian tribe named Martinique Madinina, which means island of flowers.

Banana Rama
St. Thomas, U.S. Virgin Islands

1 oz. Cruzan Banana Rum
orange juice

1 oz. dark rum
splash of Amaretto

Fill a Highball glass with ice. Pour in rums, splash of Amaretto and fill to top with orange juice. Stir.

St. Thomas is one of the most important stops on an Eastern Caribbean Cruise. The most cosmopolitan of the three U.S. Virgin Islands (four if you count the recent addition of Water Island, in St. Thomas harbor), it offers world-class shopping, dining, snorkeling, diving and of course, cocktailing!

Banana-Orange Rum Cream
Grand Cayman

1 oz. Cruzan Banana Rum
2 oz. orange juice

1 oz. Cruzan Rum Cream
martini glass

Fill a cocktail shaker with ice and shake all ingredients. Strain into a martini glass.

Grand Cayman is famous for its turtle farm. The turtles make this startling gulping sound as they come up for air. The babies fit in the palm of a child's hand. The adults have heads nearly the size of a human head.

Yeah, mon! The Bahamas are home to the largest cruise ship port in the world. Considered a Caribbean island, the archipelago of the Bahamas are actually completely within the Atlantic Ocean, stretching from the eastern tip of Florida to the southeastern tip of Cuba. The climate is relatively cool compared to the rest of the Caribbean. Well, at least I thought so. To me, it was freezing, maybe around 70 (in September). Activites on Nassau and nearby Paradise island consist of bar and casino hopping, jet-skiing, sunning and scuba diving. Nassau itself offers a good bit of history, from Victorian mansions, churches, fortresses and an ancient marketplace, full of crafts and souvenirs.

The least you need to know:

Capital: Nassau
Population: 310,000
Money: Bahamian Dollar; US$1=BA1
Official Language: English, and I did note some Patois
Political Status: Independent Nation, Member of the British Commonwealth
Just for Fun!: Ride in a horse-drawn carriage in downtown Nassau, party at Paradise Island, dive with the sea life, dolphins or sharks
Tidbit: The archipelago includes over 700 islands and more than 2,500 cays encompassing approximately 5400 square miles.

Banana Rum Cream
DOMINICA

1 1/2 oz. dark rum
1 oz. Crème de Banana
rocks glass

1 oz. Cruzan Rum Cream Liqueur
1/2 cup crushed ice

Combine all ingredients a cocktail shaker filled with ice. Strain and serve over ice in a rocks glass.

Bananas grow readily on this lush island dotted with wild orchids and waterfalls.

Bartender's Secret-Glassware Check

Beautifully crystal clear and spotless glassware adds immeasurably to the appeal of any drink. Be especially aware of lipstick, as even the most powerful electric dishwasher will not remove it. Use two towels if hand-washing. One to dry and the other to polish. For hygiene's sake, change towels frequently. If using a dishwasher, use the high heat wash and dry cycles.

Barracuda
Virgin Gorda, British Virgin Islands

1 oz. dark rum
1/2 oz. Rose's Lime Juice
champagne glass

1 oz. Cruzan Pineapple Rum
champagne

Fill a cocktail shaker with ice, rums, and limejuice. Shake and strain into a champagne glass. Fill to top with champagne.

The last time I saw a barracuda was when I was still married. What I mean is--it was in the water off the coast of Virgin Gorda, which means Fat Virgin by the way. If you look at it from a distance, it looks like a woman lying on her side.

Beachcomber
Bonaire

1 1/2 oz. white rum
1/2 oz. Cointreau
splash of lime juice

1/2 oz. Triple Sec
splash of Maraschino Liqueur
rocks glass

Fill a rocks glass full of ice and stir in all ingredients.

Bonaire is famous for its flocks of flamingos.

Beach Bum Lover
St. John, U.S. Virgin Islands

1 oz. white rum
1 oz. cranberry juice

1 1/2 oz. Midori
shooter

Fill a cocktail shaker with ice and ingredients. Shake and strain into a shooter.

St. John is home to Trunk Bay, one of the most beautiful beaches in the world.

Blue Mountain
Jamaica, mon

1 1/2 oz. Jamaican rum
1/2 oz. Tia Maria
martini glass

1/2 oz. vodka
2 oz. orange juice

Fill a strainer with ice and shake all ingredients well. Strain into a cocktail glass filled with ice.

Bermuda Triangle
BERMUDA

Bermuda really is not part of the Caribbean. However, so many cruise ships stop that I've included it anyway. Besides, did you know that anyway?

1 oz. Captain Morgan's Spice Rum
1/2 oz. Cruzan Orange Rum
freshly grated nutmeg

1 oz. Peach Schnapps
orange juice
rocks glass

Fill a rocks glass with ice. Stir in rums and schnapps. Fill to the top with orange juice and stir.

Between The Sheets
GUADELOUPE

1 oz. Junakanoo (citrus rum)
1 oz. Cointreau
sugar

1 oz. cognac
splash of fresh lemon juice
rocks glass

Wet the edge of a rocks glass with water and twist in a plate of Sugar. Fill a cocktail shaker with ice. Add rum, cognac, Cointreau and lemon juice. Shake and strain into glass.

Another fabulous drink from *Just Add Rum!* added to this book by special request for a secret friend.

KOSKELA

Berried Pleasure
St. Thomas, U.S. Virgin Islands

1 oz. white rum
1/2 oz. white Crème de Cacao
1/2 cup frozen strawberries

1/2 oz. Amaretto
1/2 oz. Cruzan Rum Cream Liqueur
1/4 cup crushed ice

Combine all ingredients in a blender until smooth. Pour into a hurricane glass.

Charlotte Amalie, the capitol of the U.S. Virgin Islands is located in St. Thomas. It is also the main shopping district on the island. Exotic boutiques offer designer clothing next to colorful tee shirt shops and stores featuring luxury items such as china, crystal, perfume, and jewelry.

Big Bamboo
St. Thomas, U.S. Virgin Islands

1 oz. white rum
1 oz. Grand Marnier
lime zest

1 oz. Junkanoo (citrus rum)
juice of one lime
rocks glass

Fill a cocktail shaker with ice. Shake all liquid ingredients. Use a strainer and pour into a rocks glass filled with ice.

If you've read one of my other books, *Just Add Rum!*, you would know that my husband named this drink. Just for the record, it's ex-husband now.

Blueberry Daiquiri

1 1/2 oz. light rum
4 oz. frozen blueberries
margarita glass

1 oz. Blueberry Schnapps
1 tsp. simple syrup

Whirl all ingredients in blender until smooth. Pour into margarita glass.

Blue Hawaiian
CLASSIC ISLAND DRINK

1 oz. white rum
1 oz. pineapple juice
1 oz. Blue Curacao

1 oz. gold rum
1 oz. lemonade
Highball glass

Fill a Highball glass with ice. Start the layers in this drink with the white rum first, then the gold rum, the juices and top with the Blue Curacao.

Yeah, mon! Barbados visitors will find everything they would ever need in a vacation to this sophisticated island. Only 14 miles wide by 21 miles long, which seems to be the standard size for a Caribbean island, there are nearly 975 miles of paved roads. Don't forget to drive on the left on this British island! The island's picturesque colonial towns are lovely, and rolling green hillsides dot the countryside.

Capital: Bridgetown

Population: nearly 300,000

Money: Barbados Dollar, US$1=BD1.98

Official Language: English and a spot of Spanish

Political Status: Independent Nation; Member of the British Commonwealth

Just for Fun!: Visit over 1,000 rum shops, see Harrison's Cave with its subterranean streams and waterfalls, visit the Flower Forest.

Tidbit: Legislators still wear powdered white wigs in one of the world's oldest Parliaments.

Bongo Drum
ST. THOMAS, U.S. VIRGIN ISLANDS

1 1/2 oz. light rum
pineapple juice

1/2 oz. Crème de Cassis
Highball glass

Fill a Highball glass with ice. First, layer the rum, then the Crème de Cassis, floating pineapple juice on top.

Borinquen
PUERTO RICO

1 1/2 oz. gold rum
1 oz. orange juice
rocks glass

1/2 oz. Rose's Lime Juice
splash Alize (passionfruit and cognac)

Fill a rocks glass with ice. Stir all ingredients.

Borinquen #2
PUERTO RICO

1 1/2 oz. light rum
1 oz. fresh limejuice
151 proof rum
martini glass

1/2 Passoa Passion Fruit Liqueur
1 oz. orange juice
1/2 cup crushed ice

Put all ingredients except 151 in blender. Blend until snowy. Pour into a martini glass and float 151 on the top.

Boston Cocktail

CLASSIC DRINK

1 oz. light rum
1 oz. brandy
martini glass

1 oz. Triple Sec
splash of Maraschino liqueur

Shake all ingredients in a cocktail shaker filled with ice. Strain into a martini glass.

Bartender's Secret–Heavenly Scents

As a writer, I was taught to evoke all the senses, especially smell. Don't underestimate the fresh, exhilarating scent of a lemon twist, orange slice or even the sweet perfume of pineapple when making drinks. Rim your glasses with citrus twists, slices, or maraschino cherry juice.

Buccaneer

ANTIGUA

A delightfully refreshing amber and emerald cocktail.

1 oz. white Crème de Menthe
1 oz. light rum
2 oz. iced tead
mint leaf

1 oz. dark rum
1 oz. simple syrup
lime twist
martini glass

In the bottom of a martini glass, place the Crème de Menthe and simple syrup, stir. Place one large ice cube in glass, and using a spoon run down the rum and ice tea, preventing the mixing with the Crème de Menthe. Garnish with lime twist and mint leaf.

Bushwhacker

ST. THOMAS-MAGEN'S BAY BEACH

1 oz. Cruzan Coconut Rum
1/2 oz. Kahlua
crushed ice
hurricane glass

1 oz. Cruzan Rum Cream Liqueur
1/2 oz. Dark Crème de Cacao
freshly grated nutmeg

Put all ingredients into blender until smooth. Pour into a hurricane glass. Sprinkle nutmeg over the top.

My 21-year-old sister drinks these when she comes down to visit. Somehow, she manages to fit into her bikini. Come to think of it, she drinks a lot of beer as well.

Caribbean Champagne

1 oz. light rum

champagne

1 oz. Crème de Banana

champagne glass

Fill a cocktail shaker with ice. Shake the rum and Crème de Banana. Strain into a martini glass. Fill to the top with champagne.

Caribbean Girl

Antigua

Caribbean girls are beautiful, but are they ever hard to catch! They'll check you out, but if you don't know the right words, you're out of there.

1 oz. light rum

1 oz. Bohemian Raspberry Liqueur by Bols

1 scoop of lime sherbert

maraschino cherry

1 oz. Stoli Razberi

4 oz. orange juice

slice of a starfruit

hurricane glass

Shake all ingredients in a cocktail shaker filled with ice, except raspberry liqueur. Pour the liqueur into the bottom of a glass. Fill halfway with ice and carefully pour rum mixture in, careful to not disturb the liqueur on the bottom.

Bartender's Secret-Ice storage for home parties

Take the bottom drawer out of your automatic dishwasher at home (make sure it's sparkling clean first) and fill with ice. I recommend that you store wine bottles, mixers and juices in the refrigerator or another ice chest unless you thoroughly wash and disinfect the outside of these containers.

Casablanca

St. Thomas, U.S. Virgin Islands

1 oz. gold rum

1/2 oz. Maraschino Liqueur

margarita glass

1 oz. Curacao

1/2 oz. Godiva Chocolate Liqueur

Fill a cocktail shaker with ice. Shake all ingredients, strain and pour into a margarita glass.

Cherry-Chocolate Rum Cream
BARBADOS

1 1/2 oz. light rum
1/2 oz. Godiva Chocolate Liqueur
rocks glass

1/2 oz. Kirshwasser
2 oz. light cream

Fill a cocktail shaker with ice. Combine and shake all ingredients until Frothy. Pour into a rocks glass filled with ice.

Cherry Coke
ST. MAARTEN, NETHERLANDS ANTILLES

1 1/2 oz. gold rum
cola
Highball glass

1 oz. cherry liqueur
lemon peel

Fill a Highball glass full of ice. Stir in rum, liqueur, and fill to top with cola. Stir gently. Twist the peel and run around rim of glass. Drop in.

Chocolate Rum
ST. BARTHS

1 oz. light rum
1/2 oz. white Crème de Menthe
splash of Amaretto

1/2 oz. dark Crème de Cacao
1 oz. light cream
splash of 151 rum

Fill a cocktail shaker with ice. Shake the rum, Crème de Cacao, Crème de Menthe and the cream. Strain into a martini glass. Float the Amaretto and 151 on the top.

St. Barth is a short ferry ride from St. Martin/St. Maarten in the Netherlands Antilles. It is a playground for the rich and reclusive.

Coqui
PUERTO RICO

2 oz. Bacardi Rum
4 oz. pineapple juice
Highball glass

1 oz. Blackberry Brandy
splash of maraschino juice

Fill a Highball glass with ice. Pour in remaining ingredients and stir.

When I had an apartment in San Juan, there was a lily pond in the front yard inhabited by tiny tree frogs, a.k.a. Coqui. They are less than an inch long and make a raucous chirping sound, cokee, cokee.

Yeah, mon! Bonaire is only 50 miles from Venezuela and very close to Aruba, part of the ABC islands, of Aruba, Bonaire and Curacao. Supposedly there are more pink flamingos than people. O.k., well maybe more than tourists. Scuba diving here is ranked among the best in the world. The capital is very quiet with only one main street, colorful colonial buildings and lined with divine shops and restaurants. The most popular attraction on the island lines the entire coast of Bonaire and its tiny offshore cay, Klein Bonaire-Bonaire Marine Park.

The least you need to know:

Capital: Kralendijk
Population: 16,000
Money: Netherlands Antilles Florin, US$1=NAF$1.78
Official Language: Dutch, English, Spanish, Patois and Papiamento
Political Status: Member of the Netherlands Antilles
Just for Fun!: Diving in water so clear you can look a fish straight in the eye; watching pink flamingos fly at sunset at Rode Pan; riding a mountain bike around the island.
Tidbit: Bonaire's Marine Park includes roughly its entire coastline, from the high water mark to a depth of 200 feet.

Coquito
PUERTO RICO

Coquito is made at home in Puerto Rico for traditional and holiday gatherings.

20 oz. 151 proof rum
1 14-oz. can sweetened-condensed milk
1 teaspoon ground cinnamon
5 egg yolks, beaten

2 ripe coconuts
1 5-oz. can evaporated milk
1/8 teaspoon ground nutmeg

With a hammer, crack open the coconuts and place in 250° oven for five minutes. The brown husk should be easy to remove from heat. Grate or put in food processor. Place grated coconut in saucepan with just enough water to cover, allow to stand for ten minutes. Place coconut in clean cheesecloth, twist, and strain milk back into saucepan.

In a large bowl, combine milks, spices, and egg yolks with rum. Stir in coconut milk. Purée in blender until smooth. Refrigerate overnight and dust with cinnamon when serving.

Corkscrew
VIRGIN GORDA, BRITISH VIRGIN ISLANDS

1 1/2 oz. light rum
splash of Port wine
rocks glass

splash of cognac
splash of Rose's Lime Juice

Fill a rocks glass with ice. Stir in all ingredients.

Coconut Bang!
TRINIDAD

1 oz. Cruzan Coconut Rum
1/2 oz. Malibu Rum
1/2 oz. Rose's Lime Juice
1/2 cup crushed ice

1 oz. Cruzan Pineapple Rum
1/2 oz. Coco Lopez
4 oz. fresh coconut milk
hurricane glass

Drain the milk from a coconut by puncturing the eyes with a Phillips screwdriver and a hammer. Carefully strain into a glass to remove pieces of the husk. Measure off two ounces and put in blender with remaining ingredients. Pour into hurricane glass.

This recipe came from Café Savanna one of the best Trinidadian restaurants on the island.

Corkscrew #2
FT. LAUDERDALE

1 1/2 oz. light rum
1/2 oz. Peach Schnapps

1/2 oz. dry Vermouth
shooter

Fill a cocktail shaker with ice. Shake ingredients and strain into a shooter.

Cran-Rum Twister
PUERTO RICO

1 1/2 oz. Barcardi light rum
lemon-lime soda
Highball glass

2 oz. cranberry juice
lemon slice

Fill a Highball glass with ice, light rum, and cranberry juice. Layer the soda over the top. Garnish with a lemon slice.

Bartender's Secret-Preserve your beer

There is no need to over chill beer. It will become cloudy and the cold temperature will ruin the flavor. While visiting Germany as a child, often I would see patrons dropping a hot iron into their brew to warm it up.

Store bottled beer in a cool, dark place. Discard beer that has lost its fizz. When washing beer mugs or glasses, be sure to rinse away every speck of soap, as it will ruin the head.

Cream Puff

St. John, U.S. Virgin Islands

2 oz. light rum
1 tsp. Powdered sugar
Club soda

1 oz. light cream
splash of Frangelico (hazelnut liqueur)
Highball glass

Fill a shaker with ice. Shake all ingredients except the Club soda. Strain into a Highball glass filled with ice. Fill with Club soda and gently stir.

Much of this jewel-like island is U.S. National Park. Some of the most beautiful beaches in the world are here.

Creole

St. Kitts

1 1/2 oz. light rum
splash of Tabasco™ or habanero hot sauce
salt and pepper to taste
old-fashioned glass

1 1/2 oz. beef bouillon
splash of fresh lemon juice
lemon twist

Fill an old fashioned glass with ice. Stir in the rum, bouillon, hot sauce, and lemon juice. Season to taste with salt & pepper.

Cube Libre

Cuba

1 1/2 oz. white Cuban rum
1/4 oz. fresh limejuice
Highball glass

Cola
lime wedge

Fill a highball glass with ice and add rum. Add lime juice. Fill glass to top with Cola. Stir gently. Garnish with lime wedge.

For true authentic flavor, use Cuban rum.

Daiquiri

Cuba

1 1/2 oz. white Cuban rum
1/4 oz. simple syrup
martini glass

juice of 1/2 lime
lime slice

Fill a cocktail shaker with cracker ice and all ingredients except the lime slice. Shake well and strain into a martini glass.

Yeah, mon! Antigua has 365 white-sand beaches, one for each day of the year. The island's continuously notched and scalloped coastline offer secluded harbors, gorgeous deep blue bays, coves and inlets. Offshore, there are more than 30 islands, cays, and islets and more fabulous secluded beaches. Barbuda is very close by.

The least you need to know:

Capital: St. John's
Population: 68,000
Money: Eastern Caribbean Dollar, US$1=EC$2.68
Official Language: English
Political Status: Independent Nation, Member of the British Commonwealth
Just for Fun!: Have a blast at the biggest party of the year-Antigua Sailing Week; drive to Shirley Heights for a spectacular view of English Harbour; head southwest on Fig Tree Drive through the rainforest and pick mangoes, pineapple and bananas.
Tidbit: The sand on Barbuda is pink.

KOSKELA

Dark and Stormy
ANTIGUA

1 oz. white rum
splash of Rose's lime juice
freshly grated ginger

1 oz. Cruzan Lime Rum
ginger ale
Highball glass

Fill a Highball glass with ice. Stir in all ingredients except for the fresh ginger. Sprinkle ginger lightly over the top.

They tell you not to open your novels with the cliché "It was a dark and stormy night." I wonder if that counts for books set in the Caribbean. Hmm.

Eye Opener
JAMAICA

1 oz. Jamaican dark rum
1/2 oz. Triple Sec
1/4 oz. Pernod
1 oz. orange juice
Highball glass

1 oz. Cruzan white rum
1/4 oz. White Crème de Cacao
1 oz. pineapple juice
splash of fresh lemon juice

Fill a cocktail shaker with ice. Shake all ingredients and strain into a Highball glass filled with ice.

Bartender's Secret-Frozen Vodka

Vodka will not freeze because of it's high alcohol content. It is rather fascinating to see it become syrupy. A neat way to serve and chill vodka is to cut off the top of a paper two-quart milk carton and fill half-way with water. Insert the vodka bottle, freeze, and remove the carton by running hot water over it.

Flamingo
ANEGADA, BRITISH VIRGIN ISLANDS

1 1/2 oz. gold rum
splash of Alize (passionfruit liqueur)
splash of fresh lime juice

splash of grenadine
2 oz. pineapple juice
rocks glass

Fill a rocks glass with ice. Stir all ingredients.

Fruit Punch
ANTIGUA

2 oz. light rum
1/2 oz. fresh limejuice
1 oz. pineapple juice
hurricane glass

1/2 oz. guava juice
1 oz. orange juice
splash of grenadine
slice of pineapple

Shake all ingredients in a cocktail shaker filled with ice. Fill a hurricane glass with ice and pour in punch. Garnish with slice of pineapple.

Goombay Smash
BAHAMAS

1 oz. dark rum
1/2 oz. Triple Sec
splash of fresh lemon juice

1 oz. Cruzan Coconut Rum
4 oz. pineapple juice

Fill a cocktail shaker with ice. Shake all ingredients and strain into a Collins glass filled with ice.

Gorilla Milk
GRENADA

1 oz. light rum
1/2 oz. Cruzan Rum Cream
1 oz. light cream

1/2 oz. Kahlua
1/2 oz. Crème de Banana
rocks glass

Fill a shaker with ice. Shake all ingredients and strain into an rocks glass filled with ice.

Grand Lucian
ST. LUCIA

Serve this refreshing drink on hot summer evenings.

1 oz. light rum
2 oz. fresh coconut milk (refer to Out At Sea)
splash of fresh limejuice
rocks glass

1 oz. Kirsch liqueur
1/2 oz. simple syrup
lime zest

Shake all ingredients in a cocktail shaker filled with ice. Fill a rocks glass with ice. Strain into glass. Garnish with lime zest.

Green Parrot
PUERTO RICO

1 1/2 oz. Barcardi light rum
1 oz. Blue Curacao
champagne glass

4 oz. orange juice
grated lemon zest

Loosely fill a champagne glass with ice. This is a layered drink, so pour carefully to not disturb the layers. Start with the rum, then the orange juice. Float the Blue Curacao on top. Sprinkle with lemon zest.

Bartender's Secret-Exotic Containers

Island-inspired drinks require creative serving ware. No container is too outlandish if impeccably clean. Try pottery bowls, ceramic vases, shaped like bamboo or parrots, flower pots (hole will have to be safely stopped), goldfish bowls, footed tiki bowls or the like. How about some of those huge, over-size brandy snifters or balloon-shaped wine glasses for rum drinks or daiquiris? Last night the wine I opened had spoiled, but I had just purchased these over-size wine glasses. I made myself a strawberry margarita and served it in the wine glass instead. Take a look in your basement or cupboard. You may just find a use for that white elephant!

Guava Daiquiri
DOMINICAN REPUBLIC

1 1/2 oz. white rum
1/2 oz. Amaretto
1/2 oz. Rose's Lime Juice
martini glass

1 oz. guava juice (local Caribbean grocery
  or gourmet section)
1/2 cup crushed ice

Mix all ingredients in blender. Pour into martini glass.

The Dominican Republic has the largest hotel inventory in the Caribbean-over 24,000 rooms and more on the way. It shares the island of Hispaniola (makes you think of pirates, doesn't it) with Haiti, which makes me think of voodoo.

Havana Special
HAVANA

2 oz. white Cuban rum
4 oz. pineapple juice
martini glass

1 oz. Maraschino liqueur
maraschino cherry

Fill a cocktail shaker with cracked ice. Shake all ingredients except the cherry. Fill a martini glass with ice. Strain and pour drink into glass. Garnish with a cherry.

Yeah, mon! Aruba is tiny, only six miles wide and 20 miles long. But if your idea of paradise is white-sand beaches, this island is for you. I was there on a cruise recently with my son, Colby. The beach was wonderful and the water sports were even better. There was a raft called the banana, which was pulled behind a speed boat, a pirate ship, parasailing and water skiing. Shopping here is world-class, rivaling St. Thomas. The bustling city if chock full of shops, quaint open-air cafés, most of which are housed in Dutch or Spanish structures.

The least you need to know:

Capital: Oranjestad
Population: 95,000
Money: Arubian Florin; US$1=Afl 1.78
Official Language: English, Spanish, Papiamento (type of Creole)
Political Status: Autonomous member of Kingdom of Netherlands
Just for Fun!: Learning to windsurf at Fisherman's Hut, shopping till you drop for duty-free goodies, i.e. china, crystal, perfume, linens, watches; playing golf at the Aruba Golf Club among the goats and cacti.
Tidbit: "No Tira Sushi" means no littering!

Hemingway Special
CUBA

2 oz. white Cuban rum
juice of 1/2 a lime
highball glass

4 oz. grapefruit juice
lime slice

Fill a cocktail shaker with ice. Add all ingredients except the lime slice and shake. Strain into a highball glass filled with ice. Garnish with lime slice.

Originally known as the "Daiquiri Com Papa", Hemingway would carry a thermos filled with his favorite drink made with Cuban rum. This liquid inspiration obviously worked. Maybe I should try it and get my novel finished.

Hurricane #1
CLASSIC ISLAND DRINK

1 oz. white rum

4 oz. pineapple juice

splash of grenadine

Maraschino cherry

1 oz. gold rum

2 oz. orange juice

orange slice

hurricane glass

Fill a hurricane glass with ice. Pour in all ingredients and stir. Garnish with orange slice and cherry.

Have I told you how many hurricanes I've survived in the Virgin Islands? Probably not. There have been so many in the last ten years; I have lost count.

Hurricane #2
CLASSIC ISLAND DRINK

1 oz. Cruzan Pineapple Rum

4 oz. pineapple juice

splash of grenadine

Maraschino cherry

1 oz. Cruzan Orange Rum

2 oz. orange juice

orange slice

hurricane glass

Fill a hurricane glass with ice. Pour in all ingredients and stir. Garnish with orange slice and cherry.

The flavored rums give an intense taste to this classic drink.

Island Iced Tea
ARUBA

1 oz. white rum

1 cup ice tea, chilled

splash of grenadine

lemon slice

1 oz. dark rum

splash of Rose's Lime Juice

splash of 151 proof rum

Highball glass

Fill a Highball glass to the top with ice. Stir in the rums (except 151), ice tea, limejuice, and grenadine. Float the 151 on the top.

Aruba is the "A" in the ABC islands of Aruba, Bonaire, and Curacao all close to Venezuela.

Island Sunrise

St. Maarten-Holland House

1 1/2 oz white rum
1 oz. grenadine

4 oz. orange juice
lime wedge

Fill a rocks glass with ice. Pour Grenadine into bottom of glass. Carefully pour orange juice over the Grenadine, trying not to disturb the red layer. Remember, you are making a beautiful layered drink here. Float rum on top. Garnish with a lime wedge.

Holland House is located on the Dutch side of St. Maarten in Phillipsburg. Perfect place to stay for bargain hunters as it is in the heart of the shopping district.

KOSKELA

Jade
St. John, U.S. Virgin Islands

1 1/2 oz. light rum
1/2 oz. Cointreau
1/2 tsp. powdered sugar

1/2 oz. green Crème de Menthe
1/2 oz. fresh limejuice

Fill a cocktail strainer with ice. Shake all ingredients and strain into a cock-tail glass.

Jou Jou
Haiti

1 oz. Haitian rum (Barbancourt)
1 oz. Southern Comfort
1/2 oz. Rose's Lime Juice
1/2 cup crushed ice
hurricane glass

1/2 oz. Cruzan Orange Rum
1 oz. orange juice
1/2 banana
grated nutmeg

Blend until smooth in blender. Pour into a hurricane glass. Sprinkle with grated nutmeg.

Jou jou is local slang for a voodoo spell. You may be spell bound for other reasons when you drink this.

Juicey Fruit
St. Croix, U.S. Virgin Islands

1 oz. Cruzan Orange Rum
1 oz. Passoa Passion Fruit Liqueur
rocks glass

1 oz. Cruzan Pineapple Rum
1 oz. Kirsch Liqueur

Fill a rocks glass with crushed ice. Add liquor and stir.

This drink is sneaky. It packs a powerful wallop.

Key West Sunset
Key West

1 1/2 oz. white rum
orange juice
orange slice
highball glass

1 1/2 oz. Peach Schnapps
grenandine
maraschino cherry

Fill a highball glass with ice. This is a layered drink, so go slowly. First, pour white rum into bottom of glass. Then using a long bar spoon inserted into ice, pour the Peach Schnapps next. Do not disturb or muddle with rum. Do the same for the orange juice, leaving about an inch of room at the top. Float grenadine on top. Garnish with orange slice and cherry.

Latin Love
PUERTO RICO

1 oz. Cruzan Banana Rum
1 oz. Chambord
pineapple juice
hurricane glass

1 oz. Cruzan Coconut Rum
1 oz. Coco Lopez
1/2 cup crushed ice

Pour all ingredients into a blender. Blend until smooth and pour into a hurricane glass.

Old San Juan is where the cruise ships dock in Puerto Rico. This old has a restored fortress dating back to the 16th century, cobblestone streets, venerable churches, museums, and shops.

Limbo Nana
ST. MARTIN, FRENCH WEST INDIES

1 oz. Cruzan Banana Rum
1/2 oz. Cruzan Rum Cream Liqueur
1/2 banana
hurricane glass

1 oz. Amaretto
juice of one lime
crushed ice

Place all ingredients in blender and combine until smooth. Pour into a hurricane glass.

This island has a Dutch side, spelled St. Maarten, and a French side, spelled St. Martin. All of the island's ten miles of beaches are gorgeous.

Bartender's Secret-Coconut Patrol

Fresh coconut is delicious, inexpensive, and readily available. Despite its trouble to prepare, the intense flavor is worth it. Select a coconut (really a seed, not a fruit), which is heavy and full of liquid. With an ice pick and a hammer, punch in the two eyes and drain the liquid. Strain through a cheesecloth and freeze or refrigerate for a couple of days. The shell can be used as a decorative container. Saw in half and pry out the meat. Grate meat with a grater.

Another method is to drain the milk as mentioned above and then bake the coconut in a 325° oven for 15 minutes. The shell will crack readily.

Prepare coconut milk by grating and then placing in a blender with about 1/4 to 1/2 cup water depending on size of coconut. Use milk for a rich coconut cream and/or add the originally drained coconut liquid.

Lounge Lizard
PUERTO RICO

1 1/2 oz. dark rum
cola

1/2 oz. Amaretto

Fill a Highball glass with ice. Pour in the rum and Amaretto. Fill to top with cola and stir gently.

Love Potion
GRENADA

Grenada is known as the spice island. While on a cruise, I visited their lovely open-air market. The heady scent of spices filled the air.

1 1/2 oz. white rum
1 oz. light cream
1/2 cup crushed ice

1 1/2 oz. Amaretto
1/2 cup frozen strawberries
hurricane glass

Combine all ingredients in blender until smooth. Pour into a hurricane glass.

M & M 151
ST. MAARTEN, NETHERLANDS ANTILLES

1 part Kahlua
1 part 151 proof rum

1 part Amaretto
shooter

Layer the Amaretto over the Kahlua. Float the 151 on the top.

Macarena
ST. THOMAS, U.S. VIRGIN ISLANDS

1 oz. Malibu rum
3 oz. lemonade
1 oz. pineapple juice
Highball glass

1/2 oz. Tequila
1 oz. orange juice
splash of maraschino juice

Fill a cocktail shaker with ice. Shake all ingredients and strain into a Collins glass filled with ice.

Did you know? Vic Bergeron, a.k.a. Trader Vic, invented the **Mai Tai** in 1944 at his Polynesian bar.

Mai Tai
ISLAND CLASSIC

1 oz. white rum
1/2 oz. orange Curacao
1/2 oz. fresh limejuice

1/2 oz. 151 proof rum
1/2 oz. orgeat (almond syrup)
martini glass

Fill a cocktail shaker with ice. Pour in all ingredients and shake. Strain and serve straight up in a chilled martini glass.

Mango Daiquiri
ANTIGUA

Antigua is the largest of the British Leeward Islands and is located somewhat near Monteserrat.

1 oz. white rum
1/2 oz. Peach Brandy
1/2 cup fresh or frozen mango
hurricane glass

1 oz. gold rum
1/2 oz. Rose's Lime Juice
1/2 cup crushed ice

Whirl all ingredients in blender until smooth. Pour into a hurricane glass.

Mango Tango
ST. THOMAS, U.S. VIRGIN ISLANDS

1 oz. white rum
1/2 oz. Peach Schnapps
splash of cranberry juice
hurricane glass

1 oz. dark rum
1/2 cup frozen mango or peach slices
1/2 cup crushed ice

Put all ingredients in blender and combine until smooth. Pour into a hurricane glass.

There is a lovely art gallery on St. Thomas called Mango Tango.

Bartender's Secret-Flavor Intensifiers

Aromatic and flavorful liqueurs can significantly improve the flavor of many mixed drinks. See the chapter on liqueurs and cordials for a complete list which includes Crème de Cacao, Crème de Banana, Triple Sec, Cointreau, Crème de Noyaux, Amaretto, Anisette and Sloe gin, just to name a few.

Besides intense flavor and fragrance, many add lovely, jewel-like colors such as Crème de Yvette (violet), Chartreuse (green for flavor, yellow for fragrance), Galliano (yellow), Grand Marnier (orange) Curacao (in yellow, red, green, blue, and clear) Kahlua (chocolate-colored), Cherry Heering (ruby) and others.

Mel's Treasure

FLORIDA

1 1/2 oz. Captain Morgan Spiced rum
lime wedge

cola
highball glass

Fill a highball glass with ice. Pour in rum and fill glass to top with cola. Stir gently. Squeeze lime wedge into drink and drop in.

Menage a Trois

U.S. VIRGIN ISLANDS

1 oz. white rum
1/2 oz. Grand Marnier
shooter

1 oz. Cacao Creole (rum and
chocolate liqueur)

Fill a cocktail shaker full of ice. Shake all ingredients and strain into a shooter.

The three U.S. Virgin Islands have recently multiplied. On December 12, 1996, Water Island, situated in St. Thomas harbor became number four.

Mocko Jumbie

ST. THOMAS, U.S. VIRGIN ISLANDS

1 oz. Cruzan Coconut Rum
4 oz. pineapple juice
Highball glass

1 oz. Midori
splash of maraschino cherry juice

Fill a Highball glass with ice. Stir in all other ingredients.

Mocko jumbies are costumed stilt-walkers that ward off evil island spirits.

Mojito

HAVANA

1 1/2 oz white Cuban rum
1/2 oz fresh limejuice
fresh mint leaves

Soda water
1/2 teaspoon sugar
highball glass

Put the sugar and limejuice in a highball glass. Crush a couple of the mint leaves into the lime and sugar mixture with a muddler. Add the rum; fill glass to top with ice. Fill soda to top. Garnish with mint leaves.

Legend has it that Sir Frances Drake, the adventurer, concocted this drink during his passage through the West Indies.

Mulatto

ANTIGUA

This drink is smooth and sweet and will sneak up on you!

2 oz. light rum
2 oz. fresh coconut milk
fresh chocolate shavings

1 oz. Malibu coconut liqueur
1 small banana
margarita glass

Blend all ingredients except chocolate with a couple of ice cubes in blender until smooth. Pour into margarita glass and garnish with chocolate shavings.

Nelson's Blood

TORTOLA, BRITISH VIRGIN ISLANDS

1 1/2 oz Pusser's British Navy Rum
1 oz. orange juice
splash of grenadine

1 oz. cranberry juice
1 oz. pineapple juice
rocks glass

Fill a rocks glass with ice. Coat the bottom of the glass lightly with grenadine. In a cocktail shaker filled with ice, shake the rum and juices. Pour carefully over the grenadine to not dislodge it.

No Go So

ST. CROIX, U.S. VIRGIN ISLANDS

1 1/2 oz. Cruzan Orange Rum
splash of Galliano

1 1/2 oz. Cruzan Banana Rum
rocks glass

Fill a rocks glass with ice. Pour in rums and Galliano. Stir.

St. Croix is the largest of the U.S. Virgin Islands and the least mountainous. More than 100 ancient sugar mills, former plantations, dot rolling green hills.

Orange Rum Rita

ST. THOMAS, U.S. VIRGIN ISLANDS

1 oz. Cruzan Orange Rum
1/2 oz. Cointreau
crushed ice

1 oz. Cruzan Pineapple Rum
1 oz. fresh limejuice
crushed rock salt

Fill a cocktail shaker with crushed ice. Shake all ingredients well. Rim a margarita glass with crushed rock salt-wet the rim first with water. Using a strainer, pour in drink.

Charlotte Amalie, in the heart of the shopping district, has many tropical bars and restaurants in its shaded alleys. Nearly all serve these new flavored rums.

Yeah, mon! Tortola, British Virgin Islands is part of a chain of some sixty-odd islands separated by a few miles from the U.S. Virgin Islands. The BVI remind me of fifty-year-old photos I have seen of St. Thomas while it was still relatively unspoiled. With the exception of Anegada, a lime and coral island, the other British Virgin Islands are volcanic in origin.

The least you should know:

Capital: Road Town on Tortola
Population: 15,000
Money: U.S. Dollar
Official Language: English and some Papamiento
Political Status: British Overseas Territory
Just for Fun!: The 360° down-island view from Skyworld; checking out the botanical garden; boating in the sailing capital of the world.
Tidbit: The governor of the island is still appointed by the Queen of England.

Outrigger

St. Vincent

1 1/2 oz. gold rum
1/2 oz. Rose's Lime Juice
martini glass

1/2 oz. Benedictine
splash of fresh lemon juice

Fill a cocktail shaker with ice. Strain into a martini glass.

St. Vincent and the Grenadines are lush, volcanic islands filled with blooming flowers. The islands are located between Barbados and Grenada in the Windward Islands.

Bartender's Secret-Tropical Toppers and Floaters

Float a hibiscus or an orchid for a fabulous Caribbean touch to cocktails. Tiny and colorful cocktail umbrellas, palm trees, and flamingos are reminiscent of faraway exotic islands as well. A splash of 151 proof rum or a pleasantly scented and flavored liqueur will add sparkle to any drink.

Out At Sea
Jamaica

This jewel-like concoction resembles the fantasy blue of the Caribbean and has a smooth, coconut finish.

2 oz. light rum
1/2 oz. grenadine
carambola or starfruit slice

1 oz. blue Curacao
1 oz. fresh coconut milk
martini glass

Use the milk from a whole coconut by piercing the three eyes at the top with an ice pick and hammer. Strain milk into a cup.

Shake all ingredients in a cocktail shaker filled with ice, except grenadine. Pour grenadine into bottom of the martini glass. Using a spoon, carefully pour over the blue rum mixture, so as to not disturb the grenadine. Garnish with starfruit slice.

Painkiller

JOST VAN DYKE, BRITISH VIRGIN ISLANDS

1 oz. Pusser's British Navy Rum
2 oz. pineapple juice
1/2 oz. Coco Lopez
ice chunks

1 oz. Pusser's 151 Proof Rum
2 oz. orange juice
freshly grated nutmeg
old-fashioned glass

Fill a rocks glass with ice chunks. Stir in all ingredients except nutmeg. Sprinkle nutmeg over the top.

There is this bar off tiny Jost Van Dyke called Soggy Dollar Bar. There is no dock and you must swim to shore, hence the name. Favorite hang-out for Virgin Islanders on weekends. The idea behind the ice chunks as opposed to cubes is that the drink will stay cool and undiluted from melting ice.

Palm Bay

TURKS AND CAICOS

1 1/2 oz. white rum
1/2 oz. fresh lemon juice
champagne glass

1/2 oz. Cointreau
champagne

Fill a cocktail shaker with ice. Shake the rum, Cointreau and lemon juice. Strain into champagne glass. Fill with champagne.

It is said that Columbus' first landfall was on Grand Turk. The British have settled the Turks and Caicos for more than 200 years.

Partly Cloudy

GUADELOUPE-CASINO DE ST. FRANCOIS

1 1/2 oz. white rum
ginger ale
highball glass

1/4 oz. fresh limejuice
freshly grated ginger root

Fill a highball glass with ice. Add white rum and limejuice. Fill to top with ginger ale. Lightly sprinkle grated ginger over top.

Sugar is Guadeloupe's primary source of income. With the influx of cruise ships, this is rapidly changing. It is still a lovely, unspoiled island.

Passion Fruit Daiquiri

DOMINICA

1 oz. white rum
1/2 oz. Rose's Lime Juice
splash of fresh lemon juice
martini glass

1 1/2 oz. Passoa Passion Fruit Liqueur
1/2 oz. cherry liqueur
1/2 cup crushed ice

Combine all ingredients in blender until snowy. Pour into a martini glass.

Passion Potion

BARBADOS

1 oz. Malibu Rum
1 oz. Passoa Passion Fruit Liqueur
1 oz. mango juice
hurricane glass

1 oz. Captain Morgan's Spiced Rum
1/2 oz. Amaretto
1 oz. orange juice

Fill a hurricane glass with ice. Pour in all ingredients and stir.

Mango juice can be found in the frozen section of your grocer or at a Latin grocery store.

Peach Daiquiri

ST. THOMAS, U.S. VIRGIN ISLANDS

1 1/2 oz. Cruzan Lime Rum
1/2 oz. Cointreau
1/2 cup crushed ice

1/2 oz. Peach Schnapps
1/2 cup canned or frozen peaches
hurricane glass

Combine in blender until smooth. Pour into a hurricane glass.

Pearly Island

ST. LUCIA

While on a cruise, my son and I took a tour of St. Lucia. The island was primitive and gorgeous, resembling St. Thomas, our home, as it was 50 years ago. A major source of its income are huge banana plantations, which we also toured. The crop is sold to Great Britain.

2 oz. light rum
1/2 banana
1/2 oz. fresh limejuice
margarita glass

1 oz. Crème de Banana
1 oz. simple syrup
orange slice

Blend all ingredients, with a couple ice cubes in blender until smooth. Then shake in a cocktail strainer filled with ice and strain into a margarita glass. Garnish with orange slice.

Piña Colada
CLASSIC ISLAND DRINK

2 oz. white rum
1 1/2 oz. Coco Lopez
pineapple slice

2 oz. pineapple juice
1/2 cup crushed ice
hurricane glass

Combine all ingredients in blender until smooth. Pour into hurricane glass and garnish with pineapple slice.

Pineapple Daiquiri
ST. JOHN, U.S. VIRGIN ISLANDS

1 oz. Cruzan Pineapple Rum
1/2 Rose's Lime Juice
1/2 cup crushed ice

1/2 oz. Crème de Banana
1/2 cup fresh or canned pineapple
hurricane glass

Blend all ingredients until smooth in blender. Pour into a hurricane glass.

Pineapple-Rum Cooler
ST. VINCENT-THE ATTIC

1 oz. gold rum
1/2 oz. Rose's limejuice
pineapple slice

4 oz. pineapple juice
shredded fresh mint leaves

Fill a highball glass with ice. Pour in rum, juice, and limejuice. Stir. Sprinkle top with mint leaves. Garnish with pineapple slice.

The Attic is a jazz club in St. Vincent that used to be located above the Kentucky Fried Chicken on Grenville Street.

Pink Creole
FLORIDA

1 1/2 oz. light rum
splash of grenadine
Maraschino cherry

1/2 oz. Rose's Lime Juice
2 oz. light cream
martini glass

Fill a shaker with ice. Shake all ingredients until frothy. Strain into a martini glass. Garnish with a cherry.

Pink Mermaid
FLORIDA

1 1/2 oz. light rum
1/2 oz. grenadine
2 oz. light cream

1/2 oz. Crème de Noyaux
1/2 oz. Rose's Lime Juice
martini glass

Fill a cocktail shaker with ice. Strain into a martini glass.

Pirate's Punch
St. Croix, U.S. Virgin Islands

1 1/2 oz. gold rum
1/2 oz. sweet vermouth

1/2 oz. 151 proof rum
dash Angostura Bitters

Plantation Punch
Barbados

1 1/2 oz. dark rum
1 oz. fresh lemon juice
club soda
Highball glass

1/2 oz. Southern Comfort
splash of Cointreau or Triple Sec
splash of grenadine

Fill a Highball glass with ice. Stir in rum, Southern Comfort, lemon juice, and Cointreau. Fill to top with club soda, stirring gently. Float the grenadine on the top.

Planter's Punch
The Original

1 1/2 oz. Myer's Dark Rum
1 oz. limejuice
orange slice
Highball glass

3 oz. orange juice
splash of grenadine
Maraschino cherry

Fill a Highball glass with ice. Stir in the rum, orange juice, lime juice and grenadine. Garnish with orange slice and cherry.

Bartender's Secret-Spill Control

For all spills, whether on furniture, fabric, or clothing, immediately blot with a white clean cloth or paper towel. The faster you move, the less likely the stain will set. Immediately douse fabrics with club soda or water to dilute stain. Add a bit of dishwashing liquid and gently rub into a lather. Rinse with more club soda.

Rubbing can lessen white rings on furniture with a cloth dampened with turpentine. Another method is to rub with salt and lemon oil or even soak the area in lemon oil for a few hours and then buff.

Presidente
CUBA

1 1/2 oz. White Cuban rum
1/2 oz. Dry Vermouth
slice of orange
old-fashioned glass

1/2 oz. Dubonnet
1 splash Grenadine
Maraschino cherry

Fill a cocktail shaker with cracked ice. Add all ingredients except orange cherry. Shake and strain into a chilled rocks glass. Garnish with orange slice and cherry.

Puerto Rican National Cocktail
PUERTO RICO

2 oz. light rum
splash of Amaretto
splash of Rose's Lime Juice

1/2 oz. apricot brandy
1 oz. pineapple juice
cocktail glass

Mix all ingredients in a cocktail shaker filled with ice. Strain into a cocktail glass.

Rain Man
ST. CROIX, U.S. VIRGIN ISLANDS

1 oz. 151 proof rum
4 oz. orange juice

1 oz. Midori
rocks glass

Fill a rocks glass with ice. Stir rum, Midori, and orange juice.

Rum Collins
CLASSIC ISLAND DRINK

2 oz. light rum
club soda
lime wedge

1/2 oz. Rose's Lime Juice
freshly grated lime zest
Highball glass

Fill a Highball glass to the top with ice. Stir in the rum, limejuice. Fill with club soda and gently stir. Sprinkle with lime zest. Garnish with lime wedge.

Rum Kamikaze
ST. THOMAS, U.S. VIRGIN ISLANDS

1 1/2 oz 151 proof rum
shooter

1/2 oz. Rose's Limejuice

Fill a cocktail shaker full of ice. Shake ingredients and strain into a shooter.

Rum Daisy
CLASSIC DRINK

2 oz. light rum
1 tsp. Grenadine
martini glass

1/2 oz. fresh lemon juice
1 tsp. powdered sugar

Fill a cocktail shaker full of ice. Shake all ingredients and strain into a martini glass.

Rum Old-Fashioned
CLASSIC ISLAND DRINK

2 oz. gold rum
dash of Angostura Bitters
lemon twist

1/2 oz simple syrup
splash of maraschino cherry juice
rocks glass

Fill a rocks glass with ice. Stir in rum, syrup, bitters, and cherry juice. Twist the lemon peel and run around rim of glass. Drop in.

Rummy Mary
St. Croix, U.S. Virgin Islands

1 1/2 oz. white rum
dash of Worcestershire
dash of salt and pepper
celery stalk

2 1/2 oz. tomato juice
dash of Tabasco™
horseradish to taste
hurricane glass

Fill a hurricane glass with ice. Pour in rum, tomato juice, Worcestershire, Tabasco™. Season to taste with salt, pepper, and horseradish. Garnish with celery stalk.

Rum Sour
CLASSIC ISLAND DRINK

2 oz. light rum
1 oz. simple syrup
martini glass

1 oz. fresh limejuice
Maraschino cherry

Fill a cocktail strainer full of ice. Shake all ingredients except cherry. Strain into a martini glass. Garnish with a cherry.

San Juan
Puerto Rico

1 1/2 oz. Bacardi light rum
splash of Peach Brandy
splash of Rose's Lime Juice

1/2 oz. brandy
splash of grenadine
martini glass

Fill a cocktail shaker with ice. Shake all ingredients and strain into a martini glass.

San Juan is one of the first stops for cruise ships touring the Eastern Caribbean.

Yeah, mon! The Cayman Islands offer some of the best beaches in the Caribbean, over 500 private, offshore banks and superb shopping. Not only are they a short hop from Miami, they are one of the Caribbean's hottest destinations. Famous Seven-Mile Beach, lined with luxury resorts and condominiums, has movies such as The Firm filmed here.

Capital: George Town on Grand Cayman
Population: 40,000
Money: Cayman Island Dollar, US$1=approximately .80
Official Language: English
Political Status: British Independent Territory
Just for Fun!: Petting the giant turtles at the turtle farm; visiting Hell on Grand Cayman-yeah, try walking on it; diving Bloody Bay, called by Jacques Cousteau one of the world's top dives.
Tidbit: Columbus originally called the island, Las Tortugas, because of all the turtles.

Sex On The Beach
Grenada

1 oz. Cruzan Pineapple Rum
1/2 oz. Chambord

1/2 oz. Midori
shooter

Fill a cocktail shaker with ice. Pour in liquor and shake. Strain into a shooter.

Bottoms up!

Sex In The Snow
Nantucket, Massachusetts

1 oz. Cruzan Orange rum
1/2 oz. white Crème de Cacao

1/2 oz. Peach Schnapps
shooter

Fill a cocktail shaker with ice. Shake all ingredients and strain into a shooter.

Okay, okay. If you've read me before, you would know that I always put in one drink from Nantucket-my other island home.

Sewer Water
I don't think I want to credit this

1 oz. 151 proof rum
1/2 oz. Midori
splash of Rose's Lime Juice
splash of Cruzan Pineapple Rum

1/2 oz. gin
1/2 oz. Coco Lopez
splash of Grenadine
martini glass

Splash the grenadine in the bottom of a martini glass and swish around. Add ice, then rum, then gin, then Midori. Float the Coco Lopez and Cruzan Pineapple Rum on the top.

I can't say where or how I obtained this drink. It is good, though.

Spice Girl
Trinidad

1 1/2 oz. Bacardi Spice Rum
freshly grated ginger root

Ginger ale
Highball glass

Fill a Highball glass with ice. Pour in rum and gently fill to top with ginger ale. Sprinkle with grated ginger.

If you can get ginger beer, which is a non-alcoholic island-style ginger ale, try and do so. Spicy!

Sun Splash
St. Croix, U.S. Virgin Islands

1 oz. Cruzan Orange Rum
1 oz. Coco Lopez
Highball glass

1 oz. Cruzan Pineapple Rum
lemonade

Fill a cocktail shaker with ice. Pour in all ingredients and shake. Strain and pour into a Highball glass filled with ice.

Scorpion
Barbuda

2 oz. light rum
1 oz. Amaretto
1/2 oz. lemon juice

1 oz. brandy
1 oz. orange juice
Highball glass

Fill a cocktail shaker full of ice. Shake all ingredients and strain into a Highball glass filled with ice.

Barbuda is north of Antigua in the Leeward Islands. It also has pink sand.

Secret Place
Tortola, British Virgin Islands

1 1/2 oz Puerto Rican dark rum
1/2 oz. dark Crème de Cacao
splash of Cointreau

1/2 oz. Kirsch
4 oz. cold coffee
chocolate shavings

Fill a cocktail shaker with ice. Shake and strain all ingredients into a hurricane glass filled with ice. Sprinkle with chocolate shavings.

Shark's Tooth
Virgin Gorda, British Virgin Islands

1 oz. 151 proof rum
1/4 oz. Sloe Gin
Club soda

1 oz. Passoa Passion Fruit Liqueur
1/2 oz. fresh limejuice
old-fashioned glass

Fill a rocks glass with ice. Stir in the rum, liqueur, Sloe Gin, and limejuice. Fill glass to top with Club soda and stir gently.

Be sure to visit the Baths in Virgin Gorda. Giant boulders as large as houses form sunlit bathing grottos.

Slippery Nut
ARUBA

1 1/2 oz. Cruzan Irish Cream Liqueur
shooter

1 1/2 oz. Malibu Rum

Fill a cocktail shaker with ice. Shake both ingredients and strain into a shooter.

Yeah, mon! Virgin Gorda, British Virgin Islands often referred to as the fat virgin, from a distance the island appears to be in the shape of a woman lying down, is one of the most picturesque of the British Virgin Islands. Some of the most luxurious vacation-home rentals can be found here.

Capital: Actually Roadtown on Tortola, Spanish Town is the main settlement here
Population: approximately 3000
Money: U.S. Dollar
Official Language: English
Political Status: British Overseas Territory
Just for Fun!: Swimming in sunlit grottos formed by boulders the size of a small house at the Baths; diving the Wreck of the Rhone; taking a jeep trip to Virgin Gorda Peak National Park the island's highest point-1,359 feet for the view.
Tidbit: One of the best beaches is at Bitter End Yacht Club.

Soca Rita
ST. JOHN, U.S. VIRGIN ISLANDS

1 oz. Cruzan Banana Rum
1/2 oz. Cointreau
1/2 cup crushed ice
lime slice

1/2 oz Cruzan Coconut Rum
1 oz. fresh limejuice
crushed rock salt
margarita glass

Blend all ingredients until smooth in blender. Wet the edge of the margarita glass with water and twist in a plate of crushed rock salt. Pour in drink.

Soca is a type of Calypso music heard during carnival. St. John has its carnival on the fourth of July.

Third Rail
CURAÇAO

Curaçao is less than one hundred miles from Venezuela and surrounded by Aruba and Bonaire.

1 oz. light rum
1/2 oz. Sambuca or Anisette Liqueur

1 oz. Calvados
shooter

Fill a cocktail shaker full of ice. Shake all ingredients and strain into a shooter.

Tropical Breeze
St. Croix, U.S. Virgin Islands

1 oz. Cruzan Pineapple Rum
2 oz. cranberry juice
Highball glass

1/2 oz. white rum
2 oz. orange juice

Fill a Highball glass with crushed ice. Pour in all ingredients and stir.

This is an interesting island-style variation on the traditional Sea Breeze made with vodka.

Voodoo Love
Jamaica

1/2 oz. Cruzan Orange Rum
1/2 oz. Cruzan Pineapple Rum
1/2 oz. Junkanoo (citrus rum)
1 oz. pineapple juice
lemon twist

1/2 oz. Cruzan Banana Rum
1/2 oz. Cruzan Coconut Rum
1 oz. orange juice
splash of grenadine
old-fashioned

Fill a cocktail shaker with ice. Add all ingredients and shake well. Strain into a chilled rocks glass, straight up. Twist the lemon and run around the rim of the glass. Drop in.

Voodoo is still alive and strong in the islands. It comes in many forms such as Santeria, Yorba and Black Congo magic. And it is scary.

West Indies Sunset
ARUBA-THE OLD MILL

1 1/2 oz. white rum
1 1/2 oz. orange juice
hurricane glass

1 1/2 oz. cranberry juice
orange slice

Fill a hurricane glass with crushed ice. Fill bottom of glass with cranberry juice, then carefully layer orange juice and float white rum on the top. Garnish with orange slice.

Yeah, mon! Curaçao is located 35 miles north of Venezuela and part of the ABC islands of Aruba, Bonaire, and Curacao. The island has an arid, rocky terrain which has resulted in secluded and craggy coves where pirates once frequented. It is also the largest island in the Netherlands Antilles. Its capital Willemstad features pretty pastel housing reminiscent of Amsterdam.

The least you need to know:

Capital: Willemsted
Population: nearly 155,000
Money: Netherlands Antilles Florin, US$1=NAF 1.76
Official Language: Dutch, Papiamento; I was just there, so English widely spoken
Political Status: Part of the independent Netherlands Antilles
Just for Fun!: Visiting the recently opened Hato Caves and seeing the baby bats; seeing the oldest synagogue in the Western Hemisphere; walking across the floating Queen Emma Bridge, originally built in 1888.
Tidbit: The Amstel beer brewery here makes beer from distilled seawater.

Whale's Milk
ANTIGUA

This is a gorgeous tie-dyed drink of white, green and blue.

1 oz. light rum
1 oz. blue Curacao
1 oz. milk
pilsner glass

1 oz. brandy or cognac
1/2 oz. green Curacao
splash of Amaretto

Shake all ingredients except colored Curacao in a cocktail shaker filled with ice. Pour into pilsner glass. Slowly pour in Curacao; do not stir.

White Lily
DOMINICAN REPUBLIC

1 oz. light rum
1/2 oz. Sambuca or Ouzo
martini glass

1/2 oz. Triple Sec
1/2 oz. gin

Fill a cocktail shaker with ice. Shake all ingredients and strain into a Martini glass.

Wild Orchid
PUERTO RICO

1 oz. white Bacardi rum
1 oz. Passoa Passionfruit Liqueur
1 oz. pineapple juice

1 oz. vodka
1 oz. orange juice
Highball glass

Fill a Highball glass with ice. Pour in all ingredients and stir.

Puerto Rico has a huge rainforest near Luquillo beach about one hour from San Juan. It is the only tropical rainforest in the U.S. National Park system.

Yellow Bird
NEVIS

1/2 oz. Cruzan Pineapple Rum
1/2 oz. Galliano
1 oz. pineapple juice
rocks glass

1/2 oz. Cruzan Banana Rum
1 oz. Crème de Banana
1 oz. orange juice

Fill a cocktail shaker with ice and ingredients. Shake and pour over an old-fashioned glass filled with ice.

A friend of mine returned from a sail down-island with this recipe.

Zombie
THE ORIGINAL--HAITI

1 oz. light rum
1/2 oz. 151 proof rum
1 oz. limejuice
crushed ice
hurricane glass

1 oz. dark rum
2 oz. pineapple juice
1 oz. orange juice
pineapple slice

Combine the ice, light rum, dark rum, and juices in the blender until smooth. Pour into a hurricane glass. Float the 151 on the top. Garnish with pineapple slice.

For the story behind the author (myself) and Zombies, see *Just Add Rum!*

CHAPTER FOURTEEN

All the Recipes!

Abbey

1 1/2 oz. gin
1 oz. orange juice
rocks glass

1 oz. Lilletblanc
drop of orange bitters

Fill a rocks glass with ice. Shake all ingredients in a cocktail shaker filled with ice. Strain into the rocks glass.

Abbot's Dream

1 oz. Bailey's Irish Cream Liqueur
1/2 oz. Crème de Banana
1/2 cup crushed ice

1/2 oz. Frangelico
2 oz. light cream
hurricane glass

Whirl all ingredients in blender until smooth. Pour into hurricane glass.

ABC

1/2 oz. Amaretto
1/2 oz. Cointreau
shooter

1/2 oz. Bailey's Irish Cream Liqueur
orange twist

Shake all ingredients in a cocktail shaker filled with ice. Strain into a shooter. Drop in orange twist.

Bartender's Secret-Bar Mixers

Usually fresh fruit juices and mixes are the superior choice. However, sometimes speed or necessity (boating or camping trip) rule. Powdered and canned mixes can be found for sweet-and-sour mix, sweetened limejuice, (Rose's) as well as egg white. One of the advantages is the consistency of the mix.

A-Bomb
MAGEN'S BAY, ST. THOMAS

1/2 oz. vodka
1/2 oz. Bailey's Irish Cream Liqueur
Highball glass

1/2 oz. Tia Maria
1/2 oz Grand Marnier

Fill a cocktail shaker with ice. Shake all ingredients and strain into a Highball glass filled with ice.

Absolution

1 oz. Absolute Vodka
1 lemon

champagne
Highball glass

Add the shot of vodka to a fluted champagne glass. Fill champagne to the top. Cut the peel from a lemon to form a ring. Float in the champagne to form a halo.

Acapulco Gold

1 1/2 oz. tequila
juice of 1/2 lemon

1/2 oz. Grand Marnier
martini glass

Combine all ingredients in blender until smooth. Pour into martini glass.

Acacia

1 1/2 gin
splash of Kirshwasser
splash of lemon juice

3/4 oz. Benedictine
splash of maraschino cherry juice
martini glass with ice

Shake all ingredients in a cocktail shaker filled with ice. Strain into a martini glass.

Yeah, mon! Dominica is one of the few unspoiled islands in the Caribbean with its over 290 square miles of volcanic peaks, 365 rivers, and rainforest dotted with sparkling waterfalls. The Smithsonian called this island a giant plant laboratory, the island a rainbow of brilliant emerald, reds, and purples. Located between Guadeloupe to the north and Martinique to the south, it is 29 miles long and 15 miles wide. One almost expects Tarzan to sweep down on a liana vine.

The least you need to know:

Capital: Roseau
Population: 77,000
Money: Eastern Caribbean Dollar; US$1=EC$2.70
Official Language: English, but most Dominicans speak French-Creole Patois
Political Status: Independent Member of the British Commonwealth
Just for Fun!: Swimming at gorgeous Trafalgar Falls; scuba diving at Soufriere Bay; hiking up Boiling Lake.
Tidbit: Home to the popular World Creole Music Festivale.

Adios Mama!

1/2 oz. vodka
1/2 oz. gin
juice of 1/2 lemon
sugar

1/2 oz Blue Curacao
1/2 oz rum
splash of Triple Sec
cocktail

Wet the lip of a martini glass and twist in a plate of sugar. Fill a cocktail shaker with ice, shake, and strain all ingredients into the martini glass.

Admiral Cocktail

2 oz. gin
1/2 oz. Cherry Heering
low ball

1/2 oz. Grand Marnier
1/2 oz. fresh limejuice

Shake all ingredients in a cocktail shaker filled with ice. Strain into a low ball filled with ice.

After 5

1 oz. Rumple Minze
 (high proof Peppermint Schnapps)

1 oz. Bailey's Irish Cream Liqueur
shooter

Fill a cocktail shaker with ice. Shake the liqueurs and strain into a shooter.

After 8

1/2 oz. white Crème de Menthe
1/2 oz. Kahlua

1/2 oz. white Crème de Cacao
shooter

Fill a cocktail shaker with ice. Shake the liqueurs and strain into a shooter.

Afterburner

1/2 oz. vodka
shooter

1 tablespoon Tabasco™

Fill a cocktail shaker with ice. Shake all ingredients and strain into a shooter.

After Midnight

1 1/2 oz. Myer's Dark Rum
1 teaspoon instant hot chocolate powder
rocks glass

1 teaspoon instant coffee (regular of decaf)
2 oz. light cream

Shake all ingredients well in a cocktail shaker filled with ice. Fill a rocks glass with ice. Strain into glass.

Agent Orange

1/2 oz. vodka
1/2 oz. gin
1/4 oz. Galliano
splash of Calvados, Midori and Yukon Jack
hurricane glass

1/2 oz. rum
1/4 oz. Cointreau
1/4 oz. Southern Comfort
orange juice

Shake all ingredients well in a cocktail shaker, except orange juice. Fill a hurricane glass to the top with ice, pour in liquor. Float orange juice on top.

Alabama Slammer

1/2 oz Amaretto
1/4 oz. sloe gin
splash of vodka
shooter

1/2 oz. Southern Comfort
1/2 oz. lemon juice
sugar

Wet the lip of a shooter and twist in a plate of sugar. Shake all other ingredients in a cocktail shaker filled with ice. Strain into the shooter.

Alaska

2 oz. gin
splash of fresh lime juice
martini glass

1 oz. yellow Chartreuse
drop of Angostura Bitters

Shake all ingredients in a cocktail shaker filled with ice. Strain into a chilled martini glass.

Alexander's Brother

1 1/2 oz. gin
1 oz. half & half
martini glass

1 oz. white Crème de Cacao
drop of orange juice

Shake all ingredients in a cocktail shaker filled with ice. Strain into a martini glass.

Alexander's Sister

2 oz. gin
drop of white Crème de Cacao
martini glass

1/2 oz. white Crème de Menthe
1 oz. half & half

Shake all ingredients in a cocktail shaker filled with ice. Strain into a martini glass.

Alexander Nevsky

1 1/2 oz. vodka
drop of Southern Comfort
2 oz. orange juice

1 oz. Apry (apricot liqueur)
1/2 oz. lemon juice
rocks glass

Shake all ingredients in a cocktail shaker filled with ice. Strain into a rocks glass filled with ice.

Almond Cocktail

1 1/2 oz. gin
1/2 oz. Peach Schnapps
splash of Amaretto
1/2 teaspoon marzipan paste

1/2 oz. dry vermouth
splash of Persico (Bols peach liqueur
   with shades of almond)
martini glass

Warm gin over low heat, carefully. Add marzipan paste, stir, and mix well. shake with remaining ingredients in a cocktail shaker filled with ice. Strain into a martini glass.

Almond Joy

2 oz. Amaretto
1/2 oz. Coco Lopez
margarita glass

1/2 oz. dark Cream to Cacao
1/2 cup crushed ice

Whirl all ingredients in blender until smooth. Serve in a margarita glass.

Amaretto Sour

1 1/2 oz. Amaretto
1/2 oz. fresh lemon juice

2 oz. lemonade
rocks glass

Fill a rocks glass with ice. Stir all ingredients.

Ambrosia

1 oz. Calvados
splash of Triple Sec
Champagne

1 oz. brandy
splash of lemon juice
champagne glass

Fill a cocktail shaker with ice and the Calvados, brandy, Triple Sec and lemon juice. Shake and strain into a champagne glass. Float the champagne to the top.

Angel's Lips

1 oz. Benedictine
club soda

1 oz. Bailey's Irish Cream Liqueur
Highball glass

Fill a Highball glass with ice, Benedictine and Bailey's. Fill to top with club soda and stir gently.

Anti-Freeze

1 1/2 oz. vodka
splash of lemon juice
shot glass

1/2 oz. Midori
lemon twist

Fill a cocktail shaker with ice, the vodka, Midori, splash of lemon juice. Twist the lemon rind and toss in. Shake and strain into a shot glass.

Apache

1 oz. Bailey's Irish Cream Liqueur
1/2 oz. Midori

1/2 oz. Tia Maria
shooter

Pour Tia Maria into bottom of glass. Carefully layer the Bailey's, then the Midori on top.

Apple Blossom

1 1/2 oz. Calvados
shot glass

splash of Boggs Cranberry Liqueur

Shake all ingredients in a cocktail shaker filled with ice. Strain into a shot glass.

Apple Pie

1/2 oz. Calvados
1/2 oz. Cruzan Pineapple rum
shooter

1/2 oz. vodka
powdered cinnamon

Fill a cocktail shaker with ice and the liquors. Shake and strain into a shooter. Sprinkle cinnamon lightly over top.

Apricot Martini

1 oz. Godiva Liqueur
1 oz. Frangelico

1 oz. apricot brandy
martini glass

Fill a cocktail shaker with ice and liquors. Shake and strain into a martini glass.

Aviation

2 oz. gin
splash of Abricotine (French apricot liqueur)
splash of Maraschino Liqueur
martini glass

1/2 oz. of Apry (made by
    Marie Brizzard, apricot cordial)
1/2 oz. fresh lemon juice

Shake all ingredients in a cocktail shaker filled with ice. Strain into a martini glass.

B & B

1 part brandy
brandy snifter

1 part Benedictine

Pour into a brandy snifter and swirl gently.

B-52

1 oz. Bailey's Irish Cream Liqueur
1 oz. Tia Maria
rocks glass

1 oz. Grand Marnier
freshly ground nutmeg

Fill a cocktail shaker with ice and shake all ingredients. Strain into a rocks glass filled with ice.

Baby's Bottom

1 1/2 oz. Wild Turkey Kentucky Bourbon
1/4 oz. white Crème de Cacao
low-ball glass

1/2 oz. white Crème de Menthe
1/4 oz. Chambord

Fill a low-ball glass with ice. Mix in all ingredients, stirring well.

Back Street Banger

1/2 oz. Jack Daniel's Tennessee
    Sour Mash Whiskey

1 oz. Bailey's Irish Cream Liqueur
shot glass

Chill and shake both ingredients in a cocktail shaker filled with ice. Strain into a shot glass.

Bad Habit

1/2 oz. Stoli Ohranj Vodka
shot glass

1 oz. Peach Schnapps

Chill and shake both ingredients in a cocktail shaker filled with ice. Strain into a shot glass.

Bailey's Chocolate Covered Cherry

1 oz. grenadine
1 oz. Bailey's Irish Cream Liqueur Liqueur
martini glass

1 oz. Tia Maria
splash of dark Crème de Cacao

Layer first the grenadine in the bottom of the glass, then the Tia Maria, Bailey's, and gently float the Crème de Cacao on the top.

Bailey's French Dream

1 oz. Bailey's Irish Cream Liqueur
2 oz. milk
martini glass

1/2 oz. Chambord
splash of vodka

Fill a cocktail shaker with ice and shake all ingredients. Strain into a chilled martini glass.

Bailey's Truffle

1 oz. Bailey's Irish Cream Liqueur
1/2 oz. Godet Belgian White Chocolate Liqueur

1/2 oz. Grand Marnier
shooter

Fill a cocktail shaker with ice and shake all ingredients. Strain into a shooter.

Banana Balm

1 1/2 oz. vodka
splash of Poire Williams (pear brandy)
club soda

1/2 oz. Crème de Banana
1 tsp. Rose's Lime Juice
rocks glass

Shake all ingredients, except club soda, in a cocktail shaker filled with ice. Strain into a rocks glass filled with ice. Fill to top with club soda. Stir gently.

Banana Boat

1/2 oz. Cruzan Coconut Rum
splash of pineapple juice
shot glass

1/2 oz. Banana Liqueur
splash of white Crème de Cacao

Fill a cocktail shaker with ice, shaking all ingredients and straining into a shot glass.

Barbary Coast

1/2 oz. Irish Whiskey
1/2 oz. light rum
1 oz. light cream

1/2 oz. gin
1 oz. white Crème de Cacao
rocks glass

Shake all ingredients in a cocktail shaker filled with ice. Strain into a rocks glass filled with ice.

Beach Bum

1 oz. vodka
1 oz. Absolut Raspberry Vodka

1 oz. Midori
martini glass

Fill a cocktail shaker with ice. Shake all ingredients and strain into a martini glass.

Bellini

1 oz. Peach Schnapps
champagne

splash of apricot liqueur
champagne glass

Pour the schnapps and liqueur into a champagne glass. Fill to top with champagne.

Billinsky

1 oz. Peach Schnapps
champagne

1 oz. vodka
wine glass with ice

Fill a wine glass with ice. Dump the ice and pour in vodka and Peach Schnapps. fill to top with champagne. Stir gently.

Bermuda Cocktail

2 oz. gin
1/4 oz. Amaretto
1/2 oz. limejuice

1 oz. apricot brandy
1/4 oz. Maraschino liqueur
martini glass

Shake all ingredients in a cocktail shaker filled with ice. Strain into a martini glass.

Bermuda Rose

1 oz. gin
juice of 1/2 lime
shot glass

1/4 oz. apricot brandy
splash of Chambord

Fill a cocktail shaker with ice and the liquors. Shake and strain into a shot glass.

Between the Sheets

1 1/2 oz. gin
1 oz. brandy
lime wedge

1 oz. Triple Sec
splash of apricot brandy
rocks glass

Shake all ingredients in a cocktail shaker filled with ice. Strain into a rocks glass filled with ice. Squeeze a lime wedge over glass and drop in.

Bewitched

1/2 oz. B&B
1/2 half & half
shot glass

1/2 oz. vodka
splash of Bailey's Irish Cream Liqueur

Fill a cocktail shaker with ice and the liquors. Shake and strain into a shot glass.

Bitch on Wheels

1 oz. Bombay gin
1/4 oz. white Crème de Menthe
shot glass

1/4 oz. Pernod
splash of brandy

Fill a cocktail shaker with ice and the liquors. Shake and strain into a shot glass.

Yeah, mon! Dominican Republic occupies two-thirds of the island of Hispaniola and borders with Haiti. This island is rapidly becoming the hottest property in the Caribbean, especially with former President Clinton's visit. Columbus chanced to land on this island in December 1492 and on Christmas Eve his ship, the Santa Maria, shipwrecked here. Every water sport imaginable is available as well as equipment rental and lessons. Golfers and divers will also find plenty to keep them happily occupied.

Capital: Santa Domingo
Population: over 9 million, wow!
Money: Dominican Peso; US$1=RD $12.75
Official Language: Spanish
Political Status: Independent Country
Just for Fun!: Exploring the 12-block area of Santo Domingo known as the Colonial Zone and its bustling shops and restaurants; visiting the Park of the Three Eyes and its beautiful pools peering out of deep limestone caves; lounging on 20-mile long Punta Cana beach, shaded by palms.
Tidbit: The Dominican Republic has one of the largest mink and fox factories in the Western Hemisphere.

Black Ice

1 oz. Opal Nera Sambuca
splash of Cointreau
shooter

1 oz. vodka
splash of white Crème de Menthe

Fill a cocktail shaker with ice and liqueurs. Shake and strain into a shooter.

Black Magic

1 oz. Stoli Lemon Vodka
lemon twist
shot glass

1/2 oz. Tia Maria
splash of lemon juice

Fill a cocktail shaker with ice and liquors. Shake and strain into a shot glass. Twist the lemon rind and run around the rim of the glass. Drop in.

Black Manhattan

1 1/2 oz. Irish Whiskey
splash of maraschino cherry juice
martini glass

1/4 oz. vermouth
Maraschino cherry

Fill a cocktail shaker with ice, whiskey, vermouth, and cherry juice. Shake and strain into a martini glass.

Black Martini

2 oz. Stoli Razberi
martini glass

splash of Chambord

Fill a cocktail shaker with ice, vodka, and Chambord. Strain into a martini glass.

Black Orchid

1 1/2 oz. Absolut Kurant
2 oz. cranberry juice
rocks glass

1/2 oz. Blue Curacao
splash of Chambord

Fill a rocks glass with ice. Stir in all ingredients.

Black Russian

2 oz. Absolut Vodka
rocks glass

1 oz. Kahlua

Fill a rocks glass with ice. Stir in vodka and Kahlua.

Blackthorn Martini

1 1/2 oz. Irish Whiskey
splash of Pernod
martini glass

1/2 oz. dry vermouth
splash of Sambuca

Fill a cocktail shaker with ice. Shake all ingredients and strain into a martini glass.

Black Velvet

1 part champagne
lemon twist
champagne glass

1 part Guinness Stout
splash of maraschino cherry juice

Fill champagne flute halfway with stout. Float champagne on top. Rum a lemon twist around rim of glass and drop in. Add just a dot of cherry juice.

Blarney Cocktail

1 oz. Irish Whiskey
splash green Crème de Menthe

1/2 oz. vermouth
shot glass

Fill cocktail shaker with ice. Shake all ingredients and strain into a shot glass.

Bloodhound

1 1/2 oz. gin
1/2 oz. dry vermouth
1/2 cup frozen strawberries
martini glass

1 oz. strawberry liqueur
splash of Framboise (clear
    strawberry brandy)

Blend all ingredients in a blender until smooth. Pour into a martini glass.

Yeah, mon! **Greneda** with its lovely historic edifices and churches is one of the most picturesque capitals in the Caribbean. A tiny island, only 21 miles long and 12 miles wide, it is filled with the scent of spice plantations, dramatic mountains and rainforest, waterfalls and endless white-sand beaches. Ninety miles north of Trinidad, it is the most southern of the Windward Islands.

Capital: St. George's
Population: nearly 100,000
Money: Eastern Caribbean Dollar, US$1=$2.67
Political Status: Independent Member of British Commonwealth
Just for Fun!: Hiking Concord Falls and then two more miles to a second, spectacular waterfall; inhaling the delicate aroma of spices at Dougaldston Estate, a spice plantation; deep sea fishing during the annual Game Fishing Tournament in late January.
Tidbit: Largest spice producer in Western Hemisphere and second largest nutmeg producer in the world.

Blow Job

1/2 oz. Bailey's Irish Cream Liqueur
splash of Crème de Banana
shot glass

1/2 oz. Tia Maria
whipped cream

Serve straight up in a shot glass. Top with whipped cream. Place mouth over shot glass (make sure the shot glass is of a good size to prevent choking-careful!), put head back and down the shot. Do not use your hands!

Blue Devil

1 oz. gin
1/2 oz. Blue Curacao

2 oz. lemon juice
low-ball glass

Shake all ingredients in a cocktail shaker filled with ice. Strain into a low-ball glass.

Blue Kamakazi

1 oz. vodka
1/4 oz. Rose's limejuice
shooter

1/4 oz. Blue Curacao
lemon twist

Shake all ingredients, except lemon twist, in a cocktail shaker filled with ice. Strain into a shot glass. Twist the lemon rind and run around the edge of the shooter.

Blue Lagoon

1 1/2 oz. vodka
1/2 oz. Cointreau
club soda
rocks glass

1/2 Blue Curacao
1 oz. fresh lemon juice
Maraschino cherry

Shake all ingredients, except club soda and cherry, in a cocktail shaker filled with ice. Pour into a rocks glass filled with ice. Float club soda on top and garnish with cherry.

Blue Margarita

1 1/2 oz. tequila
2 oz. sour mix
salt
margarita glass

1/2 oz. Blue Curacao
splash of fresh lemon juice
lemon wedge

Squeeze and run the lemon wedge along rim of glass. Twist plate in salt. Shake all other ingredients in a cocktail shaker filled with ice. Strain into margarita glass.

Blue Ocean Martini

3/4 oz. vodka
splash of Blue Curacao
martini glass

3/4 oz. Bombay Sapphire Gin
lemon twist

Fill a cocktail shaker with ice. Twist the lemon rind over the ice and drop in. Shake with vodka and gin.

Blue Shark

1 1/2 oz. vodka
1/4 oz. Blue Curacao
salt

1 1/2 oz. tequila
lime wedge
margarita glass

Wet the lip of a margarita glass and twist in a plate of salt. Shake all other ingredients, except lime wedge, in a cocktail shaker filled with ice. Strain into the margarita glass. Squeeze lime wedge in drink. Drop in.

Blue Sky

1 oz. Stoli Razberi
4 oz. milk

1/2 oz. Blue Curacao
rocks glass

Shake all ingredients in a cocktail shaker filled with ice. Strain into a rocks glass filled with ice.

Blue Vodka Martini

2 oz. vodka
splash of fresh lemon juice
martini glass

splash of Blue Curacao
lemon twist

Shake all ingredients, except lemon twist, in a cocktail shaker filled with ice. Pour into a martini glass. Twist the lemon rind, run around edge of glass, and drop in.

Bocci Ball

1/2 oz. Amaretto
1/2 oz. orange juice
shooter

1/2 oz. vodka
dash of Grand Marnier

Shake all ingredients in a cocktail shaker filled with ice. Strain into a shooter.

Boilermaker

1 1/2 oz. Irish Whiskey
shot glass and beer mug

chilled beer (ale preferably)

Serve the whiskey in the shot glass. Pour beer into a pre-chilled beer mug.

Bonbon

1/2 oz. tequila
splash of grenadine

1/2 oz. Cointreau
shot glass

Splash the grenadine in the bottom of the glass. Layer the Cointreau over the tequila.

Bootleg

(1.) 1 oz. Jack Daniels
(3.) 1/2 oz. Southern Comfort

(2.) 1/2 oz. Ouzo
shooter

Layer in the order shown in a shooter.

Brain

1 oz. Bailey's Irish Cream Liqueur
splash of Crème de Noyaux
shooter

1 oz. Persico (made by Bols,
    peach liqueuer with shades of almond)

Shake all ingredients in a cocktail shaker filled with ice. Strain into a shooter.

Brain Hemorrhage

1 oz. Tia Maria
splash of Bailey's Irish Cream Liqueur
shooter

1/2 oz. Peach Schnapps
splash of grenadine

Layer first the Tia Maria in the bottom of the glass, then the Peach Schnapps, Bailey's. Top with grenadine.

This is your brain on alcohol.

Brain Power

1 oz. Bailey's Irish Cream Liqueur
1/2 oz. Stoli Razberi

1 oz. Fraise (strawberry liqueur)
shooter

Shake all ingredients in a cocktail shaker filled with ice. Strain into a shooter.

Brandy Alexander

1 1/2 oz. brandy
1 1/2 oz. half and half or milk
martini glass

1 oz. dark Crème de Cacao
freshly grated nutmeg

Shake all ingredients, except nutmeg, in a cocktail shaker filled with ice. Strain into a martini glass. Sprinkle with nutmeg.

Brave Bull

1 1/2 oz. tequila
splash of dark rum

1 1/2 oz. Tia Maria
rocks glass

Shake all ingredients in a cocktail shaker filled with ice. Strain into a rocks glass filled with ice.

Broken Spur

1 1/2 oz. white port
1/2 oz. sweet vermouth
1 oz. cream

1 oz. gin
splash of Sambuca
rocks glass

Mix in blender until smooth. Pour into a rocks glass.

Bronx Cocktail

2 oz. gin
splash of sweet vermouth
martini glass

1 oz. orange juice
drop of Orange Bitters

Shake all ingredients in a cocktail shaker filled with ice. Strain into a martini glass.

Bubble Gum

1/2 oz. Stoli Razberi
1/2 oz. Crème de Banana
shooter

1/2 oz. Midori
1/2 oz. orange juice

Shake all ingredients in a cocktail shaker filled with ice. Strain into a shooter.

Bulldog

1 1/2 oz. gin
splash orange juice
Highball glass

ginger ale
drop Grand Marnier

Fill a Highball glass with ice. Pour in gin. Fill 3/4 full with ginger ale. Top with orange juice and Grand Marnier.

Bullfrog

1 1/2 oz. vodka
1 oz. fresh limejuice
martini glass

1/2 oz. Lillet
1 oz. Rose's Lime Juice

Shake all ingredients in a cocktail shaker filled with ice. Strain into a martini glass.

Bullshit

1 oz. Absolut Pepper
1 tsp. fresh lemon juice
splash of Tabasco™
shooter

1 oz. tomato juice
1/2 tsp. horseradish
splash of Worcestershire

Shake all ingredients in a cocktail shaker filled with ice. Strain into a shooter.

Yeah, mon! Guadeloupe, between Antigua and Dominica, looks like a giant butterfly. The entire 659-square mile Guadeloupe archipelago consists of Basse-Terre and Grande-Terre, the two largest islands, and numerous smaller ones including Marie-Galante, La Desirade and Les Saintes. If you want nightlife and casinos, go to Grande Terre. For a tour of waterfalls and an active volcano, Basse-Terre is your best bet. All others, wanting to get away from it all, try the smaller islands.

Capital: Basse-Terre
Population: over 400,000
Money: French Franc, US$1=$5.55F
Official Language: French, Creole Patois, English in major hotels
Political Status: French possession
Just for Fun!: Oohing over the brilliant fish at the Guadeloupe Aquarium, ranked fourth best in France; lunch and a swim at the Chateau de Feuilles; bathing in the buff at Ilet du Gosier beach.
Tidbit: The island has more than 100 restaurants featuring Creole and international delicacies.

Bullshot

1 1/2 oz. vodka
splash of Tabasco™
1 tsp. fresh lemon juice
rocks glass

4 oz. beef bouillon
splash of Worcestershire™
1/2 tsp. horseradish

Shake all ingredients in a cocktail shaker filled with ice. Strain into a rocks glass filled with ice.

Buttercream

1 1/2 oz. vodka
splash of Kahlua
1 oz. cream

1 1/2 oz. butterscotch schnapps
splash of white Crème de Cacao
rocks glass

Shake all ingredients in a cocktail shaker filled with ice. Strain into a rocks glass filled with ice.

Besides rimming glasses in exotic syrups and colorful sugars, use colorful straws twisted in curly-q's, bright ribbons or raffia tied onto straws, straw huggers, accordion-like decorations shaped liked parrots, monkeys and other animals which slide onto straws, reusable glass stir sticks with fish and shells on the end, etc. Starfruit sliced lengthwise looks very pretty as well. Cinnamon sticks and empty coconuts add a festive, island touch.

Buttercup

1 oz. Mozart Liqueur
2 oz. half & half
chocolate shavings

1/2 oz. butterscotch schnapps
whipped cream
low ball

Shake all ingredients in a cocktail shaker with ice. Strain into a low-ball. Top with whipped cream and chocolate shavings.

Byron's Bongo
ST. MAARTEN, WEST INDIES
COURTESY OF SINT MAARTEN GUAVABERRY COMPANY

2 oz. Sint Maarten Guavaberry liqueur
1 oz. orange juice
1/2 oz. grenadine
grated nutmeg

2 oz. pineapple juice
1/2 of. fresh limejuice
orange slice
highball

Fill a highball glass with ice. Shake all ingredients in a cocktail shaker filled with ice. Strain into a highball and garnish with orange slice and grated nutmeg.

Cape Codder

1 1/2 oz. vodka
lime wedge

cranberry juice
Highball glass

Fill a Highball glass with ice, vodka, and cranberry juice. Stir. Squeeze lime wedge and drop in.

Cement Mixer

1 oz. Bailey's Irish Cream Liqueur
shot glass

1/2 oz. limejuice

Pour Bailey's into shot glass. Add limejuice. The acid in the limejuice will congeal the cream in the Bailey's.

Interesting texture and flavor in mouth.

Yeah, mon Jamaica is over 4,400 square miles. It's huge with a plethora of excursions, activities and places to explore such as horseback riding, beaching, waterfall climbing and visiting pirate stomping grounds. It's the third-largest island in the Caribbean after Cuba and Puerto Rico. From jungles to exotic resorts on gleaming beaches, there's a little something for everyone.

Capital: Kingston
Population: 2.6 million
Money: Jamaican Dollar, US$1=$30 JD
Official Language: English and Patois when the islanders don't want you to understand.
Political Status: Independent Member of the British Commonwealth
Just for Fun!: Eating jerk from a roadside stand and washing it down with an icy Red Stripe Beer; checking out the Bob Marley Museum in Kingston; drinking Blue Mountain Coffee.
Tidbit: Jamaica was once the world's largest sugar producer.

Chambord Colada

1 1/2 oz. Chambord   1 oz. light rum
2 oz. pineapple juice   1 oz. Coco Lopez
1/2 cup crushed ice   hurricane

Mix in blender. Serve in a hurricane glass.

Chambord Iceberg

1 oz. Chambord   1 oz. vodka
champagne   drop of Blue Curacao
champagne glass

Fill a champagne flute to the top with ice. Pour in Chambord, layer vodka next; fill to top with champagne, leaving room for a drop of Blue Curacao.

While on an Alaskan cruise, I discovered that icebergs have blue in them-a refraction from the sun.

Champagne Cocktail

champagne   1 tsp. sugar
dash of Angostura bitters   champagne glass

Fill a champagne glass to the top with champagne. Gently stir in sugar and bitters.

I recommend you do this to inexpensive champagne.

Cherry Bomb

1 1/2 oz. cherry brandy
splash of Triple Sec
rocks glass

1 oz. vodka
1 oz. sour mix

Fill a rocks glass with ice. Stir all ingredients.

China Beach

1 oz. Canton Delicate Ginger Liqueur
splash of cranberry juice

1/2 oz. vodka
shot glass

Shake in a cocktail shaker filled with ice and serve in a shot glass.

Chi-Chi

1 1/2 oz. vodka
4 oz. pineapple juice
Maraschino cherry

1 oz. Coco Lopez
orange slice
hurricane glass

Mix in blender. Serve in a hurricane glass. Garnish with orange slice and cherry.

Chihuahua

1 part gold rum
3 sugar cubes

1 part Cointreau

In a lowball glass, fill glass to top with liquors or you will burn your lips and/or break the glass. Place the sugar cubes on a fork. Light the liquor by taking a bit in a spoon, lighting it, and return to glass. Hold the sugar cubes over the flame until dissolved. When dissolved, extinguish fire by stirring fork quickly in glass without touching the sides.

Chinese Torture

1/2 oz. Canton Delicate Ginger Liqueur
1/4 tsp. powdered ginger
shot glass

1/2 oz. 151 proof rum
1/4 tsp. powdered sugar

Shake liqueur and rum in a cocktail shaker filled with ice. Strain into a shot glass and sprinkle lightly with powdered ginger and sugar (mix ginger and sugar together first).

Chiquita

1 1/2 oz. vodka
1/2 oz. Amaretto
1 oz. cream

1 oz. Crème de Banana
splash of Bailey's Irish Cream Liqueur
martini glass

Shake all ingredients in a cocktail shaker filled with ice. Strain into a martini glass.

Choco Colada

2 oz. gold rum
1/2 oz. Kahlua
1 oz. chocolate syrup
1/2 cup crushed ice

1/2 oz. dark Crème de Cacao
1/2 oz. Coco Lopez
2 oz. milk or light cream
hurricane glass

Mix in blender. Pour into hurricane glass.

Chocolate Martini

1 1/2 oz. Stoli Razberi
orange peel
martini glass

1/2 oz. Godet Belgian
White Chocolate Liqueur

Shake all ingredients except orange peel in a cocktail shaker filled with ice. Strain into a chilled martini glass. Twist the orange peel and run around rim of glass. Drop in.

Chocolate Chip

1 oz. vodka
low-ball glass

1 oz. Frangelica

Shake both ingredients in a cocktail strainer filled with ice. Strain into a lowball glass.

Chocolate Covered Banana

1 oz. vodka
1/2 oz. Crème de Banana

1/2 oz. white Crème de Cacao
2 oz. light cream

Shake both ingredients in a cocktail strainer filled with ice. Strain into a rocks glass filled with ice.

Coco Loco

1 1/2 oz. tequila
1/2 oz. Coco Lopez
1/2 cup crushed ice

1 oz. pineapple juice
splash of Cruzan Banana Rum
margarita glass

Blend all ingredients in a blender until smooth. Pour into a margarita glass.

Coconut Bellini

3 oz. champagne
1 oz. Coco Lopez
splash of Cruzan Coconut Rum

1 oz. Peach Schnapps
splash of Amaretto
margarita glass

In a cocktail shaker filled with ice, shake the schnapps, Coco Lopez, Amaretto, and rum. Pour into a margarita glass. Fill with champagne and stir gently.

Coconut Cream Pie

1 1/2 oz. Malibu (coconut rum)
sweetened coconut flakes

whipped cream
shot glass

Serve in a shot glass. Top with whipped cream. Sprinkle with sweetened coconut flakes.

Coffee Cooler

1 1/2 oz. vodka
1/2 oz. Bailey's Irish Cream Liqueur
instant coffee granules

1 oz. Tia Maria
1 oz. cream
rocks glass

Shake all ingredients in a cocktail shaker filled with ice. Strain into a rocks glass filled with ice. Garnish with instant coffee granules.

Coffee Fantasy

1 1/2 oz. Bailey's Irish Cream Liqueur
milk

1 1/2 oz. cold coffee
Highball glass

Fill a Highball glass with ice. Stir in Bailey's and coffee. Fill with milk and stir.

Coldcocked

1 oz. rum
1/2 oz. Coco Lopez
4 oz. cola
hurricane glass

1 oz. Southern Comfort
2 oz. pineapple juice
1/2 cup crushed ice

Mix in blender until smooth. Pour into a hurricane glass.

Colorado Bulldog

2 oz. vodka
2 oz. cola

1 oz. Tia Maria
Highball glass

Fill a Highball glass with ice. Stir in all ingredients.

Colorado Skies

1 1/2 oz. tequila
4 oz. grapefruit juice
highball glass

1 1/2 oz. Blue Curacao
splash of Triple Sec

Fill a Highball with ice. Stir in all ingredients.

Yeah, mon! **Martinique** is considered the island of flowers as its Arawak name, Madinina, indicates. This lush island is considered one of the most spectacular in the Caribbean with its gorgeous wild orchids, hibiscus, hummingbirds and fruit trees. To the north, sleepy Mont Pelee was once an active volcano. Beaches are fabulous, some gleaming white, others a pearly black. This 425-mile island is the largest of the Windward Islands and decidedly French in flavor.

Capital: Fort-de-France
Population: over 380,000
Money: French Franc, $US1=$5.86
Official Language: French and Creole
Political Status: French possession
Just for Fun!: Surfing at Cap Macre beach; walking Diamant, the island's longest beach (2 1/2 miles); sailing around the island at sunset.
Tidbit: Martinique's Carnival runs from January to early March!

Comfortable Brother

1 1/2 oz. Southern Comfort
splash of fresh lemon juice

1 1/2 oz. Frangelico
low ball

Fill a lowball glass with ice. Stir in all ingredients.

Comfortable Screw

1 oz. vodka
orange juice

1 oz. Southern Comfort
old-fashioned

Fill an old-fashioned glass with ice. Stir in all ingredients.

Comfortable Screw
Up Against The Wall

1 oz. vodka
1/2 oz. Galliano
old-fashioned glass

1 oz. Southern Comfort
orange juice

Fill an old-fashioned glass with ice. Stir in all ingredients, filling orange juice to top.

Cosmopolitan Martini

2 oz. vodka
splash of Cointreau
martini glass

splash of Boggs Cranberry Liqueur
(cranberry liqueur)

Shake all ingredients in a cocktail shaker filled with ice. Strain into a martini glass.

Cranapple

1 oz. Calvados
splash of Boggs Cranberry Liqueur

1 oz. cranberry juice
shooter

Pour all ingredients into a shooter.

Cranberry ZZ

2 oz. light rum
1/4 cup frozen strawberries
1 oz. fresh lime juice
hurricane glass

splash of Cointreau
1 oz. Boggs Cranberry Liqueur
1/2 cup crushed ice

Mix all ingredients except rum in blender until smooth. Pour into a hurricane glass. Top with rum.

Cranberry Chocolate Martini

1 1/2 oz. Stoli Razberi
1 oz. cranberry juice
martini glass

1 oz. Godet Belgian White Chocolate
Liqueur

Shake all ingredients in a cocktail shaker filled with ice. Strain into a martini glass.

Creamsicle

1 oz. Galliano
1/2 oz. Stoli Ohranj Vodka
rocks glass

1/2 oz. Bailey's Irish Cream Liqueur
orange juice

Fill a rocks glass with ice. Shake all ingredients in a cocktail shaker filled with ice. Strain and pour into rocks glass.

Creamy Bush

1 oz. Bailey's
couple of drops of Amaretto

1 oz. Old Bushmills Irish Whiskey
rocks glass

Fill a rocks glass with ice. Stir in all ingredients.

Cum In A Hot Tub

1 oz. orange juice
low ball

1 oz. Bailey's Irish Cream Liqueur

Pour Bailey's Irish Cream Liqueur into orange juice to curdle.

Somewhat like a Cement Mixer.

Dances with Wenches
St. Maarten, West Indies
courtesy of Sint Maarten Guavaberry Company

2 oz. Sint Maarten Guavaberry liqueur
1 oz. fresh lime or lemon juice
fresh mint leaves

5 oz. cranberry juice
slice of lime
hurricane glass

Shake all ingredients in a cocktail shaker filled with ice. Pour into a hurricane glass. Garnish with lime slice and mint leaves.

Bartender's Secret-Fizz Saver

When using sparkling waters, soda or wines, be careful not to over stir. Nothing worse than a flat drink.

Deep Throat

1 clean empty glass salt shaker
1 oz. Tia Maria

1 oz. tequila
whipped cream

Similar to a Blow Job, but for women only. Pour liquor into shaker. Top with whipped cream. No hands! And use tongue to break whipped cream seal.

Dead Nazi

1 oz. Rumple Minz
splash of green Crème de Menthe

1/2 oz. Jaegermeister
shot glass

Shake all ingredients in a cocktail shaker filled with ice. Strain into a shot glass. Top with Crème de Menthe.

Dirty Harry

1 oz. Kahlua
splash of dark Crème de Cacao

1 oz. Grand Marnier
shot glass

Serve straight up in a shot glass.

Go ahead. Make my day.

Dirty Mother

2 oz. cognac or brandy
rocks glass

2 oz. Kahlua

Fill a rocks glass with ice. Stir in all ingredients.

Dirty Sock

2 oz. Scotch
rocks glass

3 oz. pineapple juice

Fill a rocks glass with ice. Stir in all ingredients.

Double Jack

1 oz. Yukon Jack
shooter

1 oz. Jack Daniels Tennessee Whiskey

Pour both ingredients into a shooter.

Yeah, mon! Puerto Rico is blessed with gorgeous beaches, medieval fortresses, the only tropical rainforest in the U.S. Forest System, a phosphorescent bay and subterranean caverns. This 110 by 35-mile island, the size of Connecticut is one of the busiest cruise ship homeports in the world. From its glittering beaches lined with high rises in the Condado area to its fascinating Colonial heritage, the island is a definite must on any Caribbean itinerary.

Capital: San Juan, a.k.a. Old San Juan and Condado area
Population: 4 million and growing
Money: U.S. Dollar
Official Language: English and Spanish
Political Status: U.S. Commonwealth
Just for Fun!: Sliding into a pool underneath a waterfall in El Yunque Caribbean National Forest; walking among cobblestone streets and gorgeous Spanish buildings in Old San Juan; having lunch at El Conquistador while looking toward Vieques island.
Tidbit: If you're a U.S. citizen, you don't even have to clear customs at this U.S. owned paradise.

Dr. Pepper

1 1/2 oz. Amaretto   4 oz. cola
rocks glass

Fill a rocks glass with ice. Stir in both ingredients.

Electric Lemonade

1 1/2 oz. vodka   1/2 oz. Blue Curacao
4 oz. lemonade   lemon twist
Highball glass

Fill a Highball glass with ice. Stir in all ingredients. Garnish with lemon twist.

Embryo

Rumple Minz   straw
drop of half & half   shot glass

Fill a shot glass with Rumple Minz. Put a straw in the center, run down a couple drops of half and half, and watch it curdle.

Emerald

1 1/2 oz. gin
1/2 oz. Midori
martini glass

1/2 oz. dry vermouth
1/2 oz Blue Curacao

Shake all ingredients in a cocktail shaker filled with ice. Strain into a martini glass.

Emerald City Martini

2 oz. Absolut Citron
martini glass

splash of Midori

Shake all ingredients in a cocktail shaker filled with ice. Strain into a martini glass.

Eye Drop

1/2 oz. Sambuca
1/2 oz. vodka
shot glass

1/2 oz. Rumple Minze
drop of Blue Curacao

Shake all ingredients in a cocktail shaker filled with ice. Strain into a shot glass.

14

1 1/2 oz. Seagram's 7 Canadian Whiskey
Highball glass

Seven-Up

Fill a Highball glass with ice. Stir ingredients gently.

43 Amigos

1 1/2 oz. tequila
1/2 oz. Cointreau
drop of Angostura bitters

1/2 oz. Licor 43
1/2 oz. fresh limejuice
martini glass

Shake all ingredients in a cocktail shaker filled with ice. Strain into a martini glass.

Fifth Avenue

(1.) 1/2 oz. Bailey's Irish Cream Liqueur
(3.) 1/2 oz. dark Cream de Cacao

(2.) 1/2 oz. apricot brandy
shot glass

Layer this drink in the order shown.

Fire

1 1/2 oz. Stoli Ohranj Vodka
shot glass

1/2 oz. Goldschlagger (cinnamon
schnapps)

Layer the schnapps over the vodka in a shot glass.

Fire and Ice

2 oz. pepper vodka
martini glass

1/2 oz. dry vermouth

Shake both ingredients in a cocktail shaker filled with ice. Strain into a rocks glass.

Fireball

1 oz. Goldschlager (cinnamon schnapps)
shot glass

splash of habanero hot sauce

Serve straight up in a shot glass. Float the habanero hot sauce on top.

Careful! Extremely fiery.

Yeah, mon! St. Lucia majestic twin peaks are called the Pitons. This island reminded me very much of the St. Thomas of yesteryear with its charming Victorian wooden homes, lush banana plantations and rugged countryside. Parts of Romancing the Stone were filmed here. Be sure to purchase a couple of bottles of the banana ketchup when here. Excellent on chicken, meat and fish.

Capital: Castries
Population: 150,000
Money: Eastern Caribbean Dollar; US$1=$2.67
Official Language: English, Patois
Political Status: Independent British Commonwealth
Just for Fun!: Taking a jeep tour through the rough and wild countryside; visiting an extinct volcano, eating fresh, local bananas-very sweet!
Tidbit: St. Lucia grows 12 varieties of bananas.

Fire Cracker

1/2 oz. Goldschlagger (cinnamon schnapps)
splash of grenadine
shooter

1/2 oz. Kirshwasser
splash of Tabasco™

Combine all ingredients and pour into a shooter.

Fire Fly

1 1/2 oz. vodka
splash of Cuarenta y Tres
lemon wedge

4 oz. grapefruit juice
splash of grenadine
Highball glass

Fill a Highball glass with ice. Stir in all ingredients. Squeeze and garnish with lemon wedge.

Firestorm

1 oz. Firewater
1 oz. 151 Rum
rocks glass

1 oz. Rumple Minz
couple drops dark Crème de Cacao

Fill a rocks glass with ice. Stir in all ingredients.

KOSKELA

Flambé

(1.) grenadine
(3.) vodka
(5.) 151 rum
shot glass

(2.) Crème de Menthe
(4.) Cointreau
straws

Layer the ingredients in the order shown. Place two large straws in drink. Light drink with a match. Drink very quickly, before straws melt.

Be very careful with this drink. Do not try this at home. It's better to have a professional bartender assist you.

Flaming Orgasm

beer in a beer mug

151 rum

Float rum on top of beer. Light on fire. Drink after flame goes out.

Flying Dutchman

2 oz. gin
drop of Galliano

1/2 oz. Cointreau
low ball

Serve warm in a low-ball.

Flying Grasshopper

1 oz. white Crème de Cacao
2 oz. vodka
margarita glass

1 oz. green Crème de Menthe
2 oz. milk

Shake all ingredients in a cocktail shaker filled with ice. Strain into a margarita glass.

Flying Tiger

1 oz. vodka
1 oz. Galliano
rocks glass

1 oz. white Crème de Menthe
splash of white Crème de Cacao

Shake all ingredients in a cocktail shaker filled with ice. Strain into a rocks glass with ice.

Fools Gold

1 1/2 oz. vodka, chilled
lemon twist

Galliano
shot glass

Pour the vodka into a shot glass. Float Galliano on top. Garnish with lemon twist.

Bartender's Secret-Sweat and Coasters

Here in the Caribbean there is no such thing as a dripless drink. I have a scene in my novel, Almost Paradise, where I capture the moment and have condensation rivulets run down the outside of a wine glass.

I have some beautiful marble coasters with palm trees hand painted on the tops. They really don't work for cold drinks because they just stick to the bottom of the glass and clatter to the floor. The best coasters are those sandstone ones that blot up the water.

Fourth of July

(1.) 1/2 oz. grenadine
(3.) 1/2 oz. Blue Curacao

(2.) 1 oz. Stoli Strawberry Vodka
shot glass

Layer this drink in the order shown in a shot glass.

Freddy Thudpucker

1 1/2 oz. tequila
2 oz. orange juice

1 oz. Galliano
rocks glass

Fill a rocks glass with ice. Stir in all ingredients.

Freight Train

1/2 oz. Grand Marnier
1/2 oz. Jack Daniel's Tennessee
   Sour Mash Whiskey

1/2 oz. Southern Comfort
splash of fresh limejuice
shot glass

Shake all ingredients in a cocktail shaker filled with ice. Strain into a shot glass.

French Connection

4 oz. brandy
1 1/2 oz. Amaretto

1 oz. Calvados
rocks glass

Fill a rocks glass with ice. Stir in all ingredients.

French Summer

1 oz. Chambord
splash of fresh lemon juice
wine glass

3 oz. sparkling mineral water
lemon twist

Fill a wine glass with ice. Pour in Chambord, and then fill with mineral water and lemon juice. Stir gently.

Frigid Hairy Virgin

1 1/2 oz. 151 rum
3 oz. pineapple juice

1/2 oz. Cointreau
rocks glass

Fill a rocks glass with ice. Stir in all ingredients.

French 75

1 1/2 oz. cognac
1 tsp. simple syrup
splash of peach liqueur

1 tsp. fresh lemon juice
champagne
champagne glass

Shake all ingredients, except champagne, in a cocktail shaker filled with ice. Pour into a champagne flute and top with champagne.

Bartender's Secret-Opening and Storing Champagne

Remove wire fastener and then the foil from the neck of the bottle. Hold the bottle away from you, other people, pets, or valuables. Hold onto to the cork and twist the bottle. Now, most people will tell you that champagne must be drunk immediately, but sometime an entire bottle is too much. Save a couple of corks from wine bottles and enjoy the champagne the next day.

French Kiss Martini

2 oz. vodka
splash of Grand Marnier
martini glass

1/2 oz. Lillet
orange twist

Shake all ingredients in a cocktail shaker filled with ice. Pour into a champagne martini glass.

Fudgesicle

1 oz. Stoli Vanil (vanilla) Vodka
splash of cream

1/2 oz. dark Crème de Cacao
shot glass

Shake all ingredients in a cocktail shaker filled with ice. Pour into a shot glass.

Fuzzy Iranian

ice cold beer in a mug

1 1/2 oz. Peach Schnapps

Pour the schnapps into the beer.

Fuzzy Navel

1 1/2 oz. Peach Schnapps
orange juice

splash of Southern Comfort
rocks glass

Fill a rocks glass with ice. Pour in schnapps and Southern Comfort. Stir in orange juice.

Fuzzy Screw

1 oz. vodka
1/2 oz. Peach Schnapps
rocks glass

1 oz. Southern Comfort
orange juice

Fill a rocks glass with ice. Stir in all ingredients, filling orange juice to top.

Gasoline

1 1/2 oz. tequila
splash of 151 rum

1 1/2 oz. Southern Comfort
low ball

Fill a low-ball glass with ice. Stir in all ingredients.

GB Bikini
St. Maarten, West Indies
courtesy of Sint Maarten Guavaberry Company

Fresh grapefruit juice as opposed to canned makes an incredible taste different in this drink.

2 oz. Sint Maarten Guavaberry liqueur
grapefruit slice or lime
highball glass

5 oz. fresh grapefruit juice
grated cinnamon

Fill a highball glass with ice. Pour in liqueur and fill to top with grapefruit juice. Garnish with grapefruit slice or lime and grated cinnamon.

Gene Splice

1 oz. Stoli Razberi
1 oz. Cruzan Pineapple Rum
highball

1 oz. Cointreau
1 oz. fresh limejuice

Fill a highball glass with ice. Stir in all ingredients.

Get Laid

1 oz. Stoli Razberi
splash of Boggs Cranberry Liqueur
martini glass

1/2 oz. Chambord
2 oz. pineapple juice

Shake all ingredients in a cocktail shaker filled with ice. Strain into a martini glass.

Ghostbuster

1/2 oz. Bailey's Irish Cream Liqueur Liqueur
1/2 oz. vodka
shooter

1/2 oz. Kahlua
splash of cream

Shake all ingredients in a cocktail shaker filled with ice. Strain into a shooter.

Gibson

2 1/2 oz. Bombay Sapphire Gin
cocktail onions
martini glass

splash of Martini & Rossi
Extra Dry Vermouth

Shake the gin and vermouth in a cocktail shaker filled with ice. Strain into a martini glass and drop a couple cocktail onions in bottom.

Gimlet

2 oz. gin
1 tsp. powdered sugar
martini glass

1 oz. fresh limejuice
1/2 cup crushed ice

Shake all ingredients in a cocktail shaker filled with ice. Pour into a martini glass.

Gin and Sin

1 1/2 oz. gin
splash of fresh lime juice
martini glass

1 oz. lemonade
splash of grenadine

Shake all ingredients in a cocktail shaker filled with ice. Strain into a martini glass.

Gin and Tonic

2 oz. gin
lime wedge

tonic water
highball

Fill a highball with ice. Pour in gin and fill to top with tonic water. Squeeze and drop in a lime wedge.

Gin Alexander

1 1/2 oz. gin
drop of Crème de Banana
martini glass

1 oz. white Crème de Cacao
2 oz. light cream

Shake all ingredients in a cocktail shaker filled with ice. Strain into a martini glass.

Gin Cobbler

2 oz. gin
club soda
highball

1/4 oz. Amaretto
lime wedge

Fill a highball glass with ice. Pour in gin and Amaretto. Fill to top with club soda and stir gently. Squeeze a lime wedge over glass and drop in.

Gin Daisy

2 oz. gin
1 oz. fresh lemon juice
club soda
highball

1 oz. Chambord
1 tsp. grenadine
mint leaves

Shake all ingredients in a cocktail shaker filled with ice. Strain into a highball filled with ice. Fill to top with club soda and stir gently. Garnish with mint leaves.

Yeah, mon! St. Kitts and Nevis are separated by a two-mile waterway. St. Kitts, tiny and lush, manages a big bang for its buck by cramming in stunning scenery in a mere 65-square miles. Endless and brilliant verdant fields of sugarcane dip to the ocean. Nevis is known for its long white and black sand beaches and mineral spa baths.

Capital: Basseterre on St. Kitts
Population: 45,000
Money: Eastern Caribbean Dollar, $US1=2.70
Political Status: Independent British Commonwealth
Official Language: English with a heavy West Indian accent
Just for Fun!: Scoping out the twin beaches of Banana Bay and Cockleshell Bay; horseback riding at sunset at Frigate Bay; becoming PADI-certified to dive the islands gorgeous waters
Tidbit: The Bath Hotel located at Bath Springs is the first hotel built in the Caribbean in 1778 by John Huggins for European aristocrats.

Gin Fizz

2 1/2 oz. gin
1 tsp. powdered sugar
club soda

drop of Triple Sec
1 oz. fresh lemon juice
highball

Fill a highball glass with ice. Stir in all ingredients.

Gin Milk Punch

2 oz. gin
1 tsp. orgeat syrup
highball

4 oz. milk
freshly ground nutmeg

Shake all ingredients, except nutmeg, in a cocktail shaker filled with ice. Fill a highball with ice. Strain into glass and sprinkle nutmeg on top.

Gin Rickey

2 oz. gin
1 tsp. simple syrup
highball

1 oz. fresh limejuice
club soda

Shake all ingredients, except club soda, in a cocktail shaker filled with ice. Strain into a highball filled with ice. Fill to top with club soda and stir gently.

Gin Sling

2 oz. gin
1 oz. fresh lemon juice
club soda
Maraschino cherry

1/2 oz. Amaretto
1/2 oz. orgeat syrup
orange slice
rocks glass

Shake all ingredients, except club soda, in a cocktail shaker filled with ice. Fill a rocks glass with ice. Strain into glass and fill to top with club soda, stirring gently. Garnish with orange slice and cherry.

Gin Sour

2 oz. gin
1 oz. orgeat syrup
Maraschino cherry

1 oz. fresh lemon juice
orange slice
martini glass

Shake all ingredients in a cocktail shaker filled with ice. Strain into a martini glass. Garnish with an orange slice and the cherry.

Gin and Tonic

1 1/2 oz. gin

tonic water

In a rocks glass filled with ice, gently stir gin and tonic water.

Girl Scout Cookie

1 oz. dark Crème de Cacao
1 oz. Kahlua

1 oz. Rumple Minze
shot glass

Layer this drink carefully in the order shown.

Godfather

1 1/2 oz. bourbon
rocks glass

3/4 oz. Amaretto

Fill a rocks glass with ice. Stir in bourbon and Amaretto.

Godmother

1 1/2 oz. vodka
rocks glass

3/4 oz. Amaretto

Fill a rocks glass with ice. Stir in vodka and Amaretto.

Golden Cadillac

1 oz. white Crème de Cacao
splash of Bailey's Irish Cream Liqueur
champagne glass

1/2 oz. Galliano
1 oz. cream

Shake all ingredients in a cocktail shaker filled with ice. Strain and pour into champagne flute.

Golden Dawn

2 oz. gin
1/4 oz. Chambord
martini glass

1 oz. Apry (apricot liqueur)
1 1/2 oz. orange juice

Shake all ingredients in a cocktail shaker filled with ice. Strain into a martini glass.

Good and Plenty

1 oz. Black Haus (blackberry brandy)
lemon wedge

1 oz. Sambuca
shot glass

Shake all ingredients, except lemon wedge, in a cocktail shaker filled with ice. Strain and pour into shot glass. Squeeze lemon wedge over top.

Gradeal Special

2 oz. gin
1 oz. Abricotine (French apricot liqueur)
rocks glass

1 oz. light rum
drop of orange bitters

Shake all ingredients in a cocktail shaker filled with ice. Fill a rocks glass with ice. Strain into glass.

Grape Crush

1 oz. vodka
splash of Chambord
shot glass

1/2 oz. sloe gin
splash of lemon juice

Shake all ingredients in a cocktail shaker filled with ice. Strain into a shot glass.

Grapefruit Cocktail

2 oz. gin
1/4 oz. Maraschino liqueur
Maraschino cherry

1 oz. grapefruit juice
drop of grenadine
martini glass

Shake all ingredients, except cherry, in a cocktail shaker filled with ice. Strain into a martini glass. Garnish with a cherry.

Grasshopper

1 oz. white Crème de Cacao
2 oz. milk

1 oz. green Crème de Menthe
margarita glass

Shake all ingredients in a cocktail shaker filled with ice. Strain into a margarita glass.

Green Dragon

2 oz. gin
1/2 oz. Kummel
splash of Angostura Bitters

1 oz. green Crème de Menthe
1/2 oz. Peach Schnapps
martini glass

Shake all ingredients in a cocktail shaker filled with ice. Strain into a martini glass.

Green Island

1 1/2 oz. pineapple vodka
2 oz. pineapple juice
splash of Cointreau
sugar

1/2 oz. green Crème de Menthe
1 oz. limejuice
pineapple ring
margarita glass

Wet the lip of the margarita glass with limejuice. Twist in a plate of sugar. Shake all ingredients in a cocktail shaker filled with ice, except pineapple ring. Pour into a margarita glass. Float pineapple ring in center.

Green Lagoon

1/2 oz. gin
1 oz. green Crème de Menthe
colored sugar crystals
margarita glass

1/2 oz. vodka
3 oz. pineapple juice
simple syrup

Wet the lip of the margarita glass with simple syrup. Twist in the colored sugar crystals. Shake all ingredients in a cocktail shaker filled with ice. Strain into the margarita glass.

Green Stinger

1 1/2 oz. vodka
martini glass

1 oz. green Crème de Menthe

Shake all ingredients in a cocktail shaker filled with ice. Strain into a martini glass.

Greyhound

1 1/2 oz. vodka
lime wedge

grapefruit juice
Highball glass

Fill a Highball glass with ice. Stir in vodka and grapefruit juice. Squeeze and drop in a lime wedge.

Guavaberry Daiquiri
St. Maarten, West Indies
Courtesy of Sint Maarten Guavaberry Company

2 oz. Sint Maarten Guavaberry liqueur
lime slice
cocktail glass

2 oz fresh limejuice or lemon
Maraschino cherry

Shake all ingredients in a cocktail shaker filled with ice. Pour into a cocktail glass. Garnish with lime slice and cherry.

Happy Virgin

1 1/2 oz. Kahlua
splash of Cruzan Pineapple rum
rocks glass

1 1/2 oz. Bailey's Irish Cream Liqueur
3 oz. pineapple juice

Fill a rocks glass with ice. Stir in all ingredients.

Bartender's Secret-Simple Syrup

Sugar and alcohol do not mix well. Instead of using superfine sugar, make up your own simple syrup. In a saucepan, add two cups of sugar to one-cup cold water. Bring to a boil for a few minutes until sugar is dissolved. Cool and pour into a clean, sterilized glass bottle. Keeps several months in refrigerator.

Harvey Wallbanger

1 1/2 oz. vodka
orange juice

1/2 oz. Galliano
rocks glass

Fill a rocks glass with ice. Pour in vodka and Galliano. Fill to top with orange juice and stir.

Hawaii Five-O

1 1/2 oz. Finlandia Pineapple Vodka
splash of maraschino cherry juice

1/2 oz. Blue Curacao
margarita glass

Shake all ingredients in a cocktail shaker filled with ice. Fill a margarita glass with ice. Strain into glass.

Hawaiian

1 oz. gin
1 oz. orange juice

splash of Galliano
shooter

Shake all ingredients in a cocktail shaker. Strain into shooter.

Hawaiian Cocktail

1 1/2 oz. gin
drop of grenadine
martini glass

1/2 oz. Cointreau
1/2 oz. pineapple juice

Shake all ingredients in a cocktail shaker filled with ice. Strain into a martini glass.

Hawaiian Night

1 oz. vodka
pineapple juice
rocks glass

1/2 oz. Echte Kroatzbeere
   (blackberry liqueur)

Fill a rocks glass with ice. Layer the ingredients in the order shown.

Hawaiian Orange Blossom

1 1/2 oz. gin
splash of Grand Marnier
1 oz. pineapple juice

1 oz. Triple Sec
1 oz. orange juice
rocks glass

Shake all ingredients in a cocktail shaker filled with ice. Strain into a rocks glass with ice.

Hawaiian Punch

1/4 oz. gin
1/4 oz. Crème de Cassis
splash of orange juice

1/4 oz. Southern Comfort
1/4 oz. Cointreau
shooter

Shake all ingredients in a cocktail shaker filled with ice. Strain into a shooter.

Hawaii Seven-O

1 1/2 oz. Seagram's 7 Canadian Whiskey
4 oz. orange juice
Highball glass

1/2 oz. Amaretto
splash of Coco Lopez

Shake all ingredients in a cocktail shaker filled with ice. Fill a Highball glass with ice. Strain and pour into glass.

Yeah, mon! St. Maarten, Dutch West Indies and St. Martin, French West Indies are located on the same 37-square-mile island. The Dutch side is perfect for those who love lots to do, be it shopping, snorkeling, golf or tennis. The French side is definitely Parisian in flavor with its restaurants and art galleries.

Capital: Marigot and Phillipsburg (Dutch side)
Population: nearly 100,000
Money: French Franc, $US1=$6.5FF; Netherlands Antilles Guilder, $US1=1.78NAF
Official Language: French, Dutch, English, Papiamento
Political Status: French side, part of Guadeloupe; Dutch side, Member of Netherlands Antilles
Just for Fun!: Sitting in an open-air French bistro with a aromatic fresh fish chowder in front of you; shopping for French clothes in Marigot; bathing in the nude at Club Orient.
Tidbit: It's said a drunken Dutchman and a Frenchman paced off the division of the island in a walking contest. The Frenchman won.

Honolulu Hammer

1 1/2 oz. vodka
splash of gin
splash of grenadine

1/2 oz. Amaretto
splash of pineapple juice
rocks glass

Fill a rocks glass with ice. Stir in all ingredients.

Highball

1 1/2 oz. Kentucky or Tennessee whiskey
lemon twist

ginger ale
Highball glass

Fill a Highball glass with ice. Stir in ginger ale and whiskey gently. Twist the lemon rind and run around rim of glass. Drop in.

Hollywood

1 oz. Stoli Strawberry Vodka
splash of Godiva Liqueur
shot glass

1 oz. Chambord
splash of pineapple juice

Shake all ingredients in a cocktail shaker filled with ice. Strain into a shot glass.

Horny Bull

1 1/2 oz. tequila
splash of Galliano

orange juice
rocks glass

Fill a rocks glass with ice. Add tequila and splash of Galliano. Stir in orange juice.

Hot Pants

1 1/2 oz. tequila
2 oz. grapefruit juice
martini glass

1/2 oz. Peppermint Schnapps
drop of habanero hot sauce

Shake all ingredients in a cocktail shaker filled with ice. Strain into a martini glass.

Hurricane

1/2 oz. Jagermeister
splash of Bailey's Irish Cream Liqueur
shot glass

1/2 oz. Yukon Jack
drop of dark Crème de Cacao

Layer first the Jagermeister, then the Yukon Jack, Bailey's and dot the Crème de Cacao on top. Do not stir for stormy effect.

Iguana

1/2 oz. gold tequila
1/2 oz. Kahlua

1/2 oz. Stoli Citron Vodka
shot glass

Shake all ingredients in a cocktail shaker filled with ice. Strain into a shot glass.

Il Paradiso

1 oz. Tuaca
splash of Galliano
rocks glass

1 oz. white Curacao
2 oz. milk

Shake all ingredients in a cocktail shaker filled with ice. Strain into a rocks glass filled with ice.

This is very important! Paradiso is the name of the main character's estate in my novel, Almost Paradise.

Irish Horseman

1 1/2 oz Irish Whiskey
1/2 oz. fresh limejuice
drop of Goldschlagger

1/2 oz. Cointreau
splash of Chambord
shooter

Shake all ingredients in a cocktail shaker filled with ice. Strain into a shooter.

Iron Butterfly

1 oz. vodka
1/2 oz. Amaretto
low ball

1/2 oz. Tia Maria
1/2 oz. Bailey's Irish Cream Liqueur

Shake all ingredients in a cocktail shaker filled with ice. Strain into a low-ball glass.

Iron Cross

(1.) 1/2 oz. Apricot Brandy   (2.) 1/2 oz. Rumple Minze
(3.) splash of Godiva Liqueur   shot glass

Layer the ingredients in the order shown in a shot glass.

Irish Horseman

1 1/2 oz Irish Whiskey   1/2 oz. Cointreau
1/2 oz. fresh limejuice   splash of Chambord
drop of Goldschlagger   shooter

Shake all ingredients in a cocktail shaker filled with ice. Strain into a shooter.

Island Lover
St. Maarten, West Indies
courtesy of Sint Maarten Guavaberry Company

1 oz. Sint Maarten Guavaberry liqueur   cold, dry white wine
frozen wine glass

Pour liqueur into a frozen wine glass. Fill to top with cold, dry white wine.

Island Queen
St. Maarten, West Indies
courtesy of Sint Maarten Guavaberry Company

1/2 oz. Sint Maarten Guavaberry liqueur   dry French or California champagne
Maraschino cherry   frozen champagne flute

Pour the liqueur into the frozen flute. Fill to top with champagne. Garnish with a maraschino cherry.

Island Suicide

1 can concentrated orange juice   light rum

Reconstitute the orange juice using rum instead of water.

Dangerous!

Jake

1 1/2 oz. Jack Daniel's Tennessee   cola
Sour Mash Whiskey Whiskey   Highball glass

Fill a Highball glass with ice. Stir ingredients.

Jamaica Me Crazy, Mon

1 oz. Cruzan Pineapple Rum
3 oz. pineapple juice
rocks glass

1/2 oz. Kahlua
splash of Absolut Mandarin

Fill a rocks glass with ice. Stir in all ingredients.

Jell-O™ Shots

12 oz. vodka
6 oz. Jell-O™ flavor of choice

12 oz. water
splash of Cointreau

Mix half the vodka with half the water and bring to a boil. Stir in Jell-O™. Remove from heat, adding remaining vodka and water. Pour into a bowl, pour Cointreau lightly over top and chill overnight.

To serve: Place a sheet of wax paper on a clean bar or counter. With an ice cream scoop, drop one scoop of Jell-O™ onto the wax paper. Using no hands, eat/drink shot.

Jelly Bean

1/2 oz. Sambuca
splash of Stoli Razberi

1/2 oz. Black Haus
shot glass

Shake all ingredients in a cocktail shaker filled with ice. Strain into a shot glass.

Jelly Fish

1/2 oz. white Crème de Cacao
1/2 oz. Coco Lopez
splash of grenadine

1/2 oz. Amaretto
1/2 oz Malibu
margarita glass

Shake first four ingredients in a cocktail shaker filled with ice. Strain into a margarita glass. Pour grenadine in center.

Jolly Rancher

1/2 oz. Peach Schnapps
splash of Midori
shot glass

1/2 oz. Calvados
splash of Boggs Cranberry Liqueur
    (cranberry liqueur)

Shake all ingredients in a cocktail shaker filled with ice. Strain into a shot glass.

Juicy Fruit

1/2 oz. Stoli Pineapple
1/2 oz. Midori
shot glass

1/2 oz. Peach Schnapps
1/2 oz. Crème de Banana

Shake all ingredients in a cocktail shaker filled with ice. Strain into a shot glass.

Jupiter Cocktail

1 1/2 oz. gin
1/2 oz. Crème de Violet
orange twist

1/2 oz. dry vermouth
splash of orange juice
martini

Shake all ingredients in a cocktail shaker filled with ice. Strain into a martini glass. Twist the orange peel, run around rim of glass, and drop in.

Jungle Jim

1 oz. vodka
splash of Frangelico
martini glass

1 oz. Crème de Banana
1 oz. cream

Shake all ingredients in a cocktail shaker filled with ice. Strain into a martini glass.

Kahlua Sombrero

2 oz. Kahlua
rocks glass

2 oz. half and half or milk

Shake both ingredients in a cocktail shaker filled with ice. Serve straight up or over ice.

Kamikaze

1 oz. vodka
splash of Rose's Lime Juice

splash of Triple Sec
shot glass

Shake all ingredients in a cocktail shaker filled with ice. Serve straight up or over ice.

Kir

1/2 oz. Crème de Cassis
champagne flute

3 oz. champagne, sparkling wine, or wine

Pour the Crème de Cassis in the bottom of the champagne flute. Fill to top with chilled wine.

Kool-Aid

1/2 oz. gin
1/2 oz. light rum
splash of Chambord

1/2 oz. Stoli Strawberry Vodka vodka
1/2 oz. Cointreau
rocks glass

Fill a rocks glass with ice. Stir all ingredients.

Krupnik

8 oz. vodka
cinnamon
whole cloves

honey
freshly ground nutmeg

Warm vodka over gentle heat with honey and spices. Allow to steep.

Serves two.

La Bomba

1 1/2 oz. tequila
2 oz. orange juice
splash of fresh lemon juice
rocks glass

1/2 oz. Galliano
2 oz. pineapple juice
splash of grenadine

Fill a rocks glass with ice. Stir all ingredients.

Bartender's Secret-Flavor Cloud

Find a small, clean, and empty spritzer bottle, fill with vermouth, Crème de Menthe, Kirsch, Amaretto, or other costly liquors, and mist over drinks. Spraying these aromatic liquors increases the intensity and taste of the drink.

Laser Beam

1 oz. Jack Daniel's Tennessee
    Sour Mash Whiskey
few drops of Tuaca

1 oz. Galliano
1 oz. Amaretto
low ball

Fill a low ball glass with ice. Stir in all ingredients.

Latin Lover

1 1/2 oz. tequila
splash of Tuaca

1/2 oz. Amaretto
shot glass

Shake all ingredients in a cocktail shaker filled with ice. Strain into a shot glass.

Lemon Drop

1 oz. Absolut Citron
sugar
shot glass

1 tsp. Cointreau
lemon slice

Wet the rim of a shot glass and twist in a plate of sugar. Serve straight up in the shot glass. Hand the drinker a lemon slice to clean the palate.

Licorice Stick

1/2 oz. vodka
1/2 oz. Cointreau

1/2 oz. Ouzo
shot glass

Shake all ingredients in a cocktail shaker filled with ice. Strain into a shot glass.

Life Saver

(1.) 1 part Cointreau
(3.) 1 part grenadine

(2.) 1 part Midori
shot glass

Layer ingredients in order shown.

Liquid Cocaine

1/2 oz. Wild Turkey Kentucky Bourbon
1/2 oz. Amaretto
1 oz. cranberry juice
hurricane glass

1/2 oz. Absolut Cranberry
1/2 oz. Cruzan Pineapple Rum
1 oz. pine

Fill a hurricane glass with ice. Stir in all ingredients.

Lillet Noyaux

2 oz. Lillet Blanc
1/2 oz. Crème de Noyaux
martini glass

1 oz. gin
drop of orange bitters

Shake all ingredients in a cocktail shaker filled with ice. Strain into a martini glass.

Lime Lambada
St. Maarten, West Indies
courtesy of Sint Maarten Guavaberry Company

2 oz. Sint Maarten Lime liqueur
highball

cola

Fill a highball glass with ice. Pour in liqueur and fill to top with cola.

Yeah, mon! St. Vincent amd the Grenadines form a archipelago of exotic, lush and mountainous islands. It's fertile and volcanic soil is home to coconut, banana and breadfruit groves. St. Vincent is only 18 miles by 9 miles wide and the largest of these islands, some 32 in all. Bequia and Mustique are the most well-known of the smaller islands, vacation home to celebrities.

Capital: Kingstown on St. Vincent
Population: some 115,000 of which about 99,000 live on St. Vincent
Money: Eastern Caribbean Dollar, US$1=EC $2.67
Official Language: English
Political Status: Independent Member of British Commonwealth
Just for Fun!: Looking at the breadfruit tree at Kingstown's Botanical Garden grown from seedlings brought by Captain Bligh; taking a two-hour sail to Mustique and glimpsing the rich and famous; diving the 80-foot visibility on numerous reefs
Tidbit: The Ciboney Indians first inhabited St. Vincent in 4300 BC, long before King Tut ruled Egypt.

Little Devil

1 1/2 oz. gin
1/2 oz. Curacao
1/2 oz. fresh lemon juice

1/2 oz. light rum
splash of Tuaca
martini glass

Shake all ingredients in a cocktail shaker filled with ice. Strain into a martini glass.

London Cocktail

1 1/2 oz. gin
splash of Maraschino liqueur
martini glass

1/2 oz. Triple Sec
1 oz. fresh lemon juice

Shake all ingredients in a cocktail shaker filled with ice. Strain into a martini glass.

London French 75

1 1/2 oz. gin
splash of Chambord
Highball

1/2 oz. fresh lemon juice
champagne

Shake all ingredients, except champagne, in a cocktail shaker filled with ice. Strain into a highball filled with ice. Fill to top with champagne. Stir gently.

Long Beach Ice Tea

1/2 oz. vodka
1/2 oz. light rum
1/2 oz. Midori
lemon wedge

1/2 oz. gin
1/2 oz. Boggs Cranberry Liqueur
  (cranberry liqueur)
highball

Fill a highball glass with ice. Stir in all ingredients. Garnish with lemon wedge.

Long Island Iced Tea

1/2 oz. vodka
1/2 oz. light rum
1/2 oz. lemon juice
lemon wedge

1/2 oz. gin
1/2 oz. simple syrup
cola
highball

Fill a highball glass with ice. Stir in all ingredients. Garnish with lemon wedge.

Maiden's Blush

2 oz. gin
1/2 oz. fresh lemon juice
martini glass

1/2 oz. Pernod
1 tsp. grenadine

Shake all ingredients in a cocktail shaker filled with ice. Strain into a martini glass.

Maiden's Prayer

1 1/2 oz. gin
splash of orange juice
martini glass

1 oz. Tuaca
splash of lemon juice

Shake all ingredients in a cocktail shaker filled with ice. Strain into a martini glass.

Mainbrace

1 1/2 oz. gin
1 oz. grapefruit juice

1 oz. Southern Comfort
martini glass

Shake all ingredients in a cocktail shaker filled with ice. Strain into a martini glass.

Mandarin Fizz

1 1/2 oz. gin
splash of Galliano
2 oz. orange juice
rocks glass

1 oz. Mandarin Napoleon (tangerine
  liqueur with brandy base)
club soda

Shake all ingredients, except club soda, in a cocktail shaker filled with ice. Strain into a rocks glass filled with ice. Fill to top with club soda and stir gently.

M & M

(1.) splash of grenadine
(3.) 1/2 oz. Tia Maria

(2.) 1/2 oz. Amaretto
shot glass

Layer ingredients in order shown.

Madras

1 1/2 oz. vodka
2 oz. cranberry juice
lime wedge

2 oz. orange juice
splash of fresh lime juice
rocks glass

Fill a rocks glass with ice. Stir in all ingredients and garnish with lime wedge.

Mango Crush

1 1/2 oz. vodka
1 oz. Mango rum
shooter

splash Boggs Cranberry Liqueur
  (cranberry liqueur)

Shake all ingredients in a cocktail shaker filled with ice. Strain into a shooter.

Manhattan

2 oz. Tennessee whiskey
splash of maraschino cherry juice
Maraschino cherry

splash of sweet vermouth
couple of drops of Angostura Bitters
martini glass

Shake all ingredients, except cherry, in a cocktail shaker filled with ice. Strain into a martini glass. Garnish with a cherry.

Margarita

1 1/2 oz. tequila
1 oz. fresh lime juice
1/2 cup crushed ice
lime wedge

1/2 oz. Cointreau
1/2 oz. simple syrup
salt
margarita glass

Squeeze the lime wedge and run around rim of margarita glass. Twist rim in a plate of salt. Blend remaining ingredients in blender until smooth. Pour into margarita glass.

Martini

2 oz. gin
olive or lemon twist

drop of Extra Dry Vermouth
martini glass

Fill the martini glass with ice. Shake the gin and drop of Vermouth in a cocktail shaker filled with ice. Dump the ice from the chilled glass. Pour in gin quickly before ice dilutes it. Garnish with lemon twist or olive.

Melon Bell

1 oz. Midori
1/2 oz. Grand Marnier

1 oz. vodka
shooter

Shake all ingredients in a cocktail shaker filled with ice. Strain into shooter.

Melon Cocktail

1 1/2 oz. gin
1/2 oz. Maraschino liqueur
splash of fresh lemon juice

1 oz. Midori
splash of Triple Sec
martini glass with ice

Shake all ingredients in a cocktail shaker filled with ice. Strain into a martini glass.

Merry Widow

1 oz. gin
splash of Pernod
splash of Benedictine
lemon twist

1/2 oz. dry vermouth
splash of Galliano
drop of Angostura bitters
martini glass

Shake all ingredients, except for lemon twist, in a cocktail shaker filled with ice. Strain into a martini glass. Twist lemon peel and run around rim of glass. Drop in.

Metropolitan

2 oz. brandy or cognac
1/2 oz. Cointreau
martini glass

1 oz. sweet vermouth
dash of Angostura bitters

Fill a martini glass with ice. Shake all ingredients in a cocktail shaker filled with ice. Dump ice from glass. Strain into glass.

Bartender's Secret-Milk or Cream?

Many of the recipes in this book call for milk, but it should be noted that heavy cream will work better. Always use fresh cream and in the case of mixing cream with a citrus juice, such as lemon, mix shortly before serving, as the acid will thicken the cream.

Miami Beach

1 1/2 oz. Scotch
1 oz. grapefruit juice

1/2 oz. dry vermouth
low ball

Fill a low-ball glass with ice. Stir in all ingredients.

Miami Ice

1/2 oz. Stoli Ohranj
1/2 oz. white rum
1/2 oz. fresh lemon juice
rocks glass

1/2 oz. gin
1/2 oz. Peach Schnapps
1 oz. orange juice

Fill a rocks glass with ice. Stir in all ingredients.

Miami Meloni

1 oz. light rum
1 oz. cream
low ball

1 oz. Midori
splash of Bailey's Irish Cream Liqueur

Fill a low-ball glass with ice. Stir in all ingredients.

Midori Cocktail

1 oz. Midori
Rose's Lime Juice

chilled champagne
champagne glass

Pour Midori into bottom of champagne glass. Fill to top with champagne. Add a couple of drops of Rose's Lime Juice and stir gently.

Mimosa

3 oz. champagne
splash of Galliano

2 oz. orange juice
champagne flute

Gently stir all ingredients in glass.

Mint Chip

1 oz. Rumple Minz
1/2 oz. dark Crème de Cacao
low ball

1 oz. Kahlua
milk

Fill a low-ball glass with ice. Stir in all ingredients, filling milk to top.

Mint Julep

1 1/2 oz. Kentucky bourbon
fresh mint leaves

1/2 oz. simple syrup
rocks glass

Mash the mint leaves on the bottom of the glass. Pour in simple syrup, then bourbon. Fill rocks glass with ice. Stir.

Mississippi Mule

2 oz. gin
1 oz. fresh lemon juice
martini glass

1/2 oz. Crème de Cassis
1 tsp. orgeat syrup

Shake all ingredients in a cocktail shaker filled with ice. Strain into a martini glass.

Mocha Brandy

1 1/2 oz. Droste Bittersweet Chocolate liqueur
1 cup milk
1/2 tsp. instant coffee
margarita glass

1 oz. brandy
1 tsp. powdered chocolate milk mix
whipped cream

Shake all ingredients in a cocktail shaker filled with ice. Strain into a margarita glass. Top with whipped cream.

Mockingbird

1 1/2 oz. tequila
splash of white Crème de Cacao
shooter

1/2 oz. white Crème de Menthe
splash of fresh lime juice

Shake all ingredients in a cocktail shaker filled with ice. Strain into a shooter.

Monsoon

(1.) 1 oz. vodka

(2.) 1/4 oz. Kahlua

(3.) 1/4 oz. Amaretto

(4.) 1/4 oz. Crème de Cacao

(5.) 1 oz. cream

rocks glass

Fill a rocks glass with ice. Layer the ingredients in order shown. Stir half a turn to start the weather.

More Sunshine

1 oz. gin

orange juice

rocks glass

1 oz. Crème de Cassis

splash of Galliano

Fill a rocks glass with ice. Stir in gin and Crème de cassis. Fill to top with orange juice and float Galliano on top.

Morning Joy

1 1/2 oz. gin

splash of Grand Marnier

rocks glass

1 oz. Crème de Banana

2 oz. orange juice

Shake all ingredients in a cocktail shaker filled with ice. Strain into a rocks glass filled with ice.

Moscow Mule

1 1/2 oz. Russian vodka
lime wedge

ginger beer
rocks glass

Fill a rocks glass with ice. Pour in vodka and fill to top with ginger beer. Squeeze and drop in lime wedge.

This is an old favorite.

Mudslide

(1.) 1 oz. Stoli Vanil (vanilla) Vodka
(3.) 1/2 oz. Bailey's Irish Cream Liqueur Liqueur
orange twist

(2.) 1/2 oz. Tia Maria
cola
rocks glass

Fill a rocks glass with ice. Stir in first three ingredients. Fill to top with cola. Garnish with orange twist. Be sure to twist rind for that drop of orange oil.

Nadir

1 1/2 oz. gin
splash of Cruzan Pineapple Rum
splash of grenadine

1/2 oz. Maraschino liqueur
1/2 oz. fresh lemon juice
rocks glass

Fill a rocks glass with ice. Stir in all ingredients.

Nantucket

1 1/2 oz. white brandy
2 oz. cranberry juice
highball

splash of white Crème de Cacao
2 oz. grapefruit juice

Fill a highball glass with ice. Stir in all ingredients.

Bartender's Secret-Fruit Juices

I prefer fresh juices, but some people claim that liquor dilutes fresh orange juice and feel that concentrated works better.

NASDAQ

1 1/2 oz. Stoli Ohranj Vodka
1/2 oz. simple syrup
orange peel/twist

1/2 oz. fresh lemon juice
dash of Orange Bitters
rocks glass

Fill a rocks glass with ice. Add all ingredients and stir. Garnish with orange peel.

Negroni

1 oz. gin
1/2 oz. Campari
rocks glass

1/2 oz. Dry Vermouth
splash of orange juice

Fill a rocks glass with ice and stir in all ingredients.

Neutron Bomb

(1.) 1/4 oz. Tia Maria
(3.) 1/4 oz. Bailey's Irish Cream Liqueur

(2.) 1/4 oz. Poire Williams
(4.) few drops of grenadine

Layer all ingredients in order shown, i.e. earth, sky, clouds, and mushroom cloud from explosion.

New Orleans Gin Fizz

2 1/2 oz. gin
splash of Southern Comfort
1 egg white
Highball

splash of Tuaca
1 oz. cream
club soda

Shake all ingredients, except club soda, in a cocktail shaker filled with ice. Strain into a Highball filled with ice. Fill to top with club soda and stir gently.

Night Train

1 1/2 oz. gin
splash of grenadine
martini glass

1 oz. Curacao
1 oz. fresh lemon juice

Shake all ingredients in a cocktail shaker filled with ice. Strain into a martini glass.

Normandy Cocktail

2 oz. gin
1/2 oz. Persico (peach liqueur made by Bols)
martini glass

1 oz. Calvados
splash of fresh lime juice

Shake all ingredients in a cocktail shaker filled with ice. Strain into a martini glass.

Nuclear Waste

1 1/2 oz. vodka
splash of fresh limejuice

1 1/2 oz. Midori
shot glass

Pour into a shot glass.

Nutcracker

1 1/2 oz. vodka
1/2 oz. Amaretto
2 oz. cream
rocks glass

1/2 oz. Frangelico
1/2 oz. Pistacha (made by
    Cointreau/pistachio)

Shake all ingredients in a cocktail shaker filled with ice. Strain into a rocks glass filled with ice.

Oatmeal Cookie

1/2 oz. Bailey's Irish Cream Liqueur
1/2 oz. Butterscotch schnapps
shot glass

1/2 oz. Goldschlagger
splash of Tuaca

Shake all ingredients in a cocktail shaker filled with ice. Strain into a shot glass.

Old-Fashioned

2 1/2 oz whiskey
splash of maraschino cherry juice
club soda
orange slice

1/2 tsp. fine-grained sugar
dash of Angostura Bitters
maraschino cherry
rocks glass

On the bottom of a rocks glass, mix the sugar, cherry juice, and bitters. Add whiskey and stir. Fill glass with ice and pour club soda to top. Garnish with orange slice and cherry.

Opera

2 oz. gin
1/2 oz. Maraschino liqueur
orange twist

1/2 oz. Dubonnet rouge
drop of Galliano
rocks glass

Shake all ingredients, except orange twist, in a cocktail shaker filled with ice.

Orange Bang

1 1/2 oz. gin
splash of Triple Sec
orange slice

1/2 oz. Tuaca
2 oz. orange juice
martini glass

Shake all ingredients, except orange slice, in a cocktail shaker filled with ice. Strain into a martini glass.

Orange Blossom

1 1/2 oz. gin
highball

orange juice

Fill a highball glass with ice. Pour in gin and fill to top with orange juice. Stir.

Yeah, mon! St. Thomas in the U.S. Virgin Islands has world-class shopping at unbeatable, duty-free prices. This picture-postcard perfect island is home to hundreds of thousands of tourists and cruise ships each year. Red roofs dot the green hills which envelope the magnificent harbor filled with sailboats, luxury yachts and super-cruise ships.

Capital: Charlotte Amalie
Population: over 100,000
Money: U.S. Dollar
Official Language: English
Political Status: U.S. Unicorporated Territory
Just for Fun!: Taking day sail on the catamaran, Wild Thing; drinking Piña Coladas and watching the sunset in the harbor from Paradise Point; buying a Rolex at A. H. Riise gift shop at 35% off stateside prices
Tidbit: Nickname for this island, "Rock City"

Orange Blossom II

1 1/2 oz. vodka
splash of Cointreau
champagne glass

1 oz. champagne
orange juice

Shake the vodka and Cointreau in a cocktail shaker filled with ice. Strain into a champagne glass and fill to top with chilled orange juice.

Orange Crush

1 oz. Stoli Ohranj
orange juice

1/2 oz. Grand Marnier
shooter

Shake the Stoli and Grand Marnier in a cocktail shaker filled with ice. Strain and pour into a shooter. Float the orange juice on top.

Orgasm

1/2 oz. Bailey's Irish Cream Liqueur
1/2 oz. Kahlua
shooter

1/2 oz. Amaretto
1/2 oz. Stoli Vanil (vanilla) Vodka

Shake all ingredients in a cocktail shaker filled with ice. Strain into a shooter.

Outrigger

1 oz. vodka
1 oz. pineapple juice
rocks glass

1 oz. Peach Brandy
splash of Poire Williams

Fill a rocks glass with ice. Stir in all ingredients.

Paralyzer

1 oz. tequila
1/2 oz. Tia Maria
rocks glass

1/2 oz. white Crème de Cacao
splash of Frangelico

Fill a rocks glass with ice. Stir in all ingredients.

Parisian

1 1/2 oz. gin
1/2 oz. Crème de Cassis
martini glass

1/2 oz. dry vermouth
splash of Crème de Yvette

Shake all ingredients in a cocktail shaker filled with ice. Strain into a martini glass.

Passionfruit Punch
St. Maarten, West Indies
courtesy of Sint Maarten Guavaberry Company

1 1/2 oz. light rum
1 oz. orange juice
splash of grenadine
grated cinnamon

1 oz. Sint Maarten Passionfruit liqueur
1 oz. pineapple juice
orange slice
highball

Fill a highball glass with ice. Shake all ingredients in a cocktail shaker filled with ice, except liqueur, orange slice, and cinnamon. Pour into highball and float the liqueur on top. Garnish with orange slice and cinnamon.

Peach Blow Fizz

2 oz. gin
1/2 oz. lemon juice
1 oz. cream
highball

1 oz. Persico (peach liqueur made by Bols)
1/2 oz. Coco Lopez
club soda

Shake all ingredients, except club soda, in a cocktail shaker filled with ice. Strain into a highball glass filled with ice. Fill to top with club soda, stirring gently.

Peach Bunny

2 oz. Peach Brandy
splash Crème de Noyaux
martini glass

2 oz. white Crème de Cacao
2 oz. milk

Shake all ingredients in a cocktail shaker filled with ice. Strain into a martini glass.

Peachfuzz

1 1/2 oz. Peach Schnapps
splash of Boggs Cranberry Liqueur
martini glass

1 1/2 cranberry juice
splash of lime juice

Shake all ingredients in a cocktail shaker filled with ice. Strain into a martini glass.

Peanut Butter Chocolate Chip Cookie

1 oz. Frangelico
1 oz. brandy
rocks glass

1 oz. Kahlua
1 oz. cream

Fill a rocks glass with ice. Stir in all ingredients.

Peppermint Patty

1/2 oz. Peppermint Schnapps
1/2 oz. dark Crème de Cacao
rocks glass

1/2 oz. Kahlua
1/2 oz. Bailey's Irish Cream Liqueur

Shake all ingredients in a cocktail shaker filled with ice. Strain into a rocks glass filled with ice.

Pink Lady

1 1/2 oz. gin
2 oz. lemonade
splash of grenadine

1/2 oz. Cointreau
1 oz. cream
martini glass

Shake all ingredients in a cocktail shaker filled with ice. Strain into a martini glass.

Pink Panther

1 oz. gin
1/2 oz. Crème de Cassis
1 oz. orange juice

1/2 oz. dry vermouth
splash of Parfait Amour
martini glass

Shake all ingredients in a cocktail shaker filled with ice. Strain into a martini glass.

Yeah, mon! Trinidad and Tobago are two diverse twin islands and the southernmost in the West Indies chain. Trinidad is cosmopolitan, bustling with shopping, restaurants and nightlife, while Tobago, a mere 22 miles away is more like a Swiss Family Robinson-style island, laid back. Columbus reached these islands on his third voyage in 1498. Trinidad is infamous for its wonderful carnival.

Capital: Port of Spain on Trinidad
Population: 50,000 approximately on Tobago and over 1.3 million on Trinidad
Money: Trinidad and Tobago dollar, US$1=6.19
Official Language: English
Political Status: Independent British Commonwealth
Just for Fun!: Attending a wild and raucous carnival celebration held between February and early March; taking a dip in Tobabo's Nylon pool, a shallow pool in the middle of the Caribbean Sea; listening to Steel Pan music.
Tidbit: Spain controlled the island for some 200 years, until 1797, when the British took over.

Pink Pussycat

2 oz. Absolut Cranberry
splash of grenadine

2 oz. pineapple juice
rocks glass

Fill a rocks glass with ice. Stir in all ingredients.

Pink Lemonade

1 1/2 oz. vodka
2 oz. lemonade
rocks glass

1/2 oz. Boggs Cranberry Liqueur
(cranberry liqueur)

Fill a rocks glass with ice. Stir all ingredients.

Pink Mustang

1 oz. Finlandia Cranberry Vodka
splash of Godet White Belgian
    Chocolate Liqueur

1 oz. Rumple Minze
rocks glass

Fill a rocks glass with ice. Stir all ingredients.

Pink Squirrel

2 oz. Crème de Noyaux
1/2 oz. Amaretto
martini glass

1 1/2 oz. white Crème de Cacao
1 oz. cream

Shake all ingredients in a cocktail shaker filled with ice. Strain into a martini glass.

Never fill a glass more than three-quarters full or accidents will result as I found out the other day and so did my Oriental rug. Wine glasses should be filled approximately half full to allow the bouquet to diffuse properly. When making "on the rocks" drinks, place ice in glass first, then mixer, then alcohol. For beer, tilt the glass, pour down the side and then in the middle to aerate beer. Stop a bit below the three-quarter mark for the head.

Presbyterian

2 oz. rye whiskey   ginger ale
club soda   lime wedge
highball

Fill a highball glass with ice. Stir in whiskey, fill to top with ginger ale and club soda. Squeeze a lime wedge over glass and drop in.

Princess Alexandria

1 1/2 oz. vodka   1 oz. white Crème de Cacao
1 oz. Godiva Liqueur   1 oz. cream
rocks glass

Shake all ingredients in a cocktail shaker filled with ice. Strain into a rocks glass filled with ice.

Puerto Plata

1 1/2 oz. vodka   1/2 oz. Crème de Anana
1/2 oz. Crème de Banana   (pineapple liqueur)
1/2 oz. Amaretto   1 oz. orange juice
rocks glass

Shake all ingredients in a cocktail shaker filled with ice. Strain into a rocks glass filled with ice.

Ramos Fizz

1 1/2 oz. gin   drop of Galliano
1 oz. fresh limejuice   1 tsp. simple syrup
1 tsp. cream   splash of orange flower water
1 egg white   club soda
Highball

Shake all ingredients in a cocktail shaker filled with ice. Strain into a Highball filled with ice.

Red Russian

1 oz. Stoli Strawberry Vodka
2 oz. milk

1 oz. Fraise (strawberry liqueur)
rocks glass

Fill a rocks glass with ice. Stir in all ingredients.

Rob Roy

3 oz. Scotch
rocks glass

1/2 oz. dry vermouth

Fill a rocks glass with ice. Stir in all ingredients.

Rootbeer

1 1/2 oz. vodka
2 oz. beer
rocks glass

1/2 oz. Galliano
2 oz. coke

Fill a rocks glass with ice. Stir in all ingredients, gently.

Royal Orange Blossom

1 1/2 oz. gin
1/2 oz. Amaretto
martini glass

1/2 oz. Grand Marnier
2 oz. orange juice

Shake all ingredients in a cocktail shaker filled with ice. Strain into a martini glass.

Russian Banana

1 1/2 oz. vodka
1 oz. Crème de Banana
2 oz. light cream

1 oz. dark Crème de Cacao
drop of Grand Marnier
martini glass

Shake all ingredients in a cocktail shaker filled with ice. Strain into a martini glass.

Russian Cocktail

1 oz. gin
1/2 oz. white Crème de Cacao
drop of orange flower water

1 oz. vodka
1/2 oz. Amaretto
martini glass

Shake all ingredients in a cocktail shaker filled with ice. Strain into a martini glass.

Russian Bear

1 1/2 oz. Stoli Vanil
2 oz. cream

1 oz. white Crème de Cacao
rocks glass

Shake all ingredients in a cocktail shaker filled with ice. Strain into a rocks glass with ice.

Russian Quaalude

1 oz. Stoli Vanil
1/2 oz. Bailey's Irish Cream Liqueur
rocks glass

1/2 oz. Frangelico
2 oz. milk

Shake all ingredients in a cocktail shaker filled with ice. Strain into a rocks glass filled with ice.

Rusty Nail

2 oz. Scotch
low ball

1 1/2 oz. Drambuie

Fill a low-ball glass with ice. Stir in all ingredients.

Salty Dog

2 oz. vodka
highball

4 oz. grapefruit juice

Fill a highball glass with ice. Stir in vodka and grapefruit juice.

Yeah, mon! Turks and Caicos are at the end of the Bahamas chain, with a total land mass of about 230 miles, Turks to the east, and Caicos to the west. The Turks and Caicos are actually two groups of islands 575 miles southeast of Miami and 90 miles north of Haiti. Most of the islands are undeveloped surrounded by immaculate reefs.

Capital: Cockburn on Grand Turk
Population: less than 15,000
Money: U.S. Dollar
Official Language: English
Political Status: British Dependent Territory
Just for Fun!: Wall-diving along the 7,000 foot underwater trench between the Turks and Caicos and glimpsing the brilliant sealife; visiting the eerie limestone Conch Bar Caves and their underground, milky white lakes; touring Flamingo Pond and seeing the wild flamingos
Tidbit: It's claimed that Columbus' first landfall was on Grand Turk.

Scarlet O'Hara

1 1/2 oz. Southern Comfort
splash of fresh lime juice

4 oz. cranberry juice
highball

Fill a highball glass with ice. Stir in all ingredients.

Screaming Orgasm

1 oz. Bailey's Irish Cream Liqueur
1 oz. Triple Sec

1 oz. Galliano
rocks glass

Fill a rocks glass with ice. Stir in all ingredients.

Screwdriver

2 oz. vodka
highball

orange juice

Fill a highball glass with ice and vodka. Fill to top with orange juice.

Sea Breeze

2 oz. vodka
1 oz. cranberry juice
rocks glass

2 oz. orange juice
lime wedge

Fill a rocks glass with ice. Stir in all ingredients. Squeeze a lime wedge over glass and drop in.

Sewer Rat

(1.) 1 oz. vodka
(3.) 1 oz. Tia Maria
(5.) 1 oz. orange juice

(2.) 1 oz. Peach Schnapps
(4.) 1 oz. Grand Marnier
rocks glass

Fill a rocks glass with ice. Layer ingredients in order shown.

Sex

1 part Tia Maria
drop of Bailey's Irish Cream Liqueur

1 part Grand Marnier
shooter

Serve in a shooter.

Sex In A Bubblegum Factory

1/2 oz. Crème de Banana
1/2 oz. Apricot Schnapps
rocks glass

1/2 oz. Blueberry Schnapps
lemon lime soda

Fill a rocks glass with ice. Stir in all ingredients, gently.

Bartender's Secret-Floating and Layering

Many of the drinks in this book are layered or have a "float" on the top. Use a long spoon and gently dribble the liquor over the back of the spoon to avoid disturbing layers below.

Sex On The Beach

1 oz. vodka
1 oz. pineapple juice

1 oz. Peach Schnapps
martini glass

Shake all ingredients in a cocktail shaker filled with ice. Strain into a martini glass.

Shark

1 oz. tequila
splash of habanero hot sauce
shooter

1 oz. vodka
lime wedge

Splash the habanero hot sauce into the shooter. Pour the tequila and vodka. Squeeze a lime wedge over glass and drop in.

Shotgun

1 oz. Stoli Citron
1 oz. fresh limejuice

1 oz. Grand Marnier
low ball

Fill a low ball with ice. Stir in all ingredients.

Sicilian Kiss

1 1/2 oz. Bailey's Irish Cream Liqueur
1 oz. Amaretto

1 oz. Galliano
rocks glass

Fill a rocks glass with ice. Stir in all ingredients.

Sidecar

1 oz. brandy
1 oz. lemonade

1 oz. Cointreau
rocks glass

Fill a rocks glass with ice. Stir in all ingredients.

Silver Bullet

1 oz. Rumple Minz
shooter

1 oz vodka

Shake all ingredients in a cocktail shaker filled with ice. Strain into a shooter.

Singapore Sling

1 oz. gin
3 oz. lemonade or sour mix
rocks glass

1 oz. Kirsch
splash of grenadine

Fill a rocks glass with ice. Stir in all ingredients.

Sit On My Face

1 oz. Tia Maria
1 oz. Bailey's Irish Cream Liqueur
rocks glass

1 oz. Frangelica
drop of Sambuca

Fill a rocks glass with ice. Stir in all ingredients.

Sledgehammer

(1.) 1/4 oz. fresh lemon juice
(3.) 1/4 oz. Blue Curacao
(4.) 1/4 oz. Grand Marnier
shooter

(2.) 1/4 oz. Marmot or other
    chocolate liqueur
(5.) 1/4 oz. Chambord

Layer ingredients starting with the Chambord.

Slippery Nipple

(1.) 1/2 oz. Sambuca
(3.) 1/2 oz. Bailey's Irish Cream Liqueur
low ball

(2.) 1/2 oz. Kahlua
(4.) 1 drop of grenadine (nipple)

Layer the liqueurs in the order shown.

Sloe Gin Fizz

1 1/2 oz. gin
2 oz. sour mix

1 oz. sloe gin
rocks glass

Fill a rocks glass with ice. Stir in all ingredients.

Slow Comfortable Screw

1 oz. vodka
1/2 oz. Southern Comfort
rocks glass

1/2 oz. sloe gin
orange juice

Fill a rocks glass with ice. Stir in all ingredients.

Slow Comfortable Screw Between The Sheets

1 oz. Absolut Mandarin
1/2 sloe gin
splash of maraschino cherry juice
highball

1 oz. Southern Comfort
splash of Triple Sec
2 oz. orange juice

Fill a highball glass with ice. Stir in all ingredients.

Smith & Kerns

1 1/2 oz. Kahlua
1 oz. milk

4 oz. cola
highball

Fill a highball glass with ice. Stir in all ingredients, gently.

Smith & Wesson

1 oz. vodka
3 oz. cola
highball

1 oz. Kahlua
1 oz. milk

Fill a highball glass with ice. Stir in all ingredients, gently.

Snake Bite

1 oz. Jack Daniel's Tennessee
   Sour Mash Whiskey
lemon wedge

1 oz. tequila
1 oz. Southern Comfort
low ball

Shake all ingredients in a cocktail shaker filled with ice. Strain into a low-ball. Squeeze a lime wedge over glass and drop in.

Southern Comfort Stinger

1 1/2 oz. Southern Comfort
rocks glass

1 oz. white Peppermint Schnapps

Fill a rocks glass with ice. Stir in both ingredients.

South of the Border

1 1/2 oz. tequila
1/2 oz. fresh limejuice

1/2 oz. Tia Maria
low ball

Fill a low-ball glass with ice. Stir in all ingredients. Squeeze a lime wedge over glass and drop in.

Strawberry Drop

1 oz. Stoli Strawberry Vodka
splash oz. Cointreau
splash of cranberry juice

1 oz. Fraise (strawberry liqueur)
2 oz. sweet and sour mix
rocks glass

Fill a rocks glass with ice. Stir all ingredients.

Swampwater

1 oz. green Chartreuse
2 oz. pineapple juice

1 oz. vodka
rocks glass

Fill a rocks glass with ice. Stir in all ingredients.

Sweet Sex

1/2 oz. Stoli Razberi
splash of Crème de Banana
splash of Watermelon Schnapps

1/2 oz. Strawberry Tequila
splash of Malibu
shooter

Shake all ingredients in a cocktail shaker filled with ice. Strain into a shooter.

Swimming Pool

1 oz. vodka
1 oz. Coco Lopez
splash of Blue Curacao

1 oz. Cruzan Pineapple Rum
2 oz. pineapple juice
hurricane

Mix all ingredients in blender, except Curacao. Pour into a hurricane glass. Float Blue Curacao on top.

Tango

1 1/2 oz. gin
drop of Galliano
2 oz. orange juice

1/2 oz. dry vermouth
drop of Parfait Amour
martini glass

Shake all ingredients in a cocktail shaker filled with ice. Strain into a martini glass.

Bartender's Secret-Mixing

Always put the ice in the glass or cocktail shaker first, then the mixers and then other ingredients. By doing this, all the ingredients will be properly chilled.

Tasty Orgasm

1 1/2 oz. Bailey's Irish Cream Liqueur
shot glass with ice

1 oz. Rumple Minz

Pour into a shot glass.

Tennessee Mud

1 oz. Wild Turkey Kentucky Bourbon
1 oz. Amaretto
rocks glass

2 oz. Kahlua
1 oz. cream

Shake all ingredients in a cocktail shaker filled with ice. Strain into a rocks glass with ice.

Yeah, mon! St. Croix in the U.S. Virgin Islands diversity comes from its verdant rolling green hills, historical ruins of sugar plantations and Danish architecture. Also the largest of the three U.S. Virgin Islands (four if you count Water Island) it has a lush rainforest in the west and an arid tropical cacti forest to the south. St. Croix has two towns, Christiansted and Frederiksted, where the cruise ships dock.

Capital: Charlotte Amalie on St. Thomas
Population:
Money: U.S. Dollar
Official Language: English
Political Status: U.S. unincorporated Territory
Just for Fun!: Shopping at Estate Whim Museum's antique furniture store and exploring an lovingly-restored sugarcane plantation; taking Big Beard's adventure tour to nearby Buck Island and snorkeling in the crystal-clear water; horseback riding at Sprat Hall near Frederiksted on the beach.
Tidbit: It's nickname is Twin City.

Tequila Sunrise

1 1/2 oz. tequila
1/2 oz. maraschino cherry juice
maraschino cherry
rocks glass

3 oz. orange juice
splash of grenadine
orange slice

Fill a rocks glass with ice. Stir in all ingredients.

Tequini

2 1/2 oz. tequila
martini glass

1/2 oz. dry vermouth

Shake all ingredients in a cocktail shaker filled with ice. Strain into a martini glass.

Terminator

1/2 oz. Wild Turkey Kentucky Bourbon
1/2 oz. Bailey's Irish Cream Liqueur
splash of white Crème de Cacao

1/2 oz. Jagermeister
1/2 oz. Rumple Minz
rocks glass

Fill a rocks glass with ice. Layer the bourbon, Jagermeister, Rumple Minz and Crème de Cacao.

The Big Chill

1 oz. Meyer's Rum
splash of Vandermint liqueur (chocolate-mint)
2 oz. cream
hurricane

1 oz. Tia Maria
4 oz. cold, strong coffee
whipped cream

Shake all ingredients except whipped cream in a cocktail shaker filled with ice. Strain into a hurricane glass filled with ice. Top with whipped cream.

Tight Snatch

1 oz. Cruzan Pineapple Rum
low ball

1 oz. Peach Brandy

Fill a lowball glass with ice. Stir in rum and Peach Brandy.

Toasted Almond

1 oz. Amaretto
1 oz. vodka
rocks glass

1 oz. Kahlua
2 oz. milk

Shake all ingredients in a cocktail shaker filled with ice. Strain into a rocks glass.

Tom Collins

2 oz. gin
1 tsp powdered sugar
highball

1 oz. fresh lemon juice
club soda

Shake all ingredients except club soda in a cocktail shaker with ice. Pour into a highball glass. Fill with club soda.

Tootsie Roll

3 oz. Mozart Chocolate liqueur
splash of Grand Marnier

2 1/2 oz. orange juice
rocks glass

Fill a rocks glass with ice. Stir in all ingredients.

Top Banana

2 oz. vodka
1 oz. Crème de Banana
rocks glass

1 oz. Cruzan Banana Rum
splash of Amer Picon

Fill a rocks glass with ice. Stir in all ingredients.

Twister Vodka

1 1/2 oz. vodka
splash of Rose's Lime Juice

3 oz. lemonade
rocks glass

Fill a rocks glass with ice. Stir in all ingredients.

Typhoon Singapore Sling

(1.) 1 oz. gin
(3.) 1/2 oz. Cointreau
(4.) 1 oz. fresh lemon juice
(6.) splash of Orange Bitters
maraschino cherry

(2.) 1/2 oz. Black Haus (blackberry
liqueur)
(5.) splash of grenadine
(7.) 2 oz. pineapple juice
Highball glass

Fill a hurricane glass with ice. Pour ingredients in order shown, then stir slowly in front of customer. Garnish with cherry.

Velvet Hammer

2 oz. Stoli Vanil
drop of Cuarenta y Tres liqueur
rocks glass

2 oz. white Crème de Cacao
2 oz. light cream

Shake all ingredients in a cocktail shaker filled with ice. Strain into a rocks glass filled with ice.

Vodka Gimlet

2 1/2 oz. vodka
1/2 oz. fresh limejuice

1/2 oz. Rose's Lime Juice
martini glass

Shake all ingredients in a cocktail shaker filled with ice. Strain into a martini glass.

Vodka Martini

3 oz. vodka
cocktail onions or olives

drop of dry vermouth

Fill a martini glass with ice. Shake all ingredients, except onions or olives in a cocktail shaker filled with ice. Dump ice from martini glass. Strain liquor into glass. Drop a couple of cocktail onions or olives in the bottom of glass.

Vodka Sour

2 oz. vodka
1/2 oz. simple syrup
maraschino cherry

1 oz. fresh lemon juice
splash of Maraschino cherry juice
rocks glass

Shake all ingredients, except cherry, in a cocktail shaker filled with ice. Strain into a rocks glass filled with ice.

Watermelon

2 oz. Midori
4 oz. cranberry juice

splash of Cointreau
rocks glass

Fill a rocks glass with ice. Stir in all ingredients.

Whiskey Sour

2 oz. American whiskey
1/2 oz. fresh lemon juice
rocks glass

4 oz. sour mix
dash of simple syrup

Fill a rocks glass with ice. Stir in all ingredients.

White Baby

1 1/2 oz. gin
drop of Grand Marnier
martini glass

1 oz. Cointreau
1 oz. cream

Shake all ingredients in a cocktail shaker filled with ice. Strain into a martini glass.

White Lady

1 1/2 oz. gin
2 oz. milk
rocks glass

2 oz. sour mix
lemon twist

Fill a rocks glass with ice. Stir in all ingredients. Garnish with lemon twist.

White Lily

1 oz. gin
1/2 Pernod
1/2 oz. fresh lemon juice

1 oz. Triple Sec
splash of light rum
martini glass

Shake all ingredients in a cocktail shaker filled with ice. Strain into a martini glass.

Whiteout

1 oz. gin
splash of white Crème de Menthe
1 oz. cream

1 oz. white Crème de Cacao
drop of Galliano
martini glass

Shake all ingredients in a cocktail shaker filled with ice. Strain into a martini glass.

White Russian

1 1/2 oz. vodka
1 1/2 oz. milk

1 1/2 oz. Kahlua
low ball

Shake all ingredients in a cocktail shaker filled with ice. Pour into a low ball filled with ice.

Windex

1 oz. vodka
splash of fresh lemon juice

1 oz. Blue Curacao
shot glass

Shake all ingredients in a cocktail shaker filled with ice. Strain into a shot glass.

Woo Woo

1 1/2 oz. vodka
splash of Boggs Cranberry Liqueur
   (cranberry liqueur)

1 oz. Peach Schnapps
2 oz. cranberry juice
1 oz. fresh limejuice

Fill a rocks glass with ice. Stir in all ingredients.

Yeah, mon! St. John in the U.S. Virgin Islands is the smallest of the three main U.S. Virgin Islands purchased originally from the Danish for the princely sum of $300 an acre. The emerald-like island is mostly National Park and features world-famous Trunk Bay, considered one of the most beautiful beaches in the world by National Geographic.

Capital: Charlotte Amalie on St. Thomas
Population:
Money: U.S. Dollar
Official Language: English
Political Status: Unicorporated U.S. Territory
Just for Fun!: Snorkeling Trunk Bay's fabulous and colorful underwater trail; sunning on secluded and stunning Hawk's Nest Beach; camping at idyllic Cinnamon Bay Campground
Tidbit: This island's nickname is Love City.

Wrigley's Doublemint Blowjob

1 oz. Tia Maria
low ball

1 oz. Rumple Minz

Shake all ingredients in a cocktail shaker filled with ice. Strain into a lowball filled with ice.

Xanthia

1 1/2 oz. gin
1 oz. Chartreuse
martini glass

1 oz. Kirsch
splash of orange juice

Shake all ingredients in a cocktail shaker filled with ice. Strain into a martini glass.

Zipper

1 oz. Bailey's Irish Cream Liqueur
1 oz. Apricot brandy

1 oz. Sambuca
rocks glass

Shake all ingredients in a cocktail shaker filled with ice. Strain into a rocks glass filled with ice.

CHAPTER FIFTEEN

Bloody Mary Tales

The Bloody Mary has won its place among other classic American cocktails such as the martini, daiquiri, and gimlet. Contrary to popular belief, it originated at Harry's New York Bar in Paris. Ernest Hemingway , F. Scott Fitzgerald, and other American expatriates living in Paris frequented the bar. Among the famous regulars were George Gerschwin, Gertrude Stein, and the Prince of Whales.

In 1924, Fernard Petiot, created the first Bloody Mary. The recipe was rather simple and consisted of a cocktail shaker filled with ice, vodka, tomato juice, salt, and pepper. The morning client readily took to the new drink and gradually variations were added.

Other stories claim the drink came from the Bucket of Blood Club in Chicago-a place where newspapermen gathered in the 1920's. Some say that it was named after the Scottish queen, Mary of Scots.

Eventually exotic items such as Worcestershire™, Tabasco™, celery salt, horseradish, and other spicy ingredients were added.

Here is **the classic Bloody Mary recipe:**

Bloody Mary

1 1/2 oz. vodka
1 tsp. fresh lemon juice
splash of Worcestershire™
salt and pepper to taste
Highball glass

3 oz. tomato juice
1/2 tsp. horseradish
splash of Tabasco™
celery stalk

Shake all ingredients in a cocktail shaker filled with ice. Strain into a Highball glass filled with ice. Garnish with celery stalk.

The following are some very good **variations** of the Bloody Mary:

Bloodhound

1 1/2 oz. vodka
4 oz. tomato juice
pinch of celery salt
celery stalk

1/2 oz. dry sherry
1/2 oz. fresh limejuice
pinch of white pepper
highball glass

Fill a Highball with ice. Stir in all ingredients. Garnish with celery stalk.

Bartender's Secret-Attractive Pepper

Use white, finely ground pepper instead of garish black pepper when making Bloody Marys.

Bloody Blossom

1 1/2 oz. vodka
2 oz. tomato juice
drop of Tabasco™
highball glass

2 oz. orange juice
1/2 oz. fresh limejuice
orange slice

Shake all ingredients in a cocktail shaker filled with ice. Strain into a Highball with ice. Garnish with orange slice.

Bloody Brew

1 1/2 oz. vodka
3 oz. tomato juice
splash of Tabasco™
small whole dill pickle

3 oz. beer
1/2 tsp. horseradish
pinch of salt and pepper
highball glass

Fill a Highball with ice. Gently stir all ingredients. Garnish with a pickle.

Bloody Bull

1 1/2 oz. vodka
1 oz. beef bouillon
1/2 tsp. horseradish
splash Tabasco™
Highball glass

3 oz. tomato juice
1 tsp. fresh lemon juice
splash Worcestershire™
lemon slice

Fill cocktail shaker with ice. Shake all ingredients and strain into a Highball glass filled with ice. Garnish with a lemon slice.

Bloody Caesar

1 1/2 oz. vodka
1 tsp. limejuice
splash Worcestershire™
lime slice

3 oz. Clamato juice
1/2 tsp. horseradish
splash Tabasco™
Highball glass

Fill cocktail shaker with ice. Shake all ingredients and strain into a Highball glass filled with ice. Garnish with lime slice.

Bloody Eight

2 oz. vodka
1/2 oz. fresh limejuice
splash of Tabasco™
highball glass

4 oz. V-8' juice
splash of Worcestershire™
celery stalk

Fill a Highball with ice. Stir all ingredients and garnish with celery stalk.

Bloody Marie

1 1/2 oz. vodka
4 oz. tomato juice
splash of Worcestershire™
1/2 tsp. horseradish
cocktail onions

1/2 oz. Pernod
splash of fresh lime juice
splash of Tabasco™
salt and pepper
highball glass

Shake all ingredients in a cocktail shaker filled with ice. Strain into a Highball with ice. Garnish with cocktail onions.

Bloody Maru

2 oz. Sake
1/2 oz. fresh limejuice
dash of Tabasco™
celery stalk

4 oz. tomato juice
dash of Worcestershire™
1/2 tsp. horseradish
Highball glass

Shake all ingredients except celery in a cocktail shaker filled with ice. Fill a Highball glass with ice, pour in drink. Garnish with celery stalk.

Clam Digger

2 oz. vodka
1 1/2 oz. clam juice
splash of Worcestershire™
1/2 tsp. horseradish
lime wedge

2 oz. tomato juice
1/2 oz. fresh limejuice
splash of Tabasco™
salt and pepper
highball glass

Shake all ingredients except lime wedge in a cocktail shaker filled with ice. Strain into a Highball with ice. Garnish with a lime wedge.

Smoky Mary

2 oz. vodka
1/2 oz. fresh limejuice
splash of Tabasco™
1 tsp. minced onion

4 oz. tomato juice
splash of barbeque sauce
splash of Worcestershire™
highball glass

Fill a highball glass with ice. Stir all ingredients well.

CHAPTER SIXTEEN
Martini and Nouveau Martini

Just say martini and one thinks of gin and a bare hint of vermouth. These days, not only are vodka martinis gaining popularity in great strides, but also a number of pseudo martinis are rapidly cropping up. It seems if you toss the word *martini* into a drink title, you'll find plenty of people willing to shell out extra money for a drink that has no resemblance to the martini. Nonetheless, the following drinks are fabulous and lot of fun to make besides.

Bartender's Secret: Great Martinis:

The underlying trick to martinis is to have the glass crackling cold which means to fill it full of ice while mixing the martini. Dump the ice out and shake any excess water from the glass before pouring the drink. The cocktail shaker should be shook vigorously and rapidly to allow for quick chilling of the liquor and minimal melting of ice.

Traditional Martini

2 1/2 oz. gin
green pitted olives, minus pimentos

1/4 oz. dry vermouth
cocktail glass

Shake all ingredients except olives in a cocktail shaker filled with ice.

Extra-Extra-Dry Martini

3 oz. gin
cocktail glass

1 bottle of vermouth in the next room

Shake the gin in a cocktail shaker filled with ice. Strain into a chilled cocktail glass. Garnish with cocktail onions or olives.

Gibson

2 1/2 oz. gin
cocktail glass

1/4 oz. dry vermouth

Shake all ingredients in a cocktail shaker filled with ice. Strain into a chilled cocktail glass. Garnish with cocktail onions.

Vodka Martini

2 1/2 oz. vodka
cocktail glass

1/4 oz. dry vermouth

Shake all ingredients in a cocktail shaker filled with ice. Strain into a chilled cocktail glass. Garnish with olives or onions.

Tequini

2 1/2 oz. tequila
cocktail glass

1/4 oz. vermouth

Shake all ingredients in a cocktail shaker filled with ice. Strain into a chilled cocktail glass. Garnish with a jalapeño pepper.

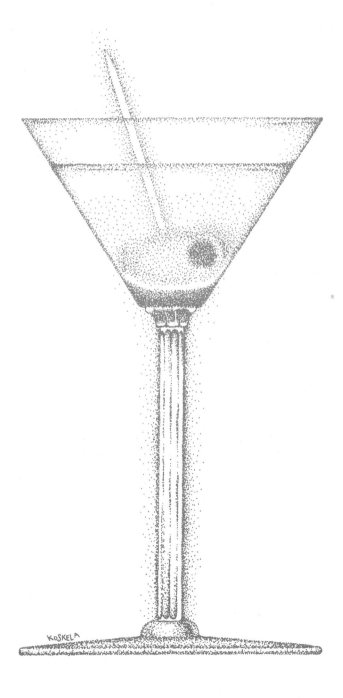

Nouveau Martinis

Almond Joy Martini

2 1/2 oz. vodka
1/4 oz. Amaretto
cocktail glass

1/4 oz. white Crème de Cacao
whole almonds

Shake all ingredients except almonds in a cocktail shaker filled with ice. Strain into a chilled cocktail glass. Drop in a couple of almonds.

Berry Martini

1 1/2 oz. Stoli Razberi
splash of cranberry juice

1 oz. Absolut Kurant
cocktail glass

Shake all ingredients in a cocktail shaker filled with ice. Strain into a chilled cocktail glass.

Blue Sky

2 oz. Skyy Vodka
cocktail glass

1 oz. Blue Curacao

Shake all ingredients in a cocktail shaker filled with ice. Strain into a chilled cocktail glass.

Caribbean Martini

1 oz. Cruzan Coconut Rum
1 oz. Cruzan Banana Rum

1 oz. Cruzan Pineapple Rum
cocktail glass

Shake all ingredients in a cocktail shaker filled with ice. Strain into a chilled cocktail glass.

Bartender's Secret-Vermouth Extender

Store all opened bottles of Vermouth in the refrigerator or the lovely flavor will disappear. Another suggestion: buy the smaller bottle and use it up more quickly.

Cappuchini

2 oz. Stoli Coffee Vodka
splash of white Crème de Cacao
cocktail glass

1 oz. Stoli Vanil Vodka
whole coffee beans

Shake all ingredients except coffee beans in a cocktail shaker filled with ice. Strain into a chilled cocktail glass. Drop in coffee beans.

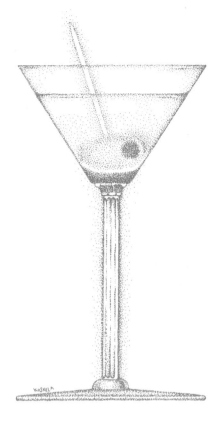

Chambortini

2 oz. Stoli Ohranj Vodka
splash of Maraschino cherry liqueur
cocktail glass

1/2 oz. Chambord
maraschino cherry

Shake all ingredients except cherry in a cocktail shaker filled with ice. Strain into a chilled cocktail glass. Drop in cherry.

Chocotini

1 1/2 oz. Stoli Vanil
1/2 oz. Kahlua

1/2 oz. white Crème de Cacao
cocktail glass

Shake all ingredients in a cocktail shaker filled with ice. Strain into a chilled cocktail glass.

Chocolate-Orange Martini

2 oz. vodka
splash of Grand Marnier

1/2 oz. white Crème de Cacao
cocktail glass

Shake all ingredients in a cocktail shaker filled with ice. Strain into a chilled cocktail glass.

Chocolate Mintini

1 1/2 oz. Stoli Chocolate Vodka
1/4 oz. white Crème de Cacao
cocktail glass

1/2 oz. Bailey's Irish Cream Liqueur
mint leaves

Shake all ingredients except mint leaves in a cocktail shaker filled with ice. Strain into a cocktail glass. Garnish with mint leaves.

Citrini

2 oz. Stoli Oranj
orange peel
cocktail glass

1/2 oz. Cointreau
whole clove

Shake all ingredients except peel and clove in a cocktail shaker filled with ice. Strain into a chilled cocktail glass. Drop in orange peel and clove.

Cosmopolitan

2 oz. vodka
1/4 oz. Triple Sec
1/4 oz. fresh limejuice

splash of Boggs Cranberry Liqueur
  (cranberry liqueur)
cocktail glass

Shake all ingredients in a cocktail shaker filled with ice. Strain into a chilled cocktail glass.

Bartender's Secret-Martini Garnishes

The traditional martini uses conventional garnishes such as an olive, cocktail onion or lemon twist. Try jalapeño peppers, capers, radishes, tiny dill pickles, mushrooms marinated in vermouth, garlic slices, onion or grapefruit or orange twists.

In the new-fangled sweeter martinis, drop in a coffee bean, colorful jelly beans, caramels or even a square of chocolate.

Creole Martini

2 oz. Absolut Pepper Vodka
jalapeño pepper

1/2 oz. Absolut Citron Vodka
cocktail glass

Shake all ingredients except jalapeño in a cocktail shaker filled with ice. Strain into a chilled cocktail glass. Drop in jalapeño pepper and a bit of the juice.

French Martini

2 oz. vodka
1/2 oz. Peach Schnapps
cocktail glass

1/2 oz. Chambord
peach slice

Shake all ingredients except peach slice in a cocktail shaker filled with ice. Strain into a chilled cocktail glass. Drop in peach slice.

Mexican Martini

2 oz. Cuervo Gold
splash of Rose's Lime Juice

1/2 oz. Cointreau
cocktail glass

Shake all ingredients in a cocktail shaker filled with ice. Strain into a chilled cocktail glass.

Orange Martini

2 oz. Stoli Oranj
cocktail glass

1 oz. Cointreau

Shake all ingredients in a cocktail shaker filled with ice. Strain into a chilled cocktail glass.

Passion Martini

2 oz. Stoli Vodka
cocktail glass

1 1/2 oz Passoa Passionfruit Liqueur

Shake all ingredients in a cocktail shaker filled with ice. Strain into a cocktail glass.

Peachini

2 oz. vodka
splash of apricot brandy

1/2 oz. Peach Schnapps
cocktail glass

Shake all ingredients in a cocktail shaker filled with ice. Strain into a chilled cocktail glass.

Raspberry Martini

2 1/2 oz. Stoli Razberi Vodka
fresh raspberries

1/2 oz. Framboise (raspberry liqueur)
cocktail glass

Shake all ingredients in a cocktail shaker filled with ice. Strain into a chilled cocktail glass. Drop in a couple of fresh raspberries.

Rising Sun

2 oz. Fris Vodka, ginger-infused
cucumber stick

1/2 oz. Sake
cocktail glass

Shake all ingredients in a cocktail shaker filled with ice. Strain into a cocktail glass. Garnish with cucumber stick.

Sint Maarten Smartini

St. Maarten, West Indies
courtesy of Sint Maarten Guavaberry Company

1 1/2 oz. Stoli vodka
1 oz. cranberry juice

1/2 oz. Sint Maarten Guavaberry liqueur
cocktail glass

Shake all ingredients in a cocktail shaker filled with ice. Strain into a chilled cocktail glass.

CHAPTER SEVENTEEN

Frozen Blender & Ice Cream Drinks

Frozen drinks are synonymous with a Caribbean vacation, extremely popular on cruise ships and hotel resorts. This section includes the basics: Banana Daiquiri, Piña Colada, Bushwhacker and exciting new favorites, i.e. Coffee-Hazelnut Float, M & M Cream Soda, and Frozen Passion to name a few. You may find some of the recipes duplicated in other chapters. Therefore, wherever possible, I have included a variation. Also note, most of these drinks are large and therefore I recommend using a hurricane glass for serving. Not for dieters!

Banana Island

1 1/2 oz. vodka
splash of Rose's Lime Juice
scoop of vanilla ice cream

1/2 oz. banana liqueur
cream soda
hurricane glass

Scoop vanilla ice cream into hurricane glass. Pour vodka and banana liqueur over ice cream. Slowly fill to top with cream soda.

Banana Daiquiri
MOUNTAINTOP, ST. THOMAS

2 oz. rum, light, or gold
1 sliced banana
cocktail glass

1/2 oz. Crème de banana
splash of Rose's Lime Juice

Mix all ingredients in blender with a cup of ice. Pour into a cocktail glass.

Bushwacker #3

1 oz. dark rum
1/2 oz. dark Crème de Cacao
splash of Amaretto
hurricane glass

1 oz. Bailey's Irish Cream Liqueur
1/2 oz. Kahlua
grated nutmeg

Whirl all ingredients in blender with 1/2-cup ice. Garnish with grated nutmeg.

Caribbean Mudslide

1 oz. dark rum
1/2 oz. Tia Maria
grated nutmeg

1 oz. Malibu coconut rum
scoop of vanilla ice cream
hurricane glass

Whirl all ingredients in blender with 1/2-cup ice. Garnish with grated nutmeg.

Coconanas

1 oz. dark rum
1/2 oz. Frangelico
splash of pineapple juice

1/2 cognac
1/2 oz. Coco Lopez
hurricane glass

Whirl all ingredients in blender with 1/2 cup ice.

Coconut Dream Pie

2 oz. Malibu coconut rum
splash of Bailey's Irish Cream Liqueur
grated coconut

1 oz. Stoli Citron
2 oz. heavy cream
hurricane glass

Whirl all ingredients in blender with 1/2-cup ice. Garnish with grated coconut.

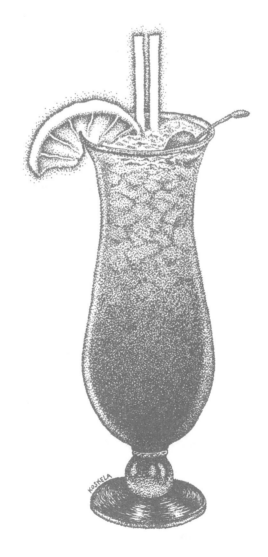

Coffee-Hazelnut Float

1 oz. Frangelico
1/2 oz. Tia Maria
1 teaspoon powdered coffee
Collins glass

1 oz. Stoli Vanil vodka
2 oz. cream soda
1 scoop coffee ice cream

Stir the powdered coffee into the cream soda, stirring well. Pour the liquor into a tall glass. Then add soda and float ice cream on top.

Cookie Monster

1 oz. gold rum
splash of Bailey's Irish Cream Liqueur
1 crumbled Oreo cookie

1 oz. dark Crème de Cacao
1 scoop vanilla ice cream

Whirl all ingredients in blender with 1/2 cup ice.

Bartender's Secret: Clear Ice:

For perfectly clear ice, use warm water instead of cold tap water.

Dreamy Monkey

1 oz. Stoli Vanil
1 oz. light Crème de Cacao
1/2 cup light cream

1 oz. Crème de Banana
1/2 fresh, ripe banana
hurricane glass

Whirl all ingredients in blender with one-cup ice.

Frozen Matador

1 1/2 oz. tequila
splash of Rose's Lime Juice
hurricane glass

2 oz. pineapple juice
pineapple wedge

Whirl all ingredients in blender with 1/2-cup ice. Garnish with pineapple wedge.

Frozen Passion

1 1/2 oz. light Puerto Rican rum
1/2 oz. orange juice
splash of Rose's Lime Juice
orange slice

1/2 oz. La Grande Passion
splash of fresh lemon juice
big splash of Coco Lopez
hurricane glass

Whirl all ingredients in blender with 1/2 cup ice. Garnish with orange slice.

Ginger Float

1 oz. ginger brandy
1 oz. Malibu
dash of ground cardamom
scoop of vanilla ice cream
Collins glass

1 oz. Amaretto
1 teaspoon crystallized ginger, chopped
dash of ground cinnamon
ginger ale

Whirl the ginger brandy, Amaretto, Malibu, and spices in a blender. Pour into the bottom of a tall glass. Add ice cream, floating ginger ale on top. Stir very gently.

Guavaberry Colada
ST. MAARTEN, WEST INDIES
COURTESY OF SINT MAARTEN GUAVABERRY COMPANY

Note that the guavaberry, a berry found high in the hills of St. Maarten, is very much different from the guavaberry. The liqueur is made from rum and local berries, having a bittersweet, fruity and woody taste.

2 oz. Sint Maarten Guavaberry liqueur
3 oz. pineapple juice
toasted coconut
hurricane glass

1 oz. Coco Lopez
pineapple slice
fresh, grated nutmeg

Blend all ingredients with 1/2 cup ice until smooth in blender. Pour into a hurricane glass. Garnish with pineapple slice, toasted coconut, and freshly grated nutmeg.

Guava Colada

1 1/2 oz. light rum
1 oz. guava nectar (found in grocery section)
splash of Coco Lopez
pineapple slice

1/2 oz. Crème de Banana
1/2 oz. fresh lime
splash of pineapple juice
hurricane glass

Whirl all ingredients in blender with 1/2-cup ice. Garnish with pineapple slice

Jungle Juice

1 oz. Apricot Brandy
1/2 oz. Crème de Cassis
orange slice

1 oz. gin
1 oz. orange juice

Whirl all ingredients in blender with 1/2-cup ice. Garnish with orange slice.

Key Lime Pie

2 oz. Liquor 43 (vanilla-flavored liqueur)
1/2 oz. fresh limejuice
lime wedge

2 oz. heavy cream
1/2 oz. Rose's Lime Juice
hurricane glass

Whirl all ingredients in blender with a cup of ice. Garnish with lime wedge.

KOSKELA

Lime Daiquiri

This is the traditional daiquiri.

2 oz. rum, light, or gold
1 1/2 oz. Rose's Lime Juice or fresh limejuice
lime slice

1/2 oz. Triple Sec or Cointreau
1 tsp. simple syrup (omit if using Rose's)
hurricane glass

Mix all ingredients in blender with a cup of ice. Garnish with lime slice.

M & M Cream Soda

4 oz. beer
1 oz. Stoli Vanil vodka
hurricane glass

1 oz. Amaretto
1 scoop vanilla ice cream

Whirl all ingredients in blender with 1/2-cup ice, except beer. Stir in beer carefully.

Mambo Me Crazy

1 oz. dark rum
1/2 oz. Blue Curacao
splash of Coco Lopez
splash of margarita mix

1/2 oz. Captain Morgan Rum
splash of orange juice
splash of pineapple juice
pineapple slice

Whirl all ingredients in blender with 1/2-cup ice. Garnish with pineapple slice.

Mango Surprise

1 1/2 oz. vodka
1/2 oz. KoKunut Rum (or any other
    coconut-flavored rum)

1 oz. Apricot Brandy
1/2 cup fresh or frozen mango
hurricane glass

Whirl all ingredients in blender with a 1/2 cup ice. Garnish with mango slice.

Mint Chocolate Chip Ice Cream

1 oz. vodka
1/2 oz. Rumpleminz schnapps
splash of Kahlua

1/2 oz. light Crème de Cacao
splash of white Crème de Menthe
hurricane glass

Whirl all ingredients in blender with 1/2-cup ice.

Mocha-Mint Creamsicle

1 oz. Kahlua
1/2 oz. light Crème de Menthe
1 oz. heavy cream

1/2 oz. light Crème de Cacao
1/2 oz. Galliano
hurricane glass

Whirl all ingredients in blender with 1/2-cup ice.

Molotov Cocktail

2 oz. Stoli Vanil vodka
1 scoop vanilla ice cream
151 Bacardi rum

1 oz. Kahlua
1 teaspoon instant coffee
hurricane glass

Whirl all ingredients in blender with 1/2-cup ice except the 151. Float the 151 on top and ignite. Cuidado! Careful!

Mudslide
CARLOS & CHARLIE'S, ARUBA

1 1/2 oz. vodka
1/2 oz. Bailey's Irish Cream Liqueur
powdered coffee

1/2 oz. Kahlua
1/2 oz. Coco Lopez
hurricane glass

Mix all in ingredients in blender with a cup of ice. Sprinkle with powdered coffee.

Orange Julius

1 oz. light rum
1/2 oz. Grand Marnier
1 oz. heavy cream
hurricane glass

1 oz. Amaretto
2 oz. orange juice
orange slice

Whirl all ingredients in blender with 1/2-cup ice. Garnish with orange slice.

Paradise Ice

1/2 oz. vodka
1/2 oz. Peach Schnapps
splash of Rose's Lime Juice
orange slice

1/2 oz. Malibu coconut rum
1/2 oz. gin
splash of orange juice
hurricane glass

Whirl all ingredients in blender with 1/2-cup ice. Garnish with orange slice.

Peach Daiquiri

2 oz. rum, light rum
1/2 cup frozen peaches
splash of Rose's Lime Juice
hurricane glass

1/2 oz. Peach Schnapps or Persico
  (made by Bols)
peach slice

Blend all ingredients with 1/2 cup ice in blender. Garnish with peach slice.

Piña Colada

2 oz. gold rum
1/2 cup fresh or canned pineapple juice
hurricane glass

2 oz. Coco Lopez
pineapple wedge

Whirl all ingredients in blender with ice cup ice. Garnish with pineapple wedge.

Bartender's Secret: Smooth Frozen Drinks:

For smooth and consistent frozen drinks, use crushed ice to avoid chunks of unbroken ice.

Pineapple Banana Cream Freeze

1 1/2 oz. Finlandia Pineapple Vodka vodka
1/2 oz. Bailey's Irish Cream Liqueur
1/2 ripe banana

1 oz. Crème de Banana
1 oz. heavy cream
hurricane glass

Whirl all ingredients in blender with 1/2-cup ice.

Raspberry Coconut Colada

1 1/2 oz. Malibu coconut rum
splash of Coco Lopez
pineapple slice

1 oz. Chambord
splash of pineapple juice
hurricane glass

Whirl all ingredients in blender with 1/2-cup ice. Garnish with pineapple slice.

Rum Almond Float

1 oz. Crème de Noyaux
scoop vanilla ice cream
Collins glass with ice

1 oz. dark rum
cream soda

Pour the Crème de Noyaux and rum into the bottom of a tall glass. Add scoop of ice cream and fill to top with cream soda.

Rum Runner II

1 oz. 151 rum
1/2 oz. Crème de Cassis
grated nutmeg

1 oz. Crème de Banana
splash Caramel Liqueur
hurricane glass

Whirl all ingredients in blender with a cup of ice. Garnish with grated nutmeg.

Seven Seas

1 oz. 7 & 7
1 oz. pineapple juice
hurricane glass

1 oz. Midori melon liqueur
pineapple slice

Whirl all ingredients in blender with 1/2-cup ice. Garnish with pineapple slice.

Strawberry Daiquiri

2 oz. rum
1/2 cup frozen strawberries
splash of Rose's Lime Juice

1/2 oz. Framboise or Fraise
strawberry liqueur
strawberry

Blend all ingredients with 1/2 cup ice in blender. Garnish with strawberry.

Bartender's Secret: Thick Frozen Drinks:

Use frozen fruit for blender-coladas. The consistency will be much thicker and the taste richer.

Strawberry Shortcake

1 1/2 oz. Amaretto
1/2 cup frozen strawberries
strawberry

1 oz. Fraise strawberry liqueur
1/2 cup milk or half-and-half
hurricane glass

Whirl all ingredients in blender with 1/3-cup ice. Garnish with a strawberry.

The Big Chill

1 oz. dark rum
1 oz. Ponche Cuba (delicious eggnog liqueur)
1 scoop vanilla ice cream
hurricane glass

1 oz. Tia Maria
splash of Pistacha (pistachio liqueur)
instant coffee

Whirl all ingredients in blender with 1/2-cup ice. Sprinkle with instant coffee.

Tropical Storm

1 oz. light rum
1 oz. orange juice
splash of Grenadine
orange slice

1 oz. Crème de Banana
splash of pineapple juice
splash of Rose's Lime Juice
hurricane glass

Whirl all ingredients in blender with 1/2-cup ice. Garnish with orange slice.

What's Up?

1 oz. vodka
1/2 oz. Amaretto
splash of pineapple juice

1/2 oz. Blue Curacao
1/2 oz. Malibu (coconut rum)
pineapple slice

Whirl all ingredients in blender with 1/2 cup ice. Garnish with pineapple slice.

Yellow Bird

1 oz. dark rum
1/2 oz. vodka
splash of orange juice
orange or pineapple slice

1 oz. Crème de Banana
1/2 oz. Galliano
splash of pineapple juice

Whirl all ingredients in blender with 1/2 cup ice. Garnish with orange or pineapple slice.

CHAPTER EIGHTEEN
Margarittaville

The fact that Margarita's have nearly taken over the martini in popularity has resulted in exotic concoctions such as Strawberry Margarita, Orange Margarita, Prickly Pear, and even a Turquoise Margarita. Follow the hints on rimming the glass with salt and try some of the jewel-like colored salts for a truly special effect.

Use a salted margarita glass for drinks in this section.

Basic Margarita

1 1/2 oz. tequila
1 oz. fresh limejuice

1/2 oz. Triple Sec

Blend with or without ice. Garnish with a lime slice. Don't forget to rim the glass with salt!

Bartender's Secret – Salting Edges

1. Pour coarse salt onto a small plate. The larger crystal will adhere to the glass better. Try some of the colored salts now available for a stunning effect.
2. Rub a lime wedge around the rim to wet it. You can also wet the rim with any assortment of liqueurs to add extra flavor: Grand Marnier, Amaretto, Kahlua, Chambord, Tuaca, etc.
3. Gently twist the rim of the glass in the salt.

Mango Margarita

2 oz. tequila
2 oz. fresh limejuice

2 oz. fresh or frozen mango
splash of Triple Sec

Whirl all ingredients in blender with 1/2-cup ice.

Midori Margarita

2 oz. tequila
3 oz. fresh limejuice

1 oz. Midori
fresh lime slice

Whirl all ingredients in blender with 1/2-cup ice. Garnish with lime slice.

Orange Margarita

2 oz. tequila
splash of Benedictine
orange slice

1 oz. Grand Marnier
3 oz. fresh limejuice

Whirl all ingredients in blender with 1/2-cup ice. Garnish with orange slice.

Raspberry Margarita

2 oz. tequila
3 oz. fresh limejuice

1 oz. Chambord

Whirl all ingredients in blender with 1/2-cup ice.

Bartender's Tip-A little salt goes a long way

Sometimes those salt-rimmed glasses are just too much and get in the way of the flavor of the cocktail. In addition, many people cannot tolerate that much salt in their system. Mix equal parts salt with sugar and use this to rim glasses.

Strawberry Margarita

2 oz. tequila
1 oz. Fraise strawberry liqueur
1/2 cup frozen strawberries

1 oz. Triple Sec
3 oz. fresh lime juice
fresh strawberry

Whirl all ingredients in blender with 1/2-cup ice. Garnish with a fresh strawberry.

CHAPTER NINETEEN
Feelin' Hot, Hot, Hot!
Coffee Drinks & Other Fire Spirits

Hot drinks have been known for their restorative properties since ancient times. Even Daniel Defoe's hero, *Robinson Crusoe*, fixed himself a hot toddy while ill. In cold climates, the hot toddy, in lieu of a central heating system, was consumed with gusto. Enormous fireplaces dominated the social center of colonial America, the tavern, where flip irons were held. Also known as loggerheads, flip irons were designed for mulling of hot drinks. "Being at loggerheads" refers to the disputes during which debaters would often point to their opponents with these pointed instruments. Libations of the time were made from wines, spirits, and ales with lusty names such as "Kill-Devil," "Hell's Vengeance," and "Whistling Skull."

Today, we no longer use a flip iron, but a flame instead. There is a certain amount of spectacle involved with pyrotechnics, and proper flaming adds flavors that cannot be obtained through conventional methods. Sugars caramelize, essential oils from citrus peals and spices are extracted, alcohol undergoes pleasant flavor changes, etc. A bit of warning though. Fire is not something to be played with by children, the inebriated, or the foolhardy. See the Bartender's Secret below for how to deal with flamed drinks elegantly, tastefully, and above all safely.

Come join us and fall under the magic charm of the fire spirits.

* = Flamed Drinks

Bartender's Secret-Firing Safely

The most important thing you need to remember is alcohol is a highly flammable substance. Use extreme caution. Alcohol when warmed gives off a flammable vapor and for the same reason, unheated alcohol, unless a high proof such as 100 to 151, will not flame. <u>Rules to be read very carefully, over and over:</u>

1. Do not use large amounts of alcohol in flaming drinks. A little, an ounce, is all that is required.
2. Flame at side cart or table. Make sure that people are not close by or sitting at the table. If the liquor spills, it could result in a lake of fire.
3. Never have a tablecloth under a flame. The same goes for flaming near draperies or combustible party decorations, such as paper, streamers, and even plastic items.
4. When flaming during daylight or in a brightly lit room, dim the lights. Not only is the display more spectacular, but safety enhanced because the flame from alcohol is nearly invisible with high lighting.
5. Keep other bottles of liquor, especially uncorked or opened, away from the flaming area.
6. Never pour alcohol directly into a dish that is already flaming. You will cause a huge ball of flame!

Aztec Coffee

1 oz. tequila
1 oz. tequila liqueur
3/4 cup hot coffee

1/2 oz. Stoli Coffee Vodka
splash of Stoli Cinnamon Vodka
whipped cream

Pour all ingredients except whipped cream into a coffee mug. Garnish with whipped cream.

Blackbeard's Café
St. Martin/Maarten
courtesy Sint Maarten Guavaberry Co.

Edward Teach, a.k.a. Thatch, or Blackbeard created the romantic and popular legend of the swashbuckling, bloodthirsty, larger-than-life, rum-drinking pirate. In his short pirate career, between 1716 to 1718, he terrorized coasts from Boston to Bonaire in the West Indies, took dozens of prizes, buried treasure, abused his crew members and wives. Before and after battle, he drank large amounts of the finest rums laced with spices and gunpowder.

1 oz. Blackbeard's Sint Maarten Coconut Rum
hot coffee
whipped cream
coffee mug

1 oz. Olde Sint Maarten Island
Almond Tropical liqueur
toasted grated coconut

Pour liquor into a mug. Fill three-quarters to top with hot coffee. Top generously with whipped cream. Garnish with grated coconut.

*Blue Blazer

2 oz. whiskey
1 tsp. honey
two coffee mugs

2 oz. boiling water
lemon twist

Pour the whiskey into one mug and the boiling water into the other. Ignite the whiskey and mix by pouring back and forth between the two mugs. Add honey and a lemon twist. Careful!

Bartender's Secret: Piping Hot Coffee Drinks:
Be sure the coffee used in coffee drinks is not only piping hot, but very strong as the liquor will dilute the strength of the coffee.

Café Anguilla

1 oz. Anguilla Rum or dark rum
hot coffee
grated orange peel

1/2 oz. Tuaca
whipped cream
coffee mug

Pour liquor into a mug. Fill three-quarters to top with hot coffee. Top generously with whipped cream. Garnish with grated orange peel.

Café Antigua

1 oz. Stoli Vanil
1/2 oz. light Crème de Cacao
whipped cream

3/4 oz. Bailey's Irish Cream Liqueur
splash of Amaretto

Pour liquor into a mug. Fill three-quarters to top with hot coffee. Top generously with whipped cream.

Café Aruba

This taste like a raspberry-chocolate truffle. Mmm!

1 oz. rum from Aruba Trading Company
    or dark rum
hot coffee
coffee mug

1 oz. dark Crème de Cacao
1 oz. Chambord
whipped cream

Pour liquor into a mug. Fill three-quarters to top with hot coffee. Top generously with whipped cream.

Café Barbados

1 oz. Lamb's Navy Rum or dark rum
1/2 oz. Vandermint
whipped cream
coffee mug

1 oz. dark Crème de Cacao
hot coffee
green Crème de Menthe

Pour liquor into a mug. Fill three-quarters to top with hot coffee. Top generously with whipped cream. Drizzle with green Crème de Menthe.

Café Bonaire

This taste just like one of those strawberry-filled chocolates from Belgian.

1 oz. dark rum
1/2 oz. Fraise (strawberry liquor)
hot coffee
Fraise

1 oz. Godet Belgian White Chocolate
    Liqueur
whipped cream
coffee mug

Pour liquor into a mug. Fill three-quarters to top with hot coffee. Top generously with whipped cream. Drizzle with Fraise.

*Café British Navy Grog

Pusser's in Roadtown, Tortola, has the most delightful shop featuring Pusser's Rum, men and women's clothing, unique gifts, and cookbooks. Mine of course!

2 tsp. butter
several pinches each: grated nutmeg, cardamom

3 tsp. coconut syrup

4 cinnamon sticks
8 oz. Pusser's Navy Rum
whipped cream

4 slices each: lemon and orange peel
hot coffee

Cream butter with coconut syrup, nutmeg, and cardamom and divide between four fireproof mugs. Place one cinnamon stick, lemon and orange peel in each. Pour two ounces of rum in each mug as well. With a long match, carefully ignite. After ten seconds, douse the flame with coffee. Garnish with whipped cream.

*Café Brulot (basic)

4 oz. cognac or dark rum, warmed
3 cinnamon sticks
4 pieces orange peel
two coffee mugs (large)

2 cups hot coffee
5 sugar cubes
4 pieces lemon peel

Place all ingredients except cognac and coffee in a chafing dish and heat. Add a few drops hot water to sugar cubes and smash into peels. Add warmed cognac or rum and stir. Ignite and then douse with hot coffee. Serve in coffee mugs.

*Café Brulot Curacao

6 sugar cubes
peel of one lemon
8 whole cloves
2 oz. Curacao
coffee mug

peel of one orange
4 cinnamon sticks
8 oz. brandy
1-quart hot coffee

In a 2-quart chafing dish, mash spices, peels and sugar. Add liquors; stir; heating gently and slowly. Ignite with a long match. Once sugar has dissolved, gradually add coffee. Strain into mugs.

*Café Diablo

2 tsp. sugar
2 oz. Kahlua
6 whole cloves
5 cups hot coffee

4 oz. dark rum or brandy
2 orange twists
One 2" cinnamon stick
coffee mug

Place all ingredients except coffee in a chafing dish. Heat slowly and gently, stirring constantly. Stand back a bit and carefully ignite, allowing to burn for one minute. Slowly stir in coffee. Serve, removing spices and peel.

Serves four.

Café Dominica

1 oz. dark rum
1/2 oz. Grand Marnier
whipped cream

1/2 oz. Stoli Vanil
hot coffee
coffee mug

Pour liquor into a mug. Fill three-quarters to top with hot coffee. Top generously with whipped cream.

Café Dominican Republic

There's a lot of liquor in this, so be sure the coffee is piping hot.

1 oz. Brugal & Co. rum or dark rum
1/2 oz. Amaretto
hot coffee
ground cinnamon

1 oz. Peach Schnapps
1/2 oz. dark Crème de Cacao
marshmallow topping
coffee mug

Pour liquor into a mug. Fill three-quarters to top with hot coffee. Top generously with whipped cream. Garnish with ground cinnamon.

Café Eustatius (Staysha)

1 oz. dark rum
hot coffee
colored sugar crystals

1 oz. Galliano
whipped cream
coffee mug

Pour liquor into a mug. Fill three-quarters to top with hot coffee. Top generously with whipped cream. Sprinkle with colored sugar crystals.

Café Francais

1 oz. Bailey's Irish Cream Liqueur
1 oz. Cointreau
whipped cream
coffee mug

1 oz. Amaretto
hot coffee
grated orange peel

Pour liquor into a mug. Fill three-quarters to top with hot coffee. Top generously with whipped cream. Garnish with grated orange peel.

Café Grenada

1 oz. Westerhill rum or dark rum
1/2 oz. Cruzan Coconut Rum
marshmallow topping

1 oz. Caramel liqueur
hot coffee
coffee mug

Pour liquor into a mug. Fill three-quarters to top with hot coffee. Top generously with marshmallow.

Café Grenadines

1 oz. dark rum
1/2 oz. Crème de Banana
whipped cream
coffee mug

1 oz. Frangelico
hot coffee
brown sugar

Pour liquor into a mug. Fill three-quarters to top with hot coffee. Top generously with whipped cream. Sprinkle with brown sugar.

Café Guadeloupe

Another delicious cherry-truffle flavored coffee.

1 oz. Beauport rum or dark rum
1 oz. Droste Bittersweet Chocolate liqueur
whipped cream
coffee mug

1 oz. Kirsch
hot coffee
grated chocolate

Pour liquor into a mug. Fill three-quarters to top with hot coffee. Top generously with whipped cream. Garnish with chocolate gratings.

Café Jamaica Me Crazy

1 oz. Appleton Estate rum or dark rum
1/2 oz. Kahlua
whipped cream
superfine sugar

1/2 oz. cognac
hot coffee
ground cinnamon and ginger
coffee mug

Pour liquor into a mug. Fill three-quarters to top with hot coffee. Top generously with whipped cream. Sprinkle with ground cinnamon, ginger, and sugar.

Café Martinique

1 oz. La Favorite rum or dark rum
1 oz. Crème de Grand Marnier
whipped cream
coffee mug

1 oz. Crème de Grande Passion
hot coffee
ground cinnamon

Pour liquor into a mug. Fill three-quarters to top with hot coffee. Top generously with whipped cream. Sprinkle with ground cinnamon.

Café Montserrat

1 oz. dark rum
splash of Goldschlager cinnamon liqueur
hot coffee

1 oz. Marmot (Swiss chocolate
    liqueur with chocolate bits)
whipped cream

Pour liquor into a mug. Fill three-quarters to top with hot coffee. Top generously with whipped cream.

Café Nevis

1 oz. dark rum
1/2 oz. cognac
whipped cream

1 oz. Toasted Almond Cream liqueur
hot coffee

Pour liquor into a mug. Fill three-quarters to top with hot coffee. Top generously with whipped cream.

Café Paradiso

This is positively decadent!

1 oz. Courvoisier
1/2 oz. Mozart Chocolate Nougat liqueur
hot coffee
grated white chocolate and cinnamon

1 oz. Tia Maria
splash of Coco Lopez
whipped cream
coffee mug

Pour liquor into a mug. Fill three-quarters to top with hot coffee. Top generously with whipped cream. Garnish with grated white chocolate and cinnamon.

Café Puerto Rico

1 oz. Barcardi or dark rum
hot coffee

1 oz. Licor 43

Pour liquor into a mug. Fill three-quarters to top with hot coffee.

*Café Royale

1 cube sugar soaked in brandy
whipped cream

1 cup hot black coffee

Place sugar cube on a long-handled spoon and ignite. Drop into coffee as sugar caramelizes. Garnish with dollop of whipped cream.

Café Saba

1 oz. dark rum
hot coffee
whipped cream

1 oz. Amontillado (sherry-based with
almond flavor)

Pour liquor into a mug. Fill three-quarters to top with hot coffee. Top generously with whipped cream.

Café St. Barths

1 oz. dark rum
1 oz. Godiva Liqueur
hot coffee

1 oz. Sabra (chocolate liqueur from
Israel flavored with orange)
whipped cream

Pour liquor into a mug. Fill three-quarters to top with hot coffee. Top generously with whipped cream.

Café St. Croix

1 oz. Cruzan Coconut Rum
1 oz. dark Crème de Cacao
whipped cream

1 oz. Cruzan Rum Cream
hot coffee
chocolate shavings

Pour liquor into a mug. Fill three-quarters to top with hot coffee. Top generously with whipped cream. Garnish with chocolate shavings.

Café St. John

1 oz. Paradise rum or gold rum
1/2 Southern Comfort
whipped cream
coffee mug

1 oz. cognac
hot coffee
chocolate shavings

Pour liquor into a mug. Fill three-quarters to top with hot coffee. Top generously with whipped cream. Garnish with chocolate shavings.

Café St. Kitts

1 oz. Baron Edmond rum or dark rum
1/2 oz. DeKuyper (cherry brandy)
very hot coffee
coffee mug

1/2 oz. brandy
1 square Hershey's chocolate
whipped cream

Place chocolate square in bottom of mug. Pour in liquor. Fill three-quarters to top with hot coffee. Stir. Top generously with whipped cream.

Café St. Lucia

1 oz. Bounty Rum
1/2 oz. Crème de Banana
1/2 oz. Seventh Heaven (ginger liqueur
    said to be an aphrodisiac)

1 oz. Crème de la Cave (St. Lucian
    rum and cream)
hot coffee
whipped cream

Pour liquor into a mug. Fill three-quarters to top with hot coffee. Top generously with whipped cream.

Café St. Thomas

1 oz. Paradise Rum, gold
1/2 oz. Pistacha (pistachio flavored rum
    produced by Cointreau in the U.S.)
whipped cream

1 oz. Malibu
1/2 oz. Cruzan Rum Cream
hot coffee
coffee mug

Pour liquor into a mug. Fill three-quarters to top with hot coffee. Top generously with whipped cream.

Café St. Vincent

1 oz. After Hour's rum or gold rum
1/2 oz. Bailey's Irish Cream Liqueur
whipped cream

1/2 oz. Pernod
hot coffee
coffee mug

Pour liquor into a mug. Fill three-quarters to top with hot coffee. Top generously with whipped cream.

Café Trinidad & Tobago

1 oz. Trinidad Distillers rum or gold rum
1/2 oz. Pineapple Rum
whipped cream

1 oz. Coconut Rum
hot coffee
coffee mug

Pour liquor into a mug. fill three-quarters with hot coffee. Top generously with whipped cream.

Café Turks and Caicos

1 oz. gold rum
1 oz. Frangelico
whipped cream

1 oz. Pasha Turkish Coffee liqueur
hot coffee

Pour liquor into a mug. Fill three-quarters to top with hot coffee. Top generously with whipped cream.

Caribbean Coffee

1 oz. Cruzan Coconut Rum
1 oz. Godiva Liqueur or dark Crème de Cacao
whipped cream
coffee mug

1 oz. Tia Maria
hot coffee
chocolate shavings

Pour liquor into mug. Fill to three-quarters with hot coffee. Top with whipped cream and garnish with chocolate shavings.

Christmas in the Islands

1 oz. Malibu Rum
1 oz. Amaretto
whipped cream
coffee mug

1 oz. Kahlua
hot coffee
toasted grated coconut

Pour liquor into mug. Fill to three-quarters with hot coffee. Garnish liberally with whipped cream and sprinkle toasted coconut on top.

Coffee Alexander

1 oz. brandy
1 oz. white Crème de Cacao
whipped cream
coffee mug

1 oz. Tia Maria
hot coffee
grated nutmeg

Pour liquor into a mug. Fill three-quarters to top with hot coffee. Top with whipped cream. Garnish with grated nutmeg.

*Flaming Hot Buttered Rum

2 oz. Cruzan Dark Rum
1 tbsp. brown sugar
cinnamon stick
2 or 3 whole cloves
grated nutmeg

1/2 oz. 151 rum
pat of butter
lemon peel
boiling water

Fill a large, heatproof mug with boiling water and let sit for one minute. Pour out and add peel, brown sugar, and butter, mashing on bottom. Add cloves and cinnamon stick and fill 2/3 full with boiling water. Stir in Cruzan dark rum. In a small fireproof ladle, ignite the 151 rum and carefully pour into mug. Sprinkle with nutmeg.

Fuzzy Nut

1 oz. Peach Schnapps
1/2 oz. white Crème de Cacao
whipped cream

1 oz. Amaretto
4 oz. very hot chocolate
cinnamon

Stir all ingredients into mug except whipped cream and cinnamon. Top generously with whipped cream. Sprinkle with cinnamon.

Gluhwein

My German parents would make this in the dead of winter. The pungent and spicy aroma would fill the house in contrast to the snow-heavy pine branches outside.

5 oz. dry red wine
lemon and orange slice
3 whole cloves

1 tsp. honey
small cinnamon stick
ground nutmeg

Heat all ingredients in a saucepan over low heat. Do not boil. Serve in a pre-heated mug.

Harbor Light

1 oz. 151 rum
1/2 oz. tequila

1/2 oz. Tia Maria
shot glass

In a shot glass, layer first the Tia Maria, tequila, and then the rum and ignite. Wait for the flame to go out before drinking.

Bartender's Secret: Preheated Mugs:

To ensure against lukewarm hot drinks, pre-heat coffee mugs by filling with boiling water and allowing to sit for one minute. Drain and carefully wipe dry (mug will be hot) just before pouring drink.

Hot Benefactor

2 oz. Cruzan rum, gold
1/2 oz. Cointreau
ground nutmeg

2 oz. dry, red wine
lemon slice

In a small saucepan, heat all ingredients over low heat except lemon slice and nutmeg. Pour into a pre-heated coffee mug. Garnish with lemon slice and nutmeg.

Hot Milk Punch

2 oz. Scotch
1 cup milk
cinnamon

1/2 oz. Drambuie
1 whole egg, beaten

Pour all Scotch, Drambuie and milk into a small saucepan over low heat. Slowly stir in beaten egg and continue to heat until slightly thickened. Pour into a pre-heated mug and top with a dash of powdered cinnamon.

Hot Toddy

2 oz. whiskey
1 pat butter
dash of ground ginger
lemon slice

1 tsp. sugar syrup
dash of ground cinnamon
boiling water
grated nutmeg

Fill a coffee mug full of hot water and allow to sit for one minute and dump out. Pour all ingredients except boiling water in mug and stir. Fill to top with boiling water. Garnish with lemon slice and grated nutmeg.

Irish Coffee (basic)

1 1/2 oz. Irish Whiskey
hot coffee
coffee mug

1 tsp. superfine sugar
whipped cream

Pour liquor and into a mug. Fill three-quarters to top with hot coffee. Stir. Top with whipped cream.

Kioki Coffee

1 oz. Kahlua
hot black coffee
coffee mug

1 oz. brandy
whipped cream

Pour liquor into a mug. Fill three-quarters to top with hot coffee. Top generously with whipped cream.

*Lighthouse

2 oz. Galliano
shot glass and cocktail glass

2 oz. dry or sweet vermouth

Pour vermouth into a cocktail glass. Pour Galliano into a shot glass and ignite, pouring over vermouth.

Bartender's Secret-Pyrotechnical Display

To add dash and flair to your party squeeze a lemon, lime, orange or grapefruit peel over a drink and ignite immediately. The volatile oils in the fruit peel will catch flame. Careful!

Mexican Chocolate Cup

1 oz. tequila
1/2 Kahlua
1 tsp. powdered cocoa

1/2 oz. Triple Sec
3/4 cup hot milk (not boiling)
whipped cream

Stir all ingredients together, except whipped cream in a heated mug. To pre-heat mug pour boiling water into cup and let sit for one minute and drain. Garnish with whipped cream.

Mexican Coffee

1 oz. Kahlua
hot coffee
grated nutmeg

1 oz. tequila
whipped cream

Pour liquor into a mug. Fill to three-quarters with hot coffee. Top generously with whipped cream.

Mexican Coffee-Caribbean Coast

1 oz. Kahlua
hot coffee
grated chocolate and cinnamon

1 oz. rum
whipped cream

Pour liquor into a mug. Fill to three-quarters with hot coffee. Top generously with whipped cream. Garnish with grated chocolate and cinnamon.

St. Lucia Royale

1 oz. Old Fort Rum or gold rum
hot coffee
whipped cream

1 oz. Liqueur Nutz n Rum (peanuts,
    spices, cream)

Pour liquor into a mug. Fill three quarters with hot coffee. Top generously with whipped cream.

CHAPTER TWENTY

Punch Me Out!

A little shy about bartending at a party? Party too large for one bartender? Too costly for an open bar? Try serving a punch.

The word punch supposedly comes from the Hindu word, panch, which means five. The rule of five is: 'one sour, two sweet, three strong, four weak, and number five consisting of spices and flavorings.

All of the following recipes should be served in a large punch bowl with a block of ice in it. Do not use ice cubes as they will melt too quickly and dilute the delicate, balanced flavors of the punch.

Bartender's Secret: Volcanic Punch Bowl:

Order a Scorpion Bowl, available from Sang-Kung in New York City. It's a large ceramic bowl with a volcano in the center that can be filled with 151 and lit!

Antigua Champagne Punch

5 bottles inexpensive, decent champagne, chilled
1 fresh, cubed pineapple, chilled
strawberries for garnish

8 oz. brandy, chilled
3 each: orange, lemon, lime, sliced
*   into thin rounds*

Mix four bottles of the champagne with the brandy in a large punch bowl with block of ice. Add fruit and dramatically pour last bottle of champagne over top. Garnish with strawberries.

Aquarium Jell-O

4 envelopes Knox plain gelatin
splash of Stoli Oranj
assorted gummi fish
a package of jelly beans
new or sterilized goldfish bowl

Blue Curacao
purple endive or other colorful,
*   ruffly foliage*
spaghetti strands, uncooked

Make gelatin according to directions, replacing water with Blue Curacao and splash of Stoli Oranj. Place jellybeans on bottom of bowl and carefully pour gelatin over them. When semi-set, add fish, speared on spaghetti and foliage. Chill until firm.

Basic Punch Recipe (without alcohol)

1 2-litre bottle of ginger ale
2 quarts orange juice

2 quarts pineapple juice
2 pints sherbet, raspberry, lime or
orange or even coconut

Mix all liquid ingredients together in a large punch bowl with a block of ice. Just prior to serving, adding sherbet.

Berry Deadly

1 pint Stoli Razberi Vodka
2 quarts orange juice

1 bottle Boone's Strawberry wine
1 2-litre bottle of ginger ale

Mix all ingredients in a large punch bowl with a block of ice.

Blackbeard's Punch

1 pint Blackbeard's Old Sint Maarten Rum
1 bottle dry red wine
2 oz. Triple Sec
1 pint orange juice

1 quart whiskey
2 oz. Benedictine
1 quart strong black tea
1 cup fresh limejuice

Combine all ingredients in large punch bowl with block of ice. Nice with the volcano bowl mentioned in Bartenders Secrets.

KOSKELA

Champagne Punch

1 bottle champagne, chilled
4 oz. Cointreau
1 quart sparkling water, chilled

4 oz. brandy
splash of Amaretto

Combine all ingredients in a punch bowl with a block of ice.

Cruzan Banana Rum Punch

1 pint Cruzan Banana Rum
1 quart orange juice
1 quart pineapple juice

1 quart ginger ale

8 ounces Crème de Banana liqueur
1 quart lemonade

Mix all ingredients in a large punch bowl, adding ginger ale last. Add a large block of ice.

Caribbean Egg Nog

4 oz. Parrot Bay rum
3 oz. Cruzan Banana Rum
2 quarts skim milk
4 eggs, beaten
2 tsp. vanilla extract
1/4 tsp. grated nutmeg, plus extra for sprinkling

3 oz. Cruzan Coconut Rum
3 oz. Cruzan Pineapple Rum
1 cup evaporated milk
2 egg whites
3/4 cup granulated sugar, plus
    two extra tablespoons

In a heavy three-quart saucepan, gently heat skim milk, 3/4 cup sugar and nutmeg, until bubbles appear. Remove from heat.

In medium bowl, whisk all eggs. Gradually stir in 2 cups of the milk and return all to saucepan. Over low heat, cook until slightly thickened.

Remove from heat and stir in all rums. Refrigerate until chilled.

AN HOUR BEFORE SERVING: Pour the evaporated milk into a bowl and freeze for 45 minutes. Remove and beat with remaining sugar until stiff peaks form. Fold into eggnog. Pour into large punch bowl and sprinkle with nutmeg.

KOSKELA

Cruzan Buck Naked Punch

1 bottle Cruzan light rum
3 cans frozen lime daiquiri mix

6 bottles of beer

Mix all ingredients until smooth. Potent!

Eggnog (traditional)

4 oz. Cruzan rum
4 oz. whiskey
1 cup milk
1 teaspoon nutmeg, plus some for dusting

4 oz. brandy
2 cups heavy cream
1 cup confectioner's sugar

Separate yolks from egg whites, setting whites aside in refrigerator. Beat the confectioner's sugar with the yolks. Stir in nutmeg, cream, milk, and liquors. Set aside.

Beat egg whites until stiff and fold into milk mixture. Refrigerate for two hours. Dust with extra nutmeg.

Floating Fruit Island

Make this sparkling delight with a colorful fruited ice ring. Easy to prepare, it makes a stunning presentation.

fruit juice of your choice (be sure to coordinate with punch) or water

1 cup seedless green grapes
1 cup whole, fresh strawberries

Pour water or fruit juice into a ring mold, which will fit inside your punch bowl. Leave about an inch from the top. Freeze until firm.

Arrange grapes, strawberries, or other fruit of your choice decoratively on top of ring. Fill to top with water or juice and freeze. Dip mold into hot water to loosen and float fruit side up in your punch bowl.

Other suggested fruits: lemon slices, orange slices, lime slices, pineapple, raspberries, maraschino cherries, mandarin orange sections, kiwi

Substitute ice tea, lemonade for water

Bartender's Secret-Punch Extenders

Sometimes the party ends up being larger than you had planned for or guests are consuming too much of a high-alcohol content punch. Do not disturb the delicate balance of flavors in the punch by adding more tea or fruit juice. Use a neutral flavor such as club soda. It will add sparkle and life to the punch and dilute the alcohol a bit.

French Island Punch

16 oz. Amaretto
6 oz. Triple Sec
2 pints vanilla ice cream

16 oz. Kahlua
6 oz. Bailey's Irish Cream Liqueur

Mix liqueurs together and put in a punch bowl with no ice. Float vanilla ice cream on top.

Goombay Punch

1 bottle Malibu Rum
1 can Hawaiian Punch

1/2 bottle Cruzan Banana Rum
2 quarts orange juice

Mix all ingredients in a punch bowl with a large block of ice.

Great Pumpkin Punch

1 part Dubonnet
.5 part Chambord
Angostura bitters

1 part Calvados
2.5 parts apple cider

Mix all ingredients in a punch bowl with block of ice, with a dash of Angostura bitters.

It's Over Punch

1 bottle vodka
8 oz. Southern Comfort
2 liters of Hawaiian Punch

8 oz. Peach Schnapps
8 oz. Chambord

Combine all ingredients in a punch bowl with a block of ice.

Mexican Eggnog

8 oz. Kahlua
powdered cinnamon

Caribbean Eggnog

Make Caribbean Eggnog recipe as directed above. Before folding in beaten evaporated milk mixture, stir in Kahlua and dust with cinnamon and nutmeg.

Paradise In A Glass

8 oz. light rum
1 bottle chilled champagne
2 tablespoons sugar

2 bottles white wine
3 cups pineapple juice
1 fresh pineapple, peeled, cored and cubed

Soak pineapple with rum and sugar overnight. Pour pineapple juice into a ring mold and freeze. Add wine to pineapple/rum mixture, and then pour into a large punch bowl. Add frozen pineapple juice ring and float champagne on top right before serving.

Piña Colada Punch

1 bottle of Cruzan Coconut Rum
1 quart pineapple juice, chilled
1 pint pineapple sherbet

2 liters pineapple soda, chilled
8 oz. Coco Lopez

Blend rum, Coco Lopez, and pineapple juice until smooth. Add pineapple soda. Pour into a punch bowl with a block of ice and float sherbet on top.

Planter's Punch

1 liter Cruzan Rum, light
2 cups fresh limejuice
1 cup pineapple juice

8 oz. Curacao
1 cup orange juice
1 quart sparkling water

Combine all ingredients in a punch bowl with a block of ice.

Bartender's Secret-Flavor Testing

Always test a punch before serving just as you would any other dish. Punches are often guilty of tasting too sweet or too sour, or even too alcoholic.

Sultry Island Sangria

1 bottle of red wine
1 cup pineapple juice
1 orange, sliced into wheels, peel and all,
    remove seeds

4 oz. Cruzan Coconut Rum
1 cup fresh limejuice
1 lemon, sliced as above
1 apple, cored and slice

Combine all ingredients in a punch bowl and marinate overnight in the refrigerator. When ready to serve, add a large block of ice.

Tipsy Strawberry-Champagne Punch

My German mother would make this when I was a child. I used to sneak the alcohol-laden strawberries when no one looked.

3 bottles chilled Moselle wine
splash of Cointreau
2 pounds, sliced strawberries

1 bottle chilled champagne
8 tablspoons sugar

Sprinkle strawberries with sugar and place in a large bowl. Add one bottle of Moselle and refrigerator for at least one day. Before serving in large punch bowl with block of ice, add remaining wine and carefully pour in champagne.

Tropical Glogg
(mulled wine, island-style)

Note, before serving, hide all the car keys for the evening.

2 bottles of cabernet or burgundy
1 bottle of light rum
1 cup raisins
1/2 cup sugar
10 cardamom pods
2 sticks cinnamon

1 bottle of vodka
1 cup water
1 cup whole blanched almonds
2 large pieces orange peel
8 whole allspice

Combine water and all other non-alcoholic ingredients in a heavy enamel or stainless steel saucepan. Bring to a boil and simmer for five minutes. Reduce heat greatly. Add wine and heat gently. Do not boil. Remove from heat and steep for a couple of hours. Before serving, add hard alcohol and reheat gently.

KOSKELA

Virgin Island Ginger Syllabub

8 oz. Cruzan Gold Rum
1 cup heavy cream
juice of 1/2 lemon
2 to 3 pieces crystallized ginger, minced

1 oz. dry sherry
2 tablespoons brown sugar
dash of ground ginger and nutmeg

Put rum, sherry, sugar, spices, and lemon juice in a large bowl and stir. Allow to sit refrigerated for an hour. Beat cream until stiff peaks form. Fold in crystallized ginger and rum mixture.

Bartender's Secret-The Making of Tea

Many punches have tea as a required ingredient. This does not mean you throw a couple of tea bags in the bottom of the punch bowl either. Tea should either be black or orange pekoe and strong to bind the punch. Don't bother with weak tea as it will only take away from the punch. Bring a pot of water to boil, remove from heat and steep tea for no longer than three minutes or it will be bitter. Cool and add to punch.

West Indies Soaked-Fruit Punch

1 bottle of 151 rum or 100 proof vodka
1 quart whole, fresh raspberries
4 firm kiwis, peeled, and cubed
1 quart pineapple juice

1 quart whole, fresh strawberries
1 cup fresh, cubed pineapple
1 quart orange juice
1 2-litre bottle ginger ale

In a large bowl, soak the fruit overnight in the alcohol. The next day, combine the fruit juice in a punch bowl. Carefully pour in fruits and alcohol mixture, stir gently. Stir in ginger ale. *Enjoy and watch out for the fruit. It holds a lot of alcohol.*

CHAPTER TWENTY-ONE

Non-Alcoholic Drinks

Just because a drink does not have alcohol in it, does not mean it cannot taste great! Non-alcoholic drinks should be an option at any party. Responsible bartenders will offer these drinks to quench thirst of non-drinkers and as a device to cut someone off who has overindulged.

Don't be afraid to experiment with some of the tropical and exotic fruit juice now available in the freezer section of your grocer.

Beach Blanket Bingo

2 oz. cranberry juice
Lime-flavored Perrier
highball

2 oz. grapefruit juice
lime slice

Fill a highball glass with ice. Stir in juices and fill to top with Perrier. Garnish with lime slice.

Bonaire Pink Flamingo

1 cup pineapple juice
2 scoops firm vanilla ice cream

1 10-oz. package frozen strawberries

Blend until smooth.

Coconut Water

Chilled unripe coconuts have their tops sliced off and a straw inserted along roadsides in the Caribbean. It's impossible to purchase unripe coconut in the States, but the ripe coconut milk is delicious also.

1 coconut

Pierce eyes of coconut with an ice pick and hammer. Watch your fingers! Strain through a cheesecloth into a glass filled with ice.

Cranberry Kooler

2 oz. cranberry juice
club soda
highball

1 oz. fresh limejuice
lime slice

Fill a highball glass with ice. Stir in juices and fill to top with club soda. Garnish with lime slice.

Ginger Beer

This traditional West Indian drink tickles the nose!

4 cups boiling water
1/2 cup fresh limejuice
scant pinch of cardamom
lime wedges

1/2 cup freshly grated ginger
1 1/4 cups sugar
1/2 teaspoon baking yeast

Combine all ingredients, except yeast. Allow to cool to 92(. Pour into a jar, along with yeast. Stir. Allow to sit 24 hours. Strain and refrigerate. Serve with a lime wedge.

Hibiscusade

30 single red hibiscus blooms (unsprayed
   with chemicals)
2 quart ginger ale

1/2 oz. freshly grated ginger
8 oz. fresh limejuice

Wash hibiscus and ginger. Boil in two quarts water for three minutes. Strain. Add to ginger ale and limejuice. Stir.

Innocent Island Passion

4 oz. passionfruit juice
splash of pineapple juice
club soda
highball

splash of cranberry juice
1/2 oz. fresh limejuice
lime slice

Fill a highball glass with ice. Stir in juices and fill to top with club soda. Garnish with lime slice.

Jumbi Monster Slime Juice

1 6 oz. package Berry Blue Kool-Aid
1 can frozen orange juice

1 can frozen lemonade
1 gallon, plus 1-quart water

Mix all ingredients with water. Watch it turn an ominous deep lagoon green color.

Jungle Kooler

4 oz. pineapple juice
1 oz. passionfruit juice
highball glass

1 oz. orange juice
1/2 oz. Coco Lopez

Fill a highball glass with ice. Stir in all ingredients.

Mock Pink Champagne

1-liter ginger ale
1 cup pineapple juice
1/2 cup sugar

2 cups cranberry juice
1/4 cup frozen orange juice concentrate
1 cup water

Boil water and sugar until dissolved. Cool and refrigerate. Combine all other ingredients, except lemon lime soda in a punch bowl with a block of ice. Add sugar syrup and ginger ale, stirring gently.

Raspberry Lemon Punch

2 cans frozen lemonade
raspberry sherbet

2 two-liter bottles raspberry seltzer

Squeeze the frozen lemonade into a punch bowl. Stir in seltzer until combined. Add a block of ice and float raspberry sherbet on top.

Roy Rogers

cola
maraschino cherry

splash of grenadine
highball glass

Fill a highball glass with ice. Drizzle in grenadine and fill to top with club soda. Garnish with cherry.

Shirley Temple

lemon-lime soda
maraschino cherry

splash of grenadine
highball glass

Fill a highball glass with ice. Drizzle in grenadine and fill to top with soda. Garnish with a cherry.

Sorrel
St. Thomas, U.S. Virgin Islands

Sorrel is an annual plant, which grows to about six feet. When the flowers wither, the sepals grow larger and this is used to make a bright red drink. This happens around December and therefore this drink is popular at Christmas time.

2 cups sorrel sepals
1 tablespoon freshly grated ginger
juice of one lime
4 cups boiling water

1 tablespoon freshly grated orange peel
5 to 6 whole cloves
1 1/2 cups sugar

Wash sorrel and place into a small saucepan along with water and all other ingredients. Heat gently, until simmering. Remove from heat, allow cooling. Refrigerate overnight.

Strawberry Lemonade

10 ripe strawberries
1 cup water

juice of one lemon
1 tablespoon sugar

Blend all ingredients with 1-cup ice in blender until smooth.

Strawberry Punch

1 10 oz. package frozen strawberries
1 pint lemon sherbet
juice of fresh lemonade

1 6 oz. container frozen lemonade
1-liter ginger ale

Thaw strawberries in refrigerator for two hours. Make lemonade, add lemon juice and chill. Pour into a large punch bowl, stir in ginger ale. Float sherbet on top.

Tamarind Iced Tea

2 tablespoons tamarind paste
1 cup cold black tea

1/4 cup granulated sugar
highball glass

It's easiest to whirl these ingredients in a blender as the paste is a bit difficult to manipulate in cold water. Fill a highball glass with ice. Pour in tamarind tea.

Did you know:? Related to the carob tree, **tamarind** is found readily throughout the tropics. Each cylindrical brown pod, can measure four to six inches and contains one to twelve hard, shiny, cinnamon colored seeds. Dense pulp surrounds these seeds. Tamarind paste can be purchased in gourmet or ethnic grocery stores.
High in potassium, magnesium, thiamin, and good source of iron.

Tea Punch

2 quarts Earl Grey tea, chilled
1 quart orange juice

2 quarts apple juice
juice of one lemon

Combine all ingredients in a punch bowl with a block of ice.

Tropical Punch

1 cup pineapple juice
1 cup fresh limejuice
1/4 cup grenadine
lemon and orange slices

1 cup orange juice
1 2-liter bottle ginger ale
1 cup strawberries

Combine all ingredients in a punch bowl with a block of ice, except ginger ale and fruit. Gently stir in ginger ale and float fruit.

Unfuzzy Navel

4 oz. orange juice
1 oz. fresh limejuice
highball glass

4 oz. peach nectar
club soda

Fill a highball glass with ice. Stir in juice and then club soda.

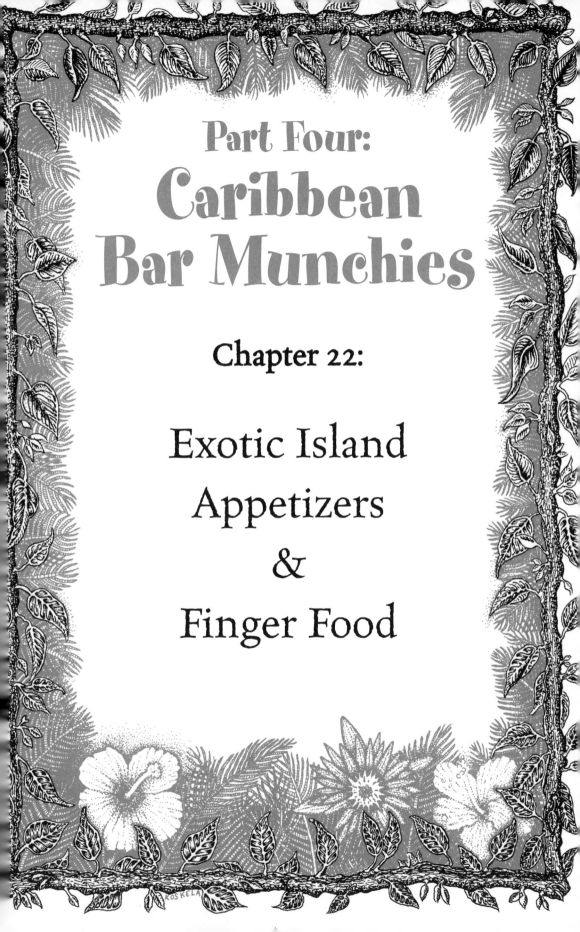

Part Four:
Caribbean
Bar Munchies

Chapter 22:

Exotic Island
Appetizers
&
Finger Food

Exotic Island Appetizers & Finger Food

A party without food? No way! A friend attended a party given in St. John the other day and told me this was the case. Guests were literally fighting over a single bag of potato chips. It's a bartender's responsibility to ensure his guests are able to travel home safely. One of the ways to do this, is to slow down the impact of alcohol imbibed by serving food. And why not make it wonderful, delicious, and exotic?

Add a colorful Caribbean element to your parties and impress your guests with these island recipes. Put on a little reggae music and you go!

BBQ Claudine Chicken Wings
ST. MAARTEN, WEST INDIES
ADAPTED FROM SINT MAARTEN GUAVABERRY COMPANY

24 chicken wings
3 oz. Sint Maarten Guavaberry liqueur
1/2 tsp. fennel seeds

6 oz. orange juice concentrate
3 oz. soy sauce
habanero, hot red pepper or any good hot sauce to taste

1. In a small bowl, combine all ingredients except the chicken.
2. Marinate the chicken in the sauce at least overnight.
3. Cook on hot barbeque, basting every minute.

Yield: 8 servings

Beef Empanadas with Mango Rum
CURACAO

Various empanada or fried turnover recipes are found all over the Caribbean.

dough:

2 cups all-purpose flour
1/2 tsp. salt
1 egg, slightly beaten
vegetable oil for frying

1 tsp. sugar
5 tbs. vegetable shortening
1/3 cup Mango-flavored rum

filling:

1 lb. ground beef
1/4 cup celery, minced
1 tbs. fresh, cracked pepper

1/4 cup yellow onion, minced
1/2 cup firm mango, slightly unripe, diced
1/2 tsp. sea salt

1. **Dough:** In a large bowl, sift together flour, salt, and sugar. With a pastry cutter or fork, cut in shortening. Mixture will look sandy and lumpy. Fold in egg and rum and form a ball. Add a bit of water if needed.

2. On a lightly floured surface, roll out the doll to about 1/8 to 1/4 inch thick. Using a jar or cookie cutter, cut out 3-inch rounds.

3. **Filling:** In a frying pan, sauté the beef, onion, and celery, about 15 minutes. Pour into heatproof colander and rinse away fat under hot water over sink. Return to skillet and fold in mango and season with salt and pepper.

4. Brush the top of each dough round with water and scoop a spoonful of filling onto center. Fold in half and pinch sides tightly together to make a turnover. Edges may be scored with a fork.

5. Pour 2 inches of oil into a deep fryer or heavy skillet and heat to 350°. Fry empanadas until golden. Drain on white paper towels, serving at once.

Yield: about 25 - 30

Cheese, Shrimp and Potato Fritters
Dominican Republic

Fritters make ideal finger food at cocktail parties and have the added benefit of being very filling.

4 cups mashed potatoes	1/4 cup freshly chopped parsley
4 tbs. melted butter	2 eggs, slightly beaten
1/2 tsp. salt	1 cup sharp cheddar cheese, grated
1 small onion, minced	1 lb. shrimp, cooked, shelled and
1 1/2 cups breadcrumbs, plain	deveined, chopped
vegetable oil for frying	

1. Mix together the mashed potatoes, parsley, onion, butter, eggs, salt and cheese. Refrigerate for two hours.

2. Grease your hands and form balls the size of ping-pongs or golf balls. Stuff the center of each balls with one teaspoon of shrimp. Roll the balls into breadcrumbs.

3. Deep fry in 2 inches of oil heated to 350° until golden. Drain on white paper towels.

Yield: about 16 to 18 fritters

Creamy Raspberry-Coconut Dip
GUADELOUPE

Serve with pineapple sticks, apple, or pear wedges.

8 oz. whipped cream cheese
1/4 tsp. ground ginger
1/2 cup fresh or frozen raspberries

1 tbs. Coco Lopez
1 1/2 tbs. raspberry vinegar
1/4 cup freshly grated coconut or
dried, unsweetened

Purée all ingredients in a food processor until smooth. Chill 4 hours before serving.

Yield: about 2 cups

Crisp-Fried Oysters
with Tropical Tartar Sauce
BONAIRE

Fried oysters are heavenly. Serve them with this exotic Tropical Tartar Sauce.

1 cup all-purpose flour
1/2 tsp. freshly cracked black pepper
1/4 tsp. nutmeg
1 egg
1 cup yellow cornmeal
16 large oysters

1/2 tsp. salt
1/4 tsp. allspice
1 tbs. habanero hot sauce
3/4 cup milk
vegetable oil for frying

sauce:

3/4 cup mayonnaise
2 jalapeño peppers, chopped (jarred is perfect)
2 tbs. capers
2 tbs. finely chopped cilantro
salt and pepper to taste

1 firm kiwi, de-fuzzed, and minced
1/4 small habanero pepper, carefully
seeded and minced
2 tbs. lime rum

1. In a small bowl, combine all ingredients for sauce. Refrigerate for at least an hour.

2. In a medium bowl, combine flour and all other ingredients except oysters, milk, egg, cornmeal, and oil.

3. Whisk together egg and milk in another bowl. Cornmeal goes in another bowl.

4. Pour 2-3 inches of oil in a deep fryer or skillet and heat to 350°. Dip each oyster in egg mixture and then dredge in flour mixture and finally in cornmeal. Place oysters on wax paper.

5. Fry until golden and drain on white paper towels. Serve with Tropical Tartar Sauce.

Yield: 16 appetizers and about 1 cup of sauce

Curried Crab, Mango, and Pear Dip
ANTIGUA

When two such decadently sweet foods such as pear and crab combine with exotic island spices and fruit, the result is a fabulous twist. Serve with pita or toast points.

2 tsp. butter
1/4 cup celery, minced
1 garlic clove, minced
1 firm mango, not green, but not overripe, peeled, seeded and finely diced
1 egg beaten
1/4 cup, plus 2 tbs. mayonnaise
1 1/2 tsp. curry powder

1/2 cup yellow onion, minced
1/4 habanero pepper, carefully seeded and minced
1 ripe pear, peeled, cored and diced
1/2 lb. fresh lump crab, cartilage pieces removed
1 tbs. Dijon mustard
2 tbs. sour cream

1. Preheat oven to 375° and lightly butter a 1-quart glass or ceramic gratin dish.

2. In a tiny skillet or pan, toast the curry powder until a slight aroma is given off, about 2-3 minutes. Set aside.

3. Melt the butter in a heavy skillet and sauté the onion, celery, habanero pepper, and garlic until the onion is just clear, 2-3 minutes. Remove from heat and allow to cool. Fold in fruit and crab.

4. Beat together the mayonnaise, egg, mustard and curry powder in a small bowl. Fold this into the crab mixture and scoop into the gratin dish.

5. In a cup, combine the sour cream and mayonnaise. Spoon over the crab. Bake for 20 minutes until bubbly.

6. In a small bowl, toss pear and mango. Spoon over crab cakes. Serve at once.

Yield: 4 to 6 servings

Curried Lobster and Cashew Patties
British Virgin Islands

pastry:
prepare as directed for Beef Empanadas with Mango Rum

filling:

1 1/2 lbs. uncooked, shelled lobster, chopped well	1/4 cup vegetable oil
1 medium onion, minced	1 clove garlic, crushed
1 1/2 tbs. curry powder	4 oz. raw cashews, roasted in oven
1/4 cup shredded parsley	for 3-4 minutes, coarsely chopped
salt and pepper to taste	

1. **Filling:** In a deep skillet, toast the curry powder over medium heat for about 2 minutes. Add oil and sauté onion and garlic, until onion is just clear. Fold in lobster, cover, reduce heat, simmering for about 10 minutes. Stir in parsley and simmer for another 2 minutes. Remove from heat and season with salt and pepper. Fold in cashews.
2. Fill and deep fry according to empanada directions.

Yield: about 18

Fiery Banana, Shrimp and Bean Dip with Garlic Crostini
St. Lucia

Serve this sweet-spicy Caribbean-inspired dish with frosty margaritas and daiquiris.

3 ripe, but firm bananas	1 cup chopped scallions
1/4 cup chopped parsley	1/4 cup chopped cilantro
1/2 habanero pepper, carefully seeded and minced	1 tablespoon habanero hot sauce
2 garlic cloves, crushed	2 cups white beans, rinsed if canned
1/4 cup olive oil	4 tbs. fresh limejuice
1 tbs. freshly cracked black pepper	1/2 tsp. sea salt
1/2 pound cooked shrimp, shelled, deveined, chopped	

1 loaf Italian or French bread	1/2 cup minced-fresh parsley
1/2 cup olive oil	sea salt to taste

1. Purée all ingredients, except shrimp, bread, 1/4 cup oil, and parsley, in food processor until smooth. Add small amounts of water if needed to blend.

2. Slice bread into 1/2 -inch-thick slices and place them on a baking sheet. Toast until golden on both sides.

3. Combine the parsley, olive oil, and salt in a small bowl. Brush over the bread.

4. Scoop bean dip onto crostini and serve.

Yield: 6 to 8 servings

Iguana Eggs with Jalapeño Sauce
ARUBA

18 fresh jalapeño peppers
1/2 cup plain breadcrumbs
1/2 cup yellow cornmeal
1/4 tsp. nutmeg
3 eggs
vegetable oil for frying

18 strips of sharp cheddar cheese
(1/2 inch x 1 inch)
1/2 cup all-purpose flour
1/4 tsp. allspice
1 tbs. habanero hot sauce

sauce:

1/2 cup frozen pineapple juice concentrate
1/4 cup rice vinegar
4 fresh jalapeño peppers, seeded and coarsely
    chopped

1/4 cup Junakanoo, lime-flavored rum
1/4 cup orange juice
2 tbs. honey

1. **To roast peppers:** Preheat oven to 450°.

2. Lightly coat peppers with olive oil and place on baking sheet in oven. Bake until skin begins to blister on peppers. Remove from oven, place in plastic bag and seal. After a few minutes, the skins should slip off easily. Cut a slit on side of each pepper and remove seeds. Stuff a cheese strip into each.

3. In a small bowl combine cornmeal, breadcrumbs, flour and spices.

4. In another bowl, beat the egg and habanero sauce. Dip each pepper in the egg mixture and then dredge with cornmeal mixture. Transfer to wax paper lined plate.

5. Pour 2-3 inches of oil into a deep fryer or heavy skillet, heating to 350°. Carefully drop in peppers and fry until golden. Drain on white paper towels.

6. **Sauce:** Bring all ingredients in a medium saucepan to boil. Lower heat and simmer for 10 minutes. Remove from heat. May be served at once or kept in refrigerator for one week.

Yield: 18 eggs and about 1 1/2 cups sauce

Island Chicken Paté
with Gingered Grapefruit

Quick, easy, inexpensive and above all, impressive.

1 lb. chicken livers, trimmed of fat and chopped	1/4 cup olive oil
1 large yellow onion, chopped	1/2 large grapefruit, peeled, seeded
2 tbs. freshly grated ginger	and diced
2 tbs. honey	

1. Preheat broiler.

2. In a small bowl, combine honey and ginger. Toss in and coat grapefruit.

3. Lightly grease broiler pan, and broil chicken livers for 8 to 10 minutes, turning once. Remove from oven and cool.

4. Heat oil in large skillet, sautéing onions until clear. Remove from heat and cool.

5. Drain grapefruit, reserving juice. Place onions, livers and grapefruit-honey liquid in food processor, puréeing until smooth. Add juice as needed to purée.

6. Transfer to attractive crock or bowl and fold in grapefruit. Serve with crostini or toast points.

Yield: about 8 to 10 servings

Jerked Ribs
JAMAICA

Jerk is the authentic Jamaican way to cook pork, beef, chicken, and seafood over a barbeque. The flavorful seasoning of Jamaican pimento (allspice), cinnamon, nutmeg, thyme, salt, peppers, onions and scallions reflect the island's lifestyle-hot, spicy and sweet. The extra brown sugar caramelizes over the barbeque heat and adds a sweet, crunchy crust.

Note: two days prep time required

jerk marinade:

1 large onion, minced	1/2 cup scallions, minced
1 habanero pepper, carefully seeded and minced	1 tsp. fresh thyme, chopped
1 tsp. allspice (Jamaican pimento)	1/2 tsp. ground nutmeg
1/2 tsp. ground cinnamon	1 tsp. fresh, cracked pepper
1 tsp. sea salt	2 tbs. brown sugar
1 tbs. olive oil	1 tbs. apple-cider vinegar
4 lbs. pork spareribs	1 cup barbeque sauce from grocer

1. Purée all ingredients for marinade and refrigerate overnight in a glass bowl.

2. Baste ribs with marinade and refrigerate overnight.

3. Over low--medium heat, grill the ribs for 1-1/2 hours, basting continuously with marinade. Serve with Jamaican Red Stripe beer and Bob Marley music.

Yield: 4 servings

Lime Rum and Coconut Shrimp
St. John, U.S. Virgin Islands

At one of the famous Caneel Bay Christmas parties, I managed to coaxed this recipe from the chef. The addition of rum livens up this otherwise traditional tropical appetizer. Packaged coconut may be substituted for the fresh if necessary.

2 eggs
1/2 cup Cruzan Junakanoo or lime-flavored rum
1 tbs. baking powder
1/4 tsp. ground ginger
2 cups freshly grated coconut
vegetable oil for frying

1 1/2 cups all-purpose flour
1/4 cup canned coconut milk
1/4 tsp. allspice
1/4 tsp. cinnamon
24 medium shrimp, peeled and deveined

1. In a large heavy bowl, stir together the eggs, 1 cup of the flour, the lime rum, baking powder, and spices. Place 1/2 cup of flour in a small bowl. Spread coconut on plate.

2. Dredge the shrimp first in the flour, then coconut milk, then the batter, then the coconut flakes. Lay the coconut shrimp on wax paper.

3. Pour 2-3 inches of oil in a deep fryer or tall, heavy skillet. Heat to 350°. Lower shrimp into oil and fry for 3-4 minutes until golden and shrimp is white and firm in center. Drain on white paper towels. Serve at once with Mango Chutney.

Yield: 8 servings

Mango Chutney
St. Croix, U.S. Virgin Islands

Bring this exotic chutney, tied up with raffia in a pretty jar, with you when invited to dinner. Compliments fish, meat, poultry dishes as well as dipping sauce for appetizers.

1 tsp. curry powder`
1 tbsp. butter
1 tbsp. freshly grated ginger
1/3 cup brown sugar
1/3 cup apple-cider vinegar
2 tablespoons almond slivers

1/4 tsp. ground cardamom
1/2 large onion, minced
1/2 small habanero pepper, carefully seeded and minced
1/4 cup golden raisins
4-5 large, firm mangoes, not green, but not too ripe either, peeled and diced

1. In a heavy saucepan, heat the curry powder and cardamom over medium heat until slightly browned and an aroma is given off.

2. Melt the butter in the same pan over medium heat and sauté the onion until just clear. Stir in ginger and habanero pepper and cook for 60 seconds. Add sugar, vinegar, and raisins, cooking for 8 minutes. Add mango, grated ginger, habanero pepper and almond slivers and cook for three more minutes. Remove from heat and cool.

3. Pour into sterilized jars and refrigerate. Keeps for one month.

Yield: about 2 cups

Phulouri (split pea) Fritters with Mango-Strawberry Salsa
Trinidad

dough:
1 cup split peas
1 clove garlic, crushed
1 tsp. black pepper
1/4 tsp. ground ginger

1 small yellow onion, minced
1/2 tsp. salt
1/4 tsp. cinnamon
vegetable oil for frying

salsa:
1 cup fresh strawberries, hulled and sliced
1/2 medium red onion, minced
1/4 cup yellow bell pepper, stemmed, seeded and diced
1/4 cup orange juice
2 tbs. fresh limejuice

1/2 cup fresh ripe mango, finely diced
1/2 small habanero pepper, carefully seeded and minced
1/4 cup green bell pepper, stemmed, seeded and diced
2 tbs. olive oil

1. **Dough:** Soak peas overnight in refrigerator. Drain the next morning and purée with onion, garlic and spices through food processor.

2. Pour 2 inches of oil in a deep fryer or skillet and heat to 375°. Forming small-flattened rounds, drop into oil and fry until golden. Drain on white paper towels.

3. **Salsa:** Combine all ingredients in a large bowl, toss gently. Refrigerate for 2 hours. Serve with Phulouri.

Yield: 2 1/2 cups salsa and about 24 phulouri fritters

Pineapple-Shrimp Mini Quiche
THE CAYMAN ISLANDS

These bite-size appetizers are incredibly easy to make, yet let an exotic flair to cocktail hour. They may be made ahead of time and frozen.

1 package (8-ounce) refrigerated buttermilk biscuits
4 tablespoons green onion, minced
1/2 teaspoon black pepper
1/4 cup fresh or canned pineapple, drained and finely diced

2 eggs
1 cup heavy cream
1/2 teaspoon sea salt
4 ounces cooked shrimp, shelled, deveined, and chopped
3/4 cup sharp cheddar, shredded

1. Preheat oven to 375°.

2. Generously grease 24 miniature muffin tins. Separate biscuits into 12 pieces and separate each one again. Press on bottom and sides, forming a miniature piecrust and place in each tin.

3. Whisk together cream, eggs, onion, salt, and pepper. Fold in shrimp and pineapple. Spoon into tin and top with cheddar.

4. Bake for 15 minutes. Serve at once.

Yield: 24 mini quiches

Plantain Chips
PUERTO RICO

Plantains are a member of the banana family and like them, are high in potassium, vitamin C, and magnesium. Choose plantains that are firm, and intact.

3 cups vegetable oil for deep-frying   *4 green plantains*
sea salt

1. Pour 3 inches of oil in a deep fryer or heavy skillet and heat to 350°.

2. Peel the plantains and slice very thinly. A mandolin works well for this.

3. Fry until golden. Drain on paper towels and sprinkle to taste with salt.

Yield: serves 8

Plantain Tostones
PUERTO RICO

4 green plantains   *4 cups water*
1-2 cloves garlic, crushed   *2 tbs. sea salt*
vegetable oil for frying

1. Peel plantains like a banana and cut into diagonal slices about 1-inch thick. In a large glass bowl, submerge plantains, garlic, and salt for 20 minutes. Drain on white paper towels.

2. Heat 2-3 inches of vegetable oil to 350° in a deep fryer or skillet with high sides. Fry plantain for about 3-4 minutes. Remove from pan and drain again on white paper towels. On a cutting board, flatten plantains either by hand or with a mallet.

3. Dip into salted water again and fry until golden. Drain on paper towels. Sprinkle lightly with salt. Serve with hot sauce or chutney.

Yield: 24 tostones

Roasted Pepper and Pear-Pineapple Dip with Shrimp
St. Barths

The contrast of sweet-smoky spiced flavors is delightful.

2 lbs. (20 to 25 per pound) cooked shrimp, shelled and deveined
1/2 cup yellow onion, minced
2 lbs. red bell peppers, roasted (see Iguana Eggs for roasting)
1 tbs. honey
1/2 cup fresh pineapple, chopped
salt and freshly ground pepper to taste

4 tbs. olive oil
2 garlic cloves crushed
1/2 small habanero pepper, seeded and coarsely chopped
1/4 cup red wine vinegar
1/2 chopped, plus one whole large ripe pear, peeled, chopped

1. Heat 2 tablespoons of olive in a small skillet and sauté the garlic, onion, and habanero pepper. Remove from heat.

2. In a food processor, purée all remaining ingredients except shrimp and whole pear, add onion mixture to food processor. Season with salt and pepper and refrigerate at least 4 hours.

3. Before serving, peel and core remaining pear. Cut into pieces. Skewer one shrimp and a piece of pear on a toothpick. Serve with Pear-Pineapple dip.

Yield: about 40 appetizers

Shrimp and Mango-Pear Satay with Peanut-Lime Sauce

St. Vincent

Also known as groundnut sauce in the West Indies, this peanut sauce can be made up to a day ahead.

1 cup unsweetened coconut milk
4 tbs. honey
1/2 cup minced green onion
1 tsp. coriander
1 cup firm, slightly unripe mango, cubed
1 ripe pear, peeled, cored and cubed

1/4 cup soy sauce
2 garlic cloves
1 tsp. cumin
2 lbs. (20-25 per pounds) large shrimp, shelled and deveined

sauce:

1/2 cup peanut butter
3 tbs. fresh limejuice
2 tsp. sesame oil
1 tsp. honey
1/2 tsp. freshly grated ginger

1/4 cup soy sauce
1 tbs. lime rum
1/2 tsp. hot, spicy sesame oil
2 garlic cloves, crushed

1. **Satay:** In a food processor, purée the coconut milk, soy sauce, honey, garlic, onion, and spices.

2. In a large bowl, place the shrimp, mango, and pear. Toss with marinade, cover, and refrigerate 2 hours.

3. Soak about 40 bamboo skewers in hot water for 1/2 hour. Preheat barbeque or broiler.

4. Thread shrimp and fruit onto skewers.

5. Grill or broil until shrimp turn pink.

6. **Sauce:** Purée all ingredients in blender or food processor until smooth. Serve with shrimp satay.

Yield: about 40 appetizers

Smoked Turkey, Starfruit and Gouda Fingers
St. Thomas, U.S. Virgin Islands

These tiny grilled sandwiches are terrific for luncheons or cocktail parties. Carambola or starfruit is tangy and pear-like in flavor.

8 slices, white, club-style bread
4 tbs. butter, softened
1/4 lb. smoked, thinly sliced turkey
8 slices, thinly sliced Gouda cheese

2 tsp. Dijon mustard
2 starfruit or carambola, cut cross-wise into star star-shaped 1/4-inch thick

1. Spread Dijon on one side of each slice of bread.

2. Layer cheese, turkey, and starfruit on four slices of the bread. Top with remaining slices. Press down.

3. Spread the outside of each sandwich with butter.

4. Heat a large griddle or frying pan over low-medium heat. Place a weight on each sandwich and grill on each side until golden and cheese is melted.

5. Cut into 4 pieces. Serve at once.

Yield: 16 appetizers

Spicy Cocktail Nuts
Barbados

1/2 lb. peanuts, shelled
1/2 lb. pecans, shelled
1 tbs. butter
1/2 tsp. sea salt or more to taste

1/2 lb. cashews, shelled
2 tbs. olive oil
1 tbs. habanero hot sauce
pepper to taste

1. Heat butter and oil in a large skillet over medium heat. Stir in hot sauce.

2. Add nuts, stirring constantly for 10 minutes.

3. Remove from heat and drain on white paper towels.

4. Season with salt and pepper.

Sweet and Fiery Coconut Chicken with Papaya-Horseradish Glaze

St. Kitts

Prepare as for Lime Rum and Coconut Shrimp (page 240), substituting 3--4 boneless, skinless chicken breasts, sliced crosswise into 1/2-inch strips-add 1 tablespoon habanero hot sauce to batter.

glaze:

1/2 cup ripe papaya	2 tbs. frozen pineapple juice concentrate
2 tbs. honey	1/4 cup fresh limejuice
2 tsp. horseradish	1/4 tsp. salt
1/4 tsp. freshly cracked blacked paper	

Whirl all ingredients in blender or food processor until smooth. Serve as dipping sauce with coconut chicken or shrimp.

Yield: about 30-40 appetizers

Stamp and Go

Jamaica, mon

These codfish cakes were once sold from seaside shacks in Jamaica, wrapped in paper and stamped, "paid," therefore *Stamp and Go.*

1/2 lb. salt cod	2 tbsp. vegetable oil
1/2 cup green onion, minced	
1 cup all-purpose flour	1 tsp. baking powder
1 tsp. cracked black pepper	1/2 tsp. salt
1/2 cup milk	1 egg
2 tbsp. melted butter	2 tbsp. Tabasco™
pinch of thyme	1/2 habanero pepper, minced (careful
1/2 cup shredded parsley	where you put your fingers, they'll burn your eyes)

1. Place cod in bowl large enough to fill with water and cover the fish. Cover and refrigerate overnight. In the morning, drain water and return to refrigerator for at least another three hours.

2. Drain and rinse fish, transferring to large, heavy saucepan. Cover fish with water and bring to boil. Reduce heat and simmer for 15-20 minutes. Drain, removing fish from water with a slotted spoon. Remove bones and skin, discarding them. With a fork, flake the cod.

3. Heat the oil in a large saucepan, adding onion. When onions are clear, remove from heat and set aside.

4. Sift together the flour, baking power, black pepper, and salt into a large bowl. Add milk, egg, and melted butter. Fold in Tabasco™, parsley, thyme, and habanero pepper. Add onion and cod. Mix well.

5. Heat 2-3 inches of vegetable oil in a deep fryer or skillet with high sides to 350°. Drop batter by tablespoonfuls into hot oil and fry until golden. Drain on white paper towels.

Yield: 24 appetizers or 8 servings

Tangy Guava-Pineapple Quesadillas

These refreshing hor d'oeuvres are filled with ripe, juicy pineapple, aromatic guava, and piquant Fontina cheese.

3/4 cup fresh ripe pineapple, minced and drained *1/2 cup guava preserves or paste*
8 flour tortillas (8-inch) *4 tbs. melted butter*
3/4 lb. Fontina cheese, shredded

1. Brush the top of each tortilla with melted butter. Spread 4 of the tortillas with guava preserves. Divide shredded cheese and pineapple between the four tortillas. Leave about a 1-inch border, as the cheese will melt out.

2. Top with four remaining tortillas and pin together with toothpicks.

3. Heat a large heavy griddle and melt a pat of butter. Cook quesadillas on each side until golden. Remove from heat and cut into eight wedges.

Yield: 32 appetizers

Virgin Island Conch Fritters
St. Thomas, U.S. Virgin Islands

These are a must at any good Caribbean party. They are absolutely the best, light, flavorful and filling. Serve with mango chutney and hot sauce.

1 lb. conch or squid, blanched and
    finely ground in food processor
1 green bell pepper, minced
1/2 cup fresh parsley, well chopped

1 egg
1 large onion, minced
1 stalk celery, minced

2 tsp. fresh coriander
1/2 tsp. thyme
1 1/2 cups self-rising flour
1/4 tsp. baking soda

1 clove garlic, crushed
1/2 tsp. freshly ground black pepper
2 tsp. baking powder
vegetable oil for frying

1. Sift the baking powder, soda, and flour together in a small bowl and set aside. In a large bowl, mix together all other ingredients, then gradually folding in flour.

2. Cover, refrigerate, and allow to marinate overnight.

3. Heat 2-3 inches of vegetable oil to 350° in the bottom of a heavy saucepan, with cover, or a deep fryer. Drop batter by tablespoonfuls into hot oil. Remove when golden and drain on white paper towels. Serve at once.

Yield: 4 servings

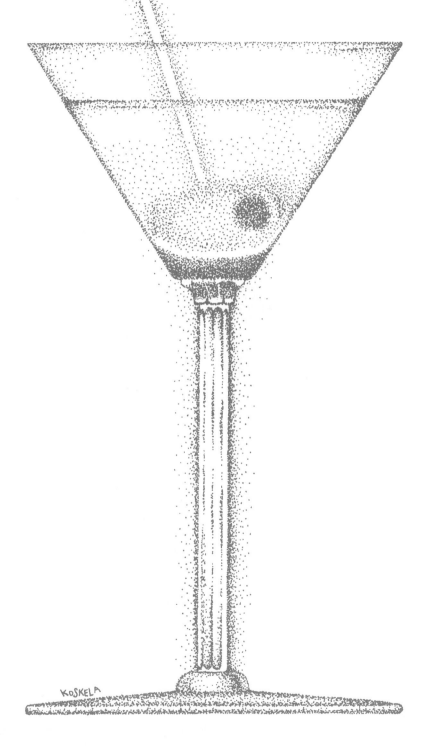

KOSKELA

Part Five:
Things to Know

Chapter 23:

Drinking to Excess

Chapter 24:

Hangovers: Causes & Tips

CHAPTER TWENTY-THREE

Drinking to Excess-Side Effects

Always do sober what you said you'd do drunk.
That will teach you to keep your mouth shut.

– Ernest Hemingway

L ike most indulgences, alcohol should be consumed in moderation. A lovely wine with a fragrant bouquet, an after-dinner cordial, or a hot coffee drink by the fireplace in winter is idyllic.

Unfortunately, alcohol can just as easily ruin as enhance life. The leading cause of teenage death in the last ten years is car accidents of which 37% are the result of drunk driving. What are the numbers? Try 68,000, nearly 7000 children whose lives have not even begun. Alcohol accounts for nearly 50% of all traffic accident fatalities. Many of these victims just innocent bystanders.

As a writer, I learn something new nearly every day. The human body produces about one ounce of ethanol each day by transforming sugars. No wonder I like chocolate cake so much!

Liquor contains ethyl alcohol, which metabolizes into fairly harmless substances. Even a small amount of isopropyl (rubbing) alcohol can cause blindness or even death.

Removing alcohol from the body is accomplished three ways: absorption, distribution, and oxidation. In absorption, alcohol passes directly into the bloodstream, bypassing digestion. Certain factors affect this. The stomach is the primary area of absorption, therefore it makes sense if you have a full stomach the effects of alcohol will be delayed. Delayed is the key word here. Once it hits the small intestine, you'll receive the full impact of the alcohol. Bubbles will make you drunk faster. The carbon dioxide hastens the movement of alcohol into the bloodstream. People of heavier bodyweight will have a larger circulatory system and not show the affects of liquor as quickly.

Once the alcohol is in the bloodstream, it affects the brain first since the brain contains a high concentration of water. When an individual's blood alcohol content (BAC) reaches 0.05%, the outer layer of the brain becomes sluggish. This is the same area that controls inhibitions, self-control, and judgment. Surprise, surprise. Ever do something under the influence you would never dream of doing while sober?

At a BAC of 0.10%, the anterior brain, a.k.a. motor area, becomes depressed and faulty coordination results. The next time you feel yourself slurring, realize that you are now at 0.10% BAC.

At 0.20% BAC, the mid-brain is affected, which controls emotional behavior. At this point, the drinker may and should be lying down as sensory and motor skills have deteriorated. You'll see drinkers laughing, crying, feeling lovey-dovey and even confused.

I'm not sure I like writing this section. I definitely recall some of these stages. At 0.30%, the lower portion of the brain becomes affected. Despite being awake, drinkers are not aware of what is going on around them. Some pass out at this stage.

After 0.35%, a drinker needs to be hospitalized. This is not to say one should plan to safely drink to this point. The body will put itself in a coma, its defense against death.

At 0.60%, the parts that control automatic function such as breathing and heart rate become affected. It's pretty easy to get to this stage by chugging a fifth of liquor. This will kill you within ten minutes. Do not ever think of doing this.

The following is a chart demonstrating the effects of BAC on a person.

BAC (%) Side Effects

.05	Relaxed, release of inhibitions, lack of self-control
.10	Slurred speech, loss of coordination, dizziness
.20	Becomes emotional, confused
.30	Awake, but not there; loss of consciousness
.35	Coma
.60	Death

Relationship Between Sex, Weight, and Amount of Alcohol Consumed indicating blood alcohol level (BAC)

alcohol (oz.)	drinks* per hour	female 150 lbs.	male 200 lbs.
1/2	1	.03	.19
1	2	.07	.38
2	4	.13	.08
3	6	.19	.12
4	8	.25	.16

Accident Risk Chart

BAC (%)	Chance of an accident
0.05	2 to 3 times normal risk
0.07	5 to 6 times
0.09	7 to 8 times
0.15	320 times

In many states, a BAC of 0.10% constitutes driving under the influence. In Massachusetts 0.08% is considered impaired, but not illegal.

Bartenders, friends, learn to discern when someone has had too much. A one-ounce drink in an average size female can cause a BAC level of 0.05%. According to the Accident Risk Chart, the chances of an accident have as much as tripled. Never serve liquor to someone intoxicated and certainly do not allow him or her to drive. Besides being morally liable, you can be held legally responsible.

CHAPTER TWENTY-FOUR

Hangovers: Causes and Valuable Tips

Have you ever had a headache that resembled a hangover, yet you had not had a drop to drink the night before? Dehydration plays a major part in this sort of headache.

Alcohol is metabolized in two ways. Through the kidneys and lungs-hence that revolting alcohol breath, and broken down in the liver.

Kidneys: Removing toxins from the bloodstream requires a great deal of water. In the case of alcohol, the toxin is ethanol. Ethanol, dissolved in water, crosses through to the kidneys and then exits via the urinary tract. Still worried about your liver? Makes you think about all the abuse your kidneys are taking when you overindulge.

Gatorade is better than water! Lot's of electrolytes are washed away as the body attempts to rid itself of ethanol.

Liver: Ethanol, broken down in the liver, is a two-step oxidation carried out by two separate enzymes. Alcohol dehydrogenase (ADH) transforms ethanol to acetaldehyde. Then acetaldehyde is converted to acetate by aldehyde dehydrogenase (ALDH).

While acetate is harmless, aldehydes are very toxic as they resemble formaldehyde. Imagine what that does to your body! Not all individuals remove alcohol as efficiently as others from their systems. Many Asians and Native Americans carry a form of the gene for ALDH, which makes a sluggish form of the enzyme. On top of that, some people carry a quick form of ADH, which dramatically increases the toxic levels of aldehyde in their bloodstream.

Alcohol poisoning is the result of a body flooded with aldehyde, which can kill. Treatment consists of a drug, which blocks ADH, thereby preventing the body from breaking down the alcohol. It allows the kidneys and lungs to excrete some of the alcohol before flooding the body with aldehyde.

Alcoholics are treated with a drug called *disulfuram,* which will make them sick if they drink alcohol. The drug inactivates ALDH which results in a toxic buildup of aldehyde. Nice, huh?

Ever drink red wine and end up with a killer hangover? The red wine and other dark and sweet drinks have additional toxins besides the alcohol, such as tannins. The metabolism of sugar in these drinks results in a reduction of B vitamins. Interestingly, and yes, I've tried this, is to ingest fructose (honey) after drinking as it slows down the sugar metabolism.

Hangover Tips

1. **100% guaranteed method:**

   Do not ever drink. Period.

2. Since most of you will not follow suggestion number one, the next most effective method is:

   Stop drinking short of intoxication. If you don't drink enough to get drunk, you won't get a hangover.

3. For those of you who absolutely cannot follow numbers one and two, the following is suggested before you pass out:

   a. Take two or three aspirin (if you can take them) with two large glasses of water. *Do not take acetaminophen as it can seriously damage your kidneys.*

   b. Have a piece of toast liberally smeared with honey and pop some B vitamins or a multi-vitamin.

4. Ever wake up and thought you were dead, but unfortunately still with the living? Stumble around so much the night before you were lucky to have found your bed, never mind the water and aspirin? The following is for those who have hopefully woken up in familiar surroundings, yet are one stop short of the emergency room:

   a. Immediately drink as much water as you can. Take two or three aspirin or ibuprofen with a quart of water is good.

   b. Your nerves are extra sensitive from coming down from a depressive drug. Soothe them by keeping the lights dimmed, having a hot bath or shower. Put on your favorite pajamas or nightie. A little aromatherapy will help. Lavender, marjoram or peppermint oil if nauseated.

   c. Avoid greasy, heavy food or dairy. Replace lost nutrients with fresh fruit and vegetables. Bananas are mild on irritated stomachs. Tomatoes salads are said to work wonders or even pasta and a light tomato sauce. A glass of tomato juice, not a Bloody Mary, is also highly recommended.

5. **Things to know before you go:** If you absolutely must go out drinking, here are a few admonitions:

   a. Do not mix your liquors, i.e. wine, beer, hard alcohol.

   b. Stay away from any colored drinks, i.e. mixed, red wine, whiskeys, liqueurs.

   c. Stay away from the sweet stuff. The end result of all that gooey sugar and alcohol is death while remaining alive in Purgatory.

Above all, remember alcohol is a drug. Exercise extreme caution when operating machinery or driving. Better yet, do not mix the two.

I certainly hope you have enjoyed our bartending cruise throughout the beautiful Caribbean islands. All the best!

Angela E. Spenceley

About the author:

Angela Spenceley has lived on St. Thomas for over fifteen years. She started writing Caribbean cookbooks after collecting thousands of recipes from all over the West Indies. *Don't Drink the Water!: A Complete Guide to Bartending in the Caribbean* is her seventh book. She is currently working on a romantic-action-thriller called *Almost Paradise*.

Her other books include: A *Walking and Driving Tour of St. Thomas*; *Guide to the U.S. Virgin Islands*, which won an award at the PCDANA show; A *Taste of the Virgin Islands*; A *Taste of Puerto Rico*; *Just Add Rum!*; and A *Taste of the Caribbean*.

She is single and lives with her two children on the south side of the island engulfed by the roar of the ocean. Her home hangs from a cliff, suspended over the azure blue Caribbean Sea.

KOSKELA

Bibliography

Foley, Ray. *Bartending for Dummies*. Foster City, California, IDG Books, 1997

Grace, Tim. *Caribbean Vacation Planner*. Coral Gables, FL, Gold Book Publishing, 2000

Laporte, Joelle. *West Indian Cocktails*. EU: Grand Sud Editions, 1995

Parkinson, Rosemary. *Shake dat Cocktail*. London: MacMillan Education Ltd, 1996

Poister, John J. *The New American Bartender's Guide*. New York: New American Library, a division of Penguin Putnam, 1999

Random House. *International Bartender's Guide*. New York: Ballantine Books, 1996

Speier, Alexander Z. *The Official Harvard Student Agencies Bartending Course*. New York: St. Martin's Press, 1999

Index

#'s

A

Appetizers

B

D

E

F

G

M

P

X

Z

Y

To Send the Gift of a Caribbean Memory

For those of you who would like to send a little paradise to friends and relatives,
for your convenience we have included this order blank.
Feel free to send us your holiday gift list and we will mail to each individual.
The price includes postage within the United States.
International orders, add $5.00 per item.
For bulk orders please call (340) 776-4208 or fax (340) 776-1400.
E-mail: vicards@islands.vi

	QUANTITY	TOTAL
CALENDARS:		
.S. Virgin Islands Calendar $13.95	_____	_____
ocket Calendar (4" X 6") $3.99	_____	_____
BOOKS:		
uerto Rico Guide Book (96 pages) $21.95	_____	_____
(available in English, Spanish, French, German and Italian)		
.S. Virgin Islands Guide Book (96 pages) $21.95	_____	_____
(available in English, Spanish, French, German, Danish and Italian)		
ritish Virgin Islands Guide Book (32 pages) $22.95	_____	_____
(available in English, French, Italian, German & Spanish)		
. Martin/St. Maarten, West Indies guide book (96 pages) $21.95	_____	_____
(English only)		
ew U.S. Virgin Islands Guide Book (32 pages) $8.95	_____	_____
(Over 90 photos 7" X 10")		
Taste of Puerto Rico Cookbook (32 pages) $10.95	_____	_____
(Over 90 photos 7" X 10")		
ew Edition: A Taste of the Virgin Islands Cookbook $8.95	_____	_____
(7" X 10" with color photographs)		
st Add Rum! Cookbook featuring appetizers, light fare and drinks $11.95	_____	_____
(100 pages, 7" X 10")		
ocket Guide Book: St. Thomas $3.99	_____	_____
(Walking and driving tour with color photos)		
Taste of the Caribbean Cookbook (over 300 pages) $24.99	_____	_____
(A complete A-Z reference for traditional and nouvelle Caribbean cuisine)		
on't Drink The Water! (over 250 pages) $24.99	_____	_____
(The Complete Guide to Bartending in the Caribbean)		
ew! St. Thomas Address Book $5.99	_____	_____

**VIRGIN ISLANDS CUSTOMERS
LEASE SHOP WITH YOUR LOCAL RETAILER.**

Please Make Check or Money Order payable to:
Virgin Islands Postcard Company Inc.
Nisky Mail P58
St. Thomas, VI 00802

AME: _____

REET ADDRESS OR BOX: _____

TY: _____ STATE: _____ ZIP: _____

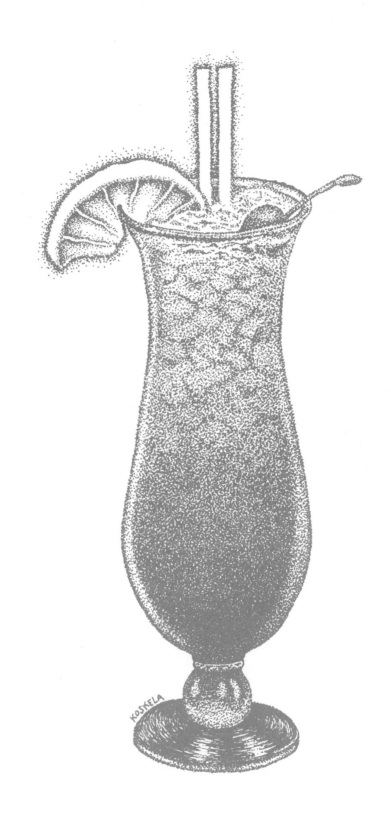